THE ICE BOWL

THE ICE BOWL

THE GREEN BAY PACKERS AND DALLAS COWBOYS SEASON OF 1967

MIKE SHROPSHIRE

Donald I. Fine Books
New York

Donald I. Fine Books
Published by the Penguin Group
Penguin Putnam Inc., 375 Hudson Street,
New York, New York 10014, U.S.A.
Penguin Books Ltd, 27 Wrights Lane,
London W8 5TZ, England
Penguin Books Australia Ltd, Ringwood,
Victoria, Australia
Penguin Books Canada Ltd, 10 Alcorn Avenue,
Toronto, Ontario, Canada M4V 3B2
Penguin Books (N.Z.) Ltd, 182–190 Wairau Road,
Auckland 10, New Zealand

Penguin Books Ltd, Registered Offices:
Harmondsworth, Middlesex, England

First published by Donald I. Fine Books,
an imprint of Penguin Putnam Inc.

First Printing, October, 1997
10 9 8 7 6 5 4 3 2 1

LIBRARY OF CONGRESS CATALOGING-IN-PUBLICATION DATA
Shropshire, Mike.
The ice bowl : the Dallas Cowboys and the Green Bay Packers
season of 1967 / Mike Shropshire.
p. cm.
ISBN 1-55611-532-6
1. National Football League—History. 2. Dallas Cowboys (Football team)—History.
3. Green Bay Packers (Football team)—History.
I. Title.
GV955.5.N35S57 1997
796.332′64′09046—dc21 97-17801
CIP

Printed in the United States of America
Set in 11/13 New Caledonia

This book is printed on acid-free paper. ♾

Acknowledgments

Last winter a Green Bay football player from the Vince Lombardi era told me (off the record), "Every couple of years I go back to a Packers' reunion. A lot of those guys can't even remember their ex-wife's first name, but they could tell you what they had for breakfast on the morning of the Ice Bowl game."

In the course of compiling the research for this book, the topic of the players' wives, ex or otherwise, never came up. But I was astonished at how vividly the players of both the Green Bay Packers and the Dallas Cowboys recalled the details of a day and a football game that happened almost thirty years earlier. As a historical episode in American sports culture, the 1967 Green Bay–Dallas NFL championship clash not only withstands the test of time but in the minds of many stands out as the most memorable pro football game ever played.

The bulk of the material in this book was assembled from interviews, some in person but most on the telephone, with a few dozen individuals who were somehow involved with that game.

Other details and quotes were collected from four books: *The Crunch,* by Pat Toomay, *Vince Lombardi on Football, The Packer Scrapbook,* by George Flynn, and *Vince,* by Michael O'Brien.

Additional source material previously appeared in *Time, Newsweek,* and *Marketplace* magazines, and one quote was taken from an article by Tom Peeler that appeared in *D Magazine* that he, in turn, had extracted from a book, *The Murchisons,* by Jane Wolfe. Also, substantial information was collected from the following newspapers: *Chicago Tribune, New York Herald-Tribune, Saint Paul Pioneer Press, Sacramento Bee, St. Louis Post-Dispatch, Houston Chronicle, Milwaukee Journal, Milwaukee Sentinel, Green Bay Press-Gazette, Dallas Morning News, Dallas Times-Herald, Los Angeles Times,* and *Fort Worth Press.*

Finally, a few parts of this book were the product of my own recollections and from several exhibits at the Packer Hall of Fame in Green Bay.

I wish to acknowledge the considerable assistance of personnel at the public libraries in Green Bay, Milwaukee, and Dallas and offer special gratitude to Tex Schramm, Forrest Gregg, Lee Remmel, Bart Starr, and his administrative assistant, Michelle Warren, who were particularly generous with their time. It is important, too, that I thank my wife and personal trainer, Karen G. Shropshire, whose technical American language expertise absolutely blows me away.

PROLOGUE

DALLAS, GREEN BAY, AND ME—BACK TO THE FUTURE

A SIMPLE DECLARATION of intention—that I planned to view 1997's Super Bowl XXXI on a big-screen television set from some location in the saloon district of Green Bay, Wisconsin—attracted gapes and stares of pure bemusement from colleagues and uninvolved onlookers in Dallas. They would break off eye contact and shake their heads, as if I had announced plans to begin clog-dancing lessons.

Why would anybody venture *up there* to witness this event when he could experience an on-site viewing down in N'awlins, where the practitioner of hedonist pursuit can experience the titillation of having his billfold lifted on a stroll through the French Quarter?

In a year in which the top sports movie of the year, *Jerry Maguire,* depicts the story of a sports agent (key line in the movie: "Show me the money"), that good old Pride of Yankees mentality continues to prevail in Green Bay. Entry into a time warp like this can serve only to resuscitate the jaded soul of the city boy.

My desire to journey to Green Bay in January, on the eastern shore of the No-Frills State, was twofold. First, I felt that I could easily obtain seating, or at least standing room, in the saloon district of Green Bay. Information persisted that the entire community was composed of nothing much *other* than a saloon district. Some locals themselves describe Green Bay as "a drinking town with a football problem." So at least I could get in. The same could not be said for the actual Packers-Patriots game, the Super Bowl in the Super Dome, and in recent years, I've been told, that the game itself has become a party that is harder and harder to crash.

Reason number two for the Green Bay journey: Now that the Super Bowl annually takes on spiritual implications, the choice seemed aesthetically realistic. Where would you rather encounter the rapture of Easter Sunday—Vatican City or Las Vegas?

Because of the long-awaited Packers appearance in pro football's winter carnival, the spirit of resurrection reigned rich across the land, or at least in Green Bay, where the holy specter of Vince Lombardi appeared poised to live again. After a twenty-nine-year hiatus, the Pack was returning to the January spectacle that it had inaugurated. Somehow the notion of witnessing something like that emerged as a pageant more meaningful in the lengthening shadows of Lambeau Field than amid the sounds of Dixieland clarinets and the smell of crawfish gumbo.

Beyond that, another and much more profound urge had taken form. For a football fan (well, let's not use the word "fan"—"keenly interested observer" is closer to the case), a yearning to transfuse the soul with something wholesome was becoming hard to resist.

A stifling soot had settled over life in the football streets of Dallas. Cowboys owner Jerry Jones, a man seemingly consumed by a profound measure of hubris, had attained a new negative popularity rating. The nature of the cupidity attached to the attainment of the endorsement contracts with Pepsi and Nike had soured even some Cowboys fans, and this in a city not exactly renowned for begrudging a man trying to make a buck.

So when Michael Irvin was indicted and facing trial after being nailed in a hotel room with a parcel of drugs and two topless dancers, the civic anthem became: "Didja hear what Jones told Irvin? He said, 'No, no, Michael. I said Pepsi and Nike, not coke and nookie.' Haw. Haw. Haw." Irvin, alleged national role model and a living end-zone idol in North Texas, presented himself before a grand jury attired in furs and baubles that he appeared to have obtained at a Zsa Zsa Gabor estate sale. One wondered whether the grand jury had leveled its indictment against an alleged drug offender or his fashion statement.

In July, my job for the month was to cover Irvin's trial for a Dallas–based sports-talk radio station. Prosecution evidence came delivered daily to the courtroom in a brown paper Food Lion grocery bag. The jury got to see a fair-sized bundle of white powder and some baggies of dope. After Irvin entered a no-contest plea at midtrial, the jury was deprived of the chance to inspect other items in the grocery bag—some sex toys confiscated by the cops on the night of the bust. Notable among the inventory was a vibrator device that could be operated via remote control, a tribute to the cutting-edge technology from Pacific Rim nations.

A member of the battalion of lawyers representing the man known as the Playmaker informed me: "Michael's problem isn't drugs. It's women. So finally I told him, 'Look, Wilt Chamberlain has claimed that he slept with over twenty thousand women. That's the world record, and not you or anybody else is ever going to break it, so why try?' Michael looked disappointed at first and said, 'Look, man. I'm only thirty.' I'll say this for Michael," the lawyer went on, "he's got a world of pride."

It was during the Irvin drug investigation that the public learned of a facility known as the White House, a small mansion on Tony Dorsett Avenue near the team's practice area that some players had rented for recreational purposes. "So they ran a few whores in and out of there. What's wrong with that?" declared Nate Newton, a guard regarded as one of the more straitlaced representatives of the modern-era Cowboys. His only mentions in life's universal book of small crimes and great mistakes include a drunk-driving arrest (no conviction) and a citation for his presence at an illegal dogfight in East Texas.

By the end of the 1996 season, the Cowboys' coast-to-coast identity had taken on the aspects of the sidewalks of New York during a garbage strike. Irvin and a brontosaurus of an offensive tackle named Erik Williams returned to the headlines and were named in a rape allegation forwarded by, yes, another topless dancer. Irvin contended that he was someplace else on the evening of the event in question, a legal defense plea known in Texas criminal courtrooms as *corpus non premises.* Police later determined that the charges had been fabricated. Apparently the dancer could not comprehend the difference between rape and rough sex on a billiard table.

Additional troubling subplots for the Dallas-area football fans surrounded the strange persona of the head coach, Barry Switzer, the man handpicked by Jerry Jones to replace Jimmy Johnson. With the proud Cowboys falling into rapid disrepair, Jones's status among the elite and effete of the Dallas cotillion set has taken on a jaundiced tint. The business genius who brought Deion Sanders to Dallas now stands portrayed as just another refugee from the Hormel provinces. As construction work was completed on Jones's mansion in Highland Park, the Dallas equivalent of Nob Hill, neighbors expressed genuine dismay at the arrival of big trucks from a furniture discount warehouse.

Some of the old Dallas Cowboys, the players who were around in the Ice Bowl era, express open contempt for the Switzer regime. "The failure all falls on [Switzer's] shoulders," George Andrie told me two weeks before the Super Bowl. Andrie was the man who scooped up a Bart Starr fumble and scored a defensive touchdown for the Cowboys in that minus-70 degree chill-factor epic played and performed on New Year's Eve afternoon in 1967. "Don't put the blame on the salary cap and poor draft positioning, either. What about player development? What ever happened to that? What really got me was after the Cowboys lost the playoff game at Carolina and some of the players said that they were glad they got beat. What does that tell you?" While many of the Cowboys of the Tom Landry era choose not to comment on the modern Dallas disaster, George Andrie has spoken out.

So has Pete Gent, a former Cowboys receiver whose essential claim to immortality happened through his novel entitled *North Dallas 40.* Gent's description of the backstage world of the National Football League of the mid- to late 1960s can hardly be described as a work of warmth with a cheerful ending. Even Gent now claims to be beyond perplexed by the rapid rise and ricochet fall of the Jerry Jones Cowboys. "I've got a son up here who is a die-hard Dallas Cowboys fan, to the max," says Gent, now living in western Michigan. "What do I tell the boy? This is appalling."

Beyond the obvious and lurid jailhouse headlines and the dubious on-the-field performance of the team, another malevolent element bedevils these Cowboys, and I finally identified it while listening to a radio sports-talk show in Dallas.

Norm Hitzges, the talk-show host, has been described as the HAL 9000 (the computer in the movie *2001: A Space Odyssey)* of sports radio. During the season, with Barry Switzer as his guest, Hitzges questioned a Cowboys coaching strategy in the previous week's game. Switzer, who attempts to maintain his manicured self-perception as a players' coach, a man of the people and a Great Communicator, suffered a telling lapse on that weekday morning.

"Do you think I give a damn about what Norm Hitzges thinks?" Switzer demanded. "Do you think I give a damn what the guy pumping gas at the Texaco station thinks?" In the span of two and a half seconds Barry Switzer provided the necessary clue as to the genuine nature of the Cowboys' demise: the virus known as terminal arrogance.

By momentarily dismissing the voice of the fan, Switzer revealed the one flaw that no coach in the spotlight can hope to overcome. These fans. They vote with their pocketbooks. Perhaps Switzer should have been listening to one of those talk shows after his apparent twin goofs in Philly late in 1995, when two fourth-and-one plunges from his own 29-yard line handed the game to the Eagles. A guy called in and talked about how, after the Cowboys had won their first Super Bowl game a quarter of a century earlier, he had planted a tree in his front yard. His Cowboys Tree, the guy called it. After the Philly game, the guy told of stomping into his front yard and chopping down the Cowboys Tree—"not with a chain saw either. With an ax."

Now the bunker mentality at the team headquarters known as Valley Ranch has become pervasive, as the Cowboys' owner has imposed a gag order on the coaching staff, forbidding them to speak to the media. "Gag order?" says Randy Galloway, a Dallas sports columnist. "Gag reflex is more like it. The only downside to this is Jones didn't put a gag on Switzer six months ago."

Frank Luksa, another columnist with close ties to the Valley Ranch inner sanctum, pondered the impact of Jones's affinity for a beverage containing vermouth and other optional additives. "Jones, I heard, had quit drinking at the start of the '96 season, but he said he did it to lose weight more than anything else," declared Luksa. "But from what I've been hearing lately . . ."

This is what has become of America's Team. Of course, that sobriquet was destined to bite the Cowboys on the ass from day one. The Cowboys' old regime has been quick to point out that it was NFL Films, and not the team, that produced that grandiose bit of packaging after the 1978 season. But it has been my experience in traveling throughout the land that the public popularity of Dallas—on the roster of world cities—ranks just ahead of Sodom and slightly behind Gomorrah.

Dallas Cowboys—America's Team. Why not John Dillinger—America's Sweetheart? Or Three Mile Island—America's Vacationland?

So, given the sulfuric nature of the prevailing football atmosphere in North Texas, my motivation to experience a spiritual reawakening by watching Super Bowl XXXI from a tavern setting in Green Bay had become impossible to resist.

The idea received the endorsement of no less a luminary than Vince Lombardi, Jr. Now fifty-four and living outside Seattle, Lombardi offered a measure of caution. "It's a good idea as long as you choose the right saloon," he said. "I'd recommend the Blurry Ears Tavern in the Northland Hotel."

That settled it. On the Saturday before Super Bowl Sunday, I was off into the white blue yonder. The most cost-efficient method of traveling from Dallas to Green Bay (the whole town of Green Bay could fit inside the D/FW airport, but so could the state of Massachusetts) was to fly to Chicago, rent a car at O'Hare, and drive the rest of the way, about three hours.

One thing I learned right away. The Green Bay Packers under Mike Holmgren might qualify as the new America's Team, but they sure as hell aren't Chicago's team. On a radio talk show, former Chicago Bears lineman Jimbo Covert reluctantly predicted that the Pack would probably beat the New England Patriots but quickly added that he could never find it in his heart to root for Green Bay. This is something that people from Dallas need to realize. Long before there were any football Cowboys, a Bears-Packers rivalry had been in place for decades, and that runs deeper than any franchise antagonisms that have sprouted during the television era.

When I finally arrived in Green Bay, the first thing I noticed was that everything was green and gold. No tree, no standing physical structure, no living person, and hardly a house pet remained unadorned with some Packers ornamental display. That involvement included the medical industry. St. Thomas Hospital on Webster Street displayed a huge banner: "Packer Fever . . . There Is No Cure." The Petal Pusher Florist on the same street offered special green and gold Valentine displays.

As I registered at the Residence Inn on St. Joseph's Street, along with the other guests, I was requested to sign a "no excessive partying" agreement in which I promised that during and after the football game on Sunday I would not attempt to burn the place down or create any disturbance that would require the presence of the cops.

When I tried to call, I learned that the Northland Hotel was no longer operational, meaning that the Blurry Ears Tavern was gone as well. So now the selection of the right saloon required advance scouting.

The Stadium View Sports Bar, within staggering distance of Lambeau Field, had been mentioned as a possibility. On the phone, the manager sounded cordial and was helpfully candid. "This place maintains a seating and standing capacity of 2,400 people, and the fire department stands at the door and counts everybody coming and going. Kickoff tomorrow afternoon is at 5:18. We're opening at 10:00 in the morning. If you're not here by 10:10 or 10:15, you won't get in."

A guy at Fuzzy's Shenanigans, another acclaimed beverage outlet, told me the same story. Fuzzy, naturally, is Fuzzy Thurston, the great offensive guard on the Lombardi Packers of yore. Unlike me, Fuzz has seen enough games from Green Bay, both from the football field and from saloon TV sets, so he, like 26,000 other locals, chose to travel to New Orleans for this one. All of those who had departed were now replaced in town by commuters from Rhinelander and Wausau and everywhere else in the region, eager to capture the moment—even if on a TV screen—in the shrine. Unified by standards and circumstances of relentless climate and spartan living, tempered by twenty-nine years' worth of unfulfilled faith and hope on the gridiron, the people stood poised for redemption. Emotionally, Mount St. Helens prepared to blow. In the zero-degree chill factor of the Saturday night darkness, the visitor could feel the energy.

While the Stadium View Sports Bar would no doubt be impossible on Sunday, I at least wanted to capture the mood of the joint on the night before the game. Curiously, those now famous Cheesehead adornments were nowhere on display in the Stadium View. Green and gold Mardi Gras beads happened to be the fashion rage on this unforgettable weekend in Green Bay.

Soon, however, it was time to switch saloons, since the task of successfully ordering a beer loomed as all but impossible.

Across the street a sign on a Chinese restaurant read LOUNGE. I found inside Dennis Andre, who runs Andre's Penguin City pizza restaurant in Algoma, celebrating his forty-seventh birthday. Dennis appeared gratified, although not particularly surprised, when someone presented him with a shoe box–size cardboard container filled with official Lambeau Field Frozen Tundra. When the stadium floor had been covered with new sod for the championship game against the

Carolina Panthers two weeks earlier, the team had boxed up the old turf and sold it in $10 souvenir packages, with the proceeds forwarded to charity. "Some teenagers came and tried to steal some of the sacred sod," one of the party attendees related, "so they brought in the police. Only in Green Bay will you find heavily armed men guarding dirt." To me the stuff looked a lot like the smoking material that many Cowboys fans rely on before games at Texas Stadium.

A man wearing defensive end Reggie White's jersey number 92 sat among the party guests. On a bar napkin he was planning the Pack's starting lineup for the opening game of the '97 regular season. By his calculations, the Pack would lose a couple of players via the free-agent route in the off-season. With the restrictions of the salary cap in place, he saw no way that the Pack could retain the services of kick-return magician Desmond Howard. And yet, in lockstep with the overwhelming consensus of Packers fans everywhere, he felt that as long as Brett Favre and Reggie White continue to wear the green and gold, the Pack could recruit the other twenty starters from the nearby Fort Howard paper mill and repeat as Super Bowl champions.

Mike, the man planning the next season's roster, turned out to be a Catholic priest. I suggested to him that with the extreme likelihood that the Pack would prevail on Sunday, his efforts at maintaining spiritual well-being among his Green Bay flock should be more gratifying. Obviously, he had already pondered that possibility. On the flip side, he pointed out that if, say, Brett Favre broke his leg during the pregame introductions and the Packers somehow failed to win the Super Bowl, the local priesthood would radio the home office for reinforcements. "To so many Green Bay *is* the Packers, and that's all they've got," the priest said.

By then I had identified myself as a Texan (but neglected to also mention that I was writing a book) who had stumbled into the Kingdom of Sharp Cheddar to watch the football game, and the Packers fans welcomed me to the birthday party. All of the women at the table wore green-and-gold earrings shaped like footballs and with the famous Packer G helmet logo. Dennis's older sister, who was fifty-nine, owned two season tickets near the top row in one of the end zones, the same seats she had held since 1957. The waiting list of persons wanting these or any other seats now extended to over 26,000 names. Because about three or four tickets conventionally become available each year, the person at the bottom of the list can expect to hear from the Packers' ticket office in what mathematicians now calculate will be slightly over five thousand years.

Just as Mike the priest might have owned up to occasions when he questioned the depth of his ecclesiastical commitment, Dennis's sister confessed that there had been years when she wondered what those tickets might fetch according to the dictates of a free and open marketplace. She remembered December 1988 with the same relish that stockbrokers recall October 1987. The Packers, marching into the abyss of a 2–14 season, sprang an upset over Arizona in the final game of the season. That seemingly obscure win gave Dallas, and not the Pack, first pick in the draft. Dallas used that selection to obtain Troy Aikman. Green Bay, with the second selection, drafted tackle Tony Mandarich and paid him $4 million. Mandarich, after he arrived in training camp, began to shrink and actually disappeared after three seasons in which he didn't contribute a damn thing.

Membership in the Society of the Cheesehead, whether one chooses to wear the yellow triangular war bonnet or not, does not come cheap. To qualify for the council of elders, the apprenticeship lasts twenty-nine years.

As the party broke up, I ventured back toward the center of town, on Main Street, and selected a bistro at random for a nightcap. Entry took place through a side door only, like an old speakeasy, and it was not until after I was inside that I discovered that I was in the midst of what is known in Dallas as a gentlemen's club. No, not *that* kind of place. Two things that the visitor is certain not to locate in Green Bay are a gay bar and a Mormon temple. What I'm talking about here is a showplace for topless female performers, although this appeared to be a one-woman show. Positioned horizontally on a platform, the artist performed a dance routine that would be regarded with alarm by chaperones at a high school senior prom.

Her repertoire, by the way, proceeded entirely to the background rhythms of Packers marching songs, including one semi-rap-style masterwork sung by wide receiver Robert Brooks. A woman poked me in the ribs. "Wanna buy a pretty girl a drink?" She made Dolly Parton look like Twiggy. She wanted a tequila and tomato juice. I nodded, then tiptoed past the cigarette machine, out the side door, and into the brutal nocturnal chill of Green Bay.

Next door, in a more Christian atmosphere, a younger element of Packers fandom got primed for the big game. Entertainment consisted of a guy who climbed onto the rectangular bar and traveled an obstacle course at a full sprint without spilling anyone's drink. The stunt attracted the attention of nobody. I approached the aspiring acrobat. "Hey, I'm from, uh, outta state, Texas actually, and wonder what might be a good place to watch the Super Bowl tomorrow?"

The kid gave me the kind of look that a pot retailer would throw down on somebody he suspected might be working undercover.

"You're not from Dallas, are you?" he asked.

"Oh, hell, no," I said. "Corpus Christi. Can't stand Dallas. Nobody down there can."

"Well, in that case, watch the goddamn game in here!" Then he shouted, "Go, Pack!" and stumbled backward into a waitress, landing adroitly on the back of his head.

At that moment I realized that the decision to visit Green Bay on Super Sunday qualified as divinely inspired. Nowhere on the planet existed more ardent and more distinctly joyous, uninhibited sports fans, including those soccer wussies in Italy and Brazil. Still, with the kickoff of Super Bowl XXXI then slightly less than seventeen hours away, common sense told me to retreat to the hotel.

Sunday would bring adrenaline, and Sunday would require stamina. I had to be ready, because as Vince Lombardi himself so eloquently pointed out, fatigue makes cowards of us all.

LAMBEAU FIELD, A structure of prodigious dignity that transmits a visceral sense of grandeur and tradition, appeared to assume a fastidiously proud posture in the late-morning hours of Super Bowl Sunday. Beneath the bold lettering, GREEN BAY PACKERS, some college-age folks played touch football on the snow-and-ice surface of the parking lot. In this stately setting, a graceful quarterback with flowing golden hair pitched a touchdown pass. The quarterback was female. This kind of activity would not be found, or probably allowed, on the parking lot outside Texas Stadium.

These Dallas–Green Bay contrasts grew more extreme by the hour. Across the street, hundreds of fans poured into the Green Bay Packer Hall of Fame, the only hall of fame in the known universe devoted to only one team. Bob Harlan, the CEO of the nonprofit, fan-owned Packers, regards the essence of his job as "the preservation of a national treasure." If that's the case, this Packer museum simplifies that duty. Other than the Baseball Hall of Fame, I have never toured a better designed or more complete specialty museum in the country. The fan can find every morsel of memorabilia in here except the X rays of Paul Hornung's neck injury that forced him to retire.

While hundreds of fans toured the Packer Hall of Fame, next door thousands more streamed through the main entrance of the city arena. For a set price Pack loyalists received a package deal that included one free drink and a special Super Bowl edition of the *Milwaukee Journal.* Of course, these folks could have poured all the free drinks they wanted at home. Still, after twenty-nine years of waiting while the Miamis and the Pittsburghs and San Franciscos, and all those times they endured the booming baritone of NBC's Dick Enberg: "Dallas, your Cowboys are once again the champions of the football world," the cork was about to pop from the bottle, and many of these Pack fans wanted to be among a crowd to share the gladness.

On the topic of emancipation of corks from the necks of bottles, the man at the cash register of a spirits emporium revealed that he had sold more champagne on the morning of Super Bowl Sunday than the previous nine or ten New Year's Eves combined. Another big hit: collector bottles of a product called Packer Backer Brau. Someone at a microbrewery over in Appleton had rolled the dice before the regular season and emblazoned SUPER BOWL XXXI across the label. Another Cheesehead had passed the test of faith.

By Super Sunday even the pulpit professionals confirmed to the town that, due in no small part to the power of prayer, a Green Bay victory in New Orleans ranked as a done deal. The message board at the First United Church of Christ proclaimed: TWO SURE THINGS—GOD AND THE PACK.

Particularly the Pack. According to the morning line, Green Bay remained on the happy end of a 14-point spread over the Patriots, while God was listed as only a 9½-point favorite over Original Sin.

By two-thirty, light snow was falling on streets now mostly abandoned. All oxygen-breathing life-forms in Wisconsin had settled in to witness the pregame show now in full swing on the Fox Network. After touring the town, I had decided to watch the first half from a typical corner bar—named, in fact, the Korner Bar. Then I planned to watch the rest of the game from a sports bar right down the street—Gipper's.

All of the regulars, plus one irregular (me), stood or sat in the

Korner Bar, ready for the game, which was due to begin in ninety minutes. But the minutes ticked past slowly. Outside, the little snowflakes were becoming huge, and inside, the tension turned to raw anxiety. The mood of the flight crew on the *Enola Gay* just before they dropped the bomb must have been very much like this—the difference (I presume, at least) being that the boys in the B-29 were not totally plastered. In the Korner Bar they began to pace, like trial defendants in a courtroom hallway awaiting a jury verdict. One guy killed time by reciting the Packers' starting defensive eleven the last time Green Bay had appeared in a Super Bowl. "Front four, that's easy. Willie Davis, Henry Jordan, Ron Kostelnik and . . . goddamn. I can't think of the other guy. I'll get back to the front four in a minute. The linebackers were Ray Nitschke, of course, and Dave Robinson and Lee Roy Caffey, and the secondary, that was Bob Jeter and Herb Adderley on the corners and Tom Brown and Willie Wood at safety. Now, back to the front four. Who was that other guy? Oh, yeah. Henry Jordan."

"Nah," says his pal. "You already named Jordan."

"Goddamn, this is gonna drive me nuts," said the trivia expert, except that in Green Bay this recitation hardly qualified as sports trivia. Preschoolers are taught this material before they learn the alphabet. Soon the eleventh name came to mind. "Aldridge! That's it! Lionel Aldridge!"

Another regular, a man named Randy whom they all called Runner, watched with amusement. I had been making idle chatter with Runner, told him I was from Texas. He showed no curiosity whatsoever in what had brought me to Green Bay today.

So I asked him, "You're a lifelong Packer fan. Were you, by any chance, at the Ice Bowl game?"

"No," said Runner. "That year I was in Vietnam. I listened to the game on Armed Forces radio."

When the game finally began, the Korner Bar became racked with intense mood swings. Right away, Favre hit Andre Rison with a 54-yard touchdown strike, and the room trembled. Doug Evans accomplished a swoop-and-dive move that would have done credit to a trapeze artist and intercepted a Drew Bledsoe pass. Ecstasy in the Korner Bar.

But, as they like to say at the Wisconsin Academy of Fine Arts, football imitates life. New England held Green Bay to a field goal, then delivered two sudden touchdowns. The Packers trailed by four points, and every glass of beer in the state of Wisconsin suddenly tasted flat. Hardly anyone remained seated now, and most of the men assumed a Ray Nitschke stance on every play, leaning forward with all the weight on the balls of their feet.

Soon Favre lofted a first-down pass down the right sideline to Antonio Freeman. Antonio, on cruise control, murmured adieu to the Patriots secondary on an 81-yard touchdown journey. The Korner Bar was mystically changed into an isle of bliss. That play did not happen solely because of the expertise of the Green Bay offense. The patrons of the Korner Bar *willed* it to happen.

For my pal Runner, the thrill of the moment was embellished when he won a door-prize raffle, a Packers sweatshirt. "First thing I've ever won in my life," he said. "And imagine that. A Packer shirt on the day they win the Super Bowl."

The remainder of the half became a textbook kick-butt exhibition on the part of the Pack. After two quarters the heroes gained control, 27–14. I told Runner that I was heading to another spa for the second half. "Hey," he said, "take the Packer shirt. Take it back to Texas with you and tell 'em hello from Green Bay."

On the quick drive over to Gipper's sports bar (probably called that because Curly Lambeau played in the same Notre Dame backfield with George Gipp), the notion occurred to me that the last thing the city of Green Bay needed this time of year was about four more inches of snow. But that was what it would get. On this occasion, though, the big flakes looked like confetti pouring down in Charles Lindbergh's welcome-home parade. The rock 'n' roll Super Bowl halftime boomed from the television set. James Brown bellowed out his old hit "I Feel Good." Hell, James Brown just *thought* he felt good. He should have been inside Gipper's.

Festivities hit a lull during the third quarter. On a fourth-and-one gamble, a Packers running play got stuffed. The ball carrier, Dorsey Levens, lost seven yards.

Seven plays later, New England's Curtis Martin banged through the middle of the Packer defense for 18 yards and a touchdown to cut the Green Bay lead to 27–21. Full glasses reached awaiting mouths in world record time and grown men swallowed hard. Girlfriends and wives looked at their boyfriends and husbands with expressions of concern. These women all thought the same thing: "If the Packers blow this game, I'm in for a long winter."

One commercial later, the crowd's fears evaporated. Desmond Howard caught the kickoff from the Patriots' Adam Vinatieri, followed a blocking wedge until he found his lane of escape ("running to daylight," Vince Lombardi used to call it), and then seemed propelled into overdrive by some unseen catapult. Howard completed his 99-yard mission in what seemed like about six seconds flat. Gipper's sports bar began to vibrate.

When the Pack had finally won, 35–21, consecrating its season-long compact with its adoring support base, a fan named Al, who had driven in from New Franken, recalled, "I was in grade school when they played that Ice Bowl. My family listened to the game on the radio because in those days the TV home games were blacked out in this area. When the Cowboys took the lead in the fourth quarter, I started crying. I guess I've thought about that game maybe every day since. In some ways," Al said, "that seems like an eternity ago, and other ways it seems like only yesterday."

America's Cheeseheads jammed the thoroughfares and tangoed on the sidewalks. The Fox River, frozen into ivory concrete, would thaw before the party subsided. On Monday, they packed Lambeau Field to greet the team, which arrived late. Nobody cared. After twenty-nine years, what difference did a couple of hours make? In weather that would have sent Sir Edmund Hillary scurrying off to Palm Springs, people sat in an arena where no game was taking place and chanted, "Repeat! Repeat!"

The "drinking town" aspect of Green Bay's identity may or may not persist into eternity, but the football problem seems gone forever. And, you know, it was just what I wanted. A sort of purification process for this old sinner from Sin Town.

CHAPTER

1

A PRIME COLLECTIBLE in the archives of NFL Films shows that rarest of events, one in which the winning determinant of the annual championship game of the pro football universe teeters on one final climactic play. It's December 30, 1966, and the Green Bay Packers are playing the Dallas Cowboys for the National Football League championship. Here it comes. The Dallas Cowboys, down by seven, can force overtime by scoring from the Green Bay Packer three-yard line.

Grantland Rice, the poet laureate of American sportswriters, offered the phrase "braying bedlam" to describe the crowd scene during the storied "long-count" episode at the Jack Dempsey–Gene Tunney heavyweight rematch in Chicago in 1926. The nearest approximation to that, in my experience as a sportswriter, came with the thunder that echoed on the field at the Cotton Bowl as Don Meredith brought the Cowboys from the huddle.

Meredith took the snap and rolled to his right. Before the quarterback could locate an open receiver, Packer linebacker Dave Robinson surged through a crack in the Dallas offensive line. Instantly, Robinson found Meredith's skinny East Texas country boy neck in the grasp of his large left paw. Meredith could only fling the football sidearm into heavy crisscrossing traffic in the end zone. A Dallas quarterback who would emerge a decade later, Roger Staubach, would accomplish sports immortality by scoring miracle touchdowns with blind heaves like this one.

Don Meredith, more accustomed to a Bloody Mary than a Hail Mary, experienced no such luck. In the back of the end zone, a player wearing number 40 for the Packers, Tom Brown, intercepted the pass, and in the process preserved the historic context of the Green Bay football dynasty. Freeze-frame Tom Brown's interception. Crouched about eight feet away, just beyond the back of the end zone, there's a guy in a black London Fog overcoat. That's me. If Brown hadn't caught the ball, I would have.

My job that afternoon in Dallas was to visit the Packers locker room and gather postgame comments. Usually, the winning dressing quarters after the NFL championship game present a show of less than elegant and completely unbridled exuberance. I could remember the scene on TV just three years earlier. The Chicago Bears, having rendered New York Giants quarterback Y. A. Tittle a battered and broken heap, poured bottled beer over each other's heads and sang an anthem of praise to their coach, George Halas: "Hooray for George! Hooray at last! Hooray for George—he's a horse's ass!"

The setting that I encountered in the Packer locker room, located at the end of a ramp beneath the stands in the south end zone of the Cotton Bowl, wasn't at all that way. The Pack seemed almost subdued. Of the entire forty-player roster, the only one not smoking a cigarette was Bart Starr, the quarterback. They all appeared eager to get the hell out of Dallas.

You have to remember that the coach of this entourage was Vince Lombardi, a man with gleaming teeth and a heart allegedly forged of stainless steel. Toleration of postgame rejoicing did not rank high in the table of contents of Lombardi's book of disciplines. Not when some games remained on the Packers' schedule. For the first time in professional football history, the NFL championship game no longer stood out as the summit match. Now the winner had to trudge off to an anticlimactic contest known as the Super Bowl (although in its inaugural season it was called the NFL-AFL championship game). So the Pack's mission still not complete, the locker-room disposition presented something less than unrestrained joy. Also, the fact that the upstart, fancy-pants Cowboys had pinned them to the ropes at the finish was not easy to digest.

Offensive guard Jerry Kramer, with dried blood caked on his lips and teeth, announced that while he was certain the Packer defense would somehow keep the onrushing Cowboys out of Green Bay's fourth-quarter end zone, he conceded relief now that it was over.

Paul Hornung, the Green Bay golden boy, reflected on that. Nobody, including Hornung himself, knew at the time that he had just played his last game. Nerve damage in his neck would keep him out of the game against the AFL champion, and after that doctors would insist that he retire.

The golden boy, without his pads, presented an upper torso that defied the Adonis image. To his teammates, in fact, Hornung was known as Goat Shoulders. Now Hornung, pulling on a deep drag from his menthol Salem, remarked on the sensation of absolute anxiety that he'd felt the instant before Meredith's fourth-down pass sailed awry. "The Cowboys had all the momentum in the world there at the end and with all that incredible crowd noise, if the game had gone into overtime, well . . ."

Earlier that afternoon, Kansas City had beaten the Buffalo Bills (thus inuring Bills quarterback Jack Kemp to the sensation of major defeat later in the center ring) and now were set up as the sacrificial goat in this first ever NFL-AFL championship game. Just before leaving the press box at the Cotton Bowl to head down to the field and then into the locker room to gather my quotes, I'd ripped a story from the old AP teletype. It contained quotes from the Chiefs' Fred Williamson that predicted, "Whether we play the Packers or the Cowboys, the NFL is in for a bitter shock when they play KC."

I presented that strip of yellow wire copy to middle linebacker Ray Nitschke and asked him for a comment. From a distance, on TV, Nitschke's face looked like something that had been transported down from the side of Mount Rushmore. Up close, that countenance appeared as clusters of scar tissue situated around the cheekbones and eyebrows that surrounded a nose that was a mass of tangled cartilage.

Nitschke read Williamson's bold and, ultimately, foolhardy comments, and that face took on an even more sinister aspect. "That guy"—and here Nitschke paused ominously—"is getting ready to find out who the Green Bay Packers are and what we represent."

Lombardi, standing on a chair, presented a cheerful message to the assembled media: "All right, you guys have had enough time. Clear out. Get the hell outta here!" Lombardi, for all of his Old World, hard-guy bombast, realized that had it not been for dumb luck, his destiny as the winning coach in the first ever NFL-AFL championship match and media gala probably would have been denied him.

On that fourth-and-three crisis and the ensuing Dallas mishap that decided the game, Tom Landry, the automaton Cowboys coach, had dispatched the wrong players onto the field, and two of them were aligned in a formation that did not coincide with the play call. As a result, nobody was in a position to block the blitzing Dave Robinson, who had waltzed untouched into the Cowboys' backfield. Landry later would speculate that Bullet Bob Hayes, amid the crowd noise, had misunderstood the instructions when he went onto the field to transfer the play call to Meredith.

In the Packers' dressing room moments after the game, before the media people had been allowed to flood in, Lombardi approached Dave Robinson. The coach was grinning, and Robinson anticipated a rare postgame accolade. Instead, Robinson recalled years later, Lombardi said, "Dave, you weren't supposed to blitz on that play."

From small fiascos, they say, great plays are made. So Green Bay traveled to Southern California and made football history, stampeding the Chiefs, 34–10. Receiver Max McGee, one of the few players on the Packers' roster who could compete with Paul Hornung in the party league, had been pressed into service when Boyd Dowler got hurt. McGee wound up the star of the game, catching two touchdown passes. After the game Lombardi approached McGee and said, "Max, you drive me crazy. You make these great behind-the-back circus catches, and then you turn around and drop the passes that are thrown right on the numbers."

"Maybe that's because I don't get much practice catching passes right on the numbers," countered McGee, who could talk to the coach that way because he was not much younger than Lombardi.

Ray Nitschke's promise to Fred Williamson, that he would learn who the Packers were and what they represented, took shape in the second half. The Hammer got trampled by a Green Bay power sweep, was relieved of his senses, and left the floor of the L.A. Coliseum on a stretcher.

What the Packers did not understand after the game, and probably still don't, was that their second-string fullback, Jim Grabowski, served as the catalyst for the game's even being played in the first place. Grabowski, although he may not have realized it himself, was a principal backstage character in a sequence of events that led to the merger of the National and American Football Leagues.

One year earlier, when the NFL-AFL bidding war for prime college draft choices was at full throttle, the Dallas Cowboys wanted to sign Grabowski, who, like Ray Nitschke and Dick Butkas, was a star at Illinois. "In Dallas, we were used to signing whatever players we wanted," remembered Tex Schramm, the Cowboys' president and general manager, who for nearly three decades served as the shadow commissioner of the National Football League. Schramm had given Pete Rozelle his first job in pro football. "But Grabowski had an agent. He was one of the first players to use one. And after we learned his financial demands, we knew we couldn't sign him.

"The Packers—because of their peculiar public ownership structure by which the profits are never disbursed to the stockholders—had tons of money, a whole lot of cash. So for them drafting and signing players like Grabowski was not necessarily a problem.

"But that wasn't the case in, say, Pittsburgh. Because of this bidding war against the AFL, the teams on the low end of the finance chain were using first-round drafts on guys who should have been in the third or fourth round, because they were the only ones they could afford. By the end of the 1965 season, the draft was totally predicated on whether you could sign your player.

"After [the Cowboys] learned that we couldn't sign Jim Grabowski, we flew John Niland, a guard, from Iowa to Washington, D.C., where the Cowboys were playing the Redskins. I didn't even go to the game. I spent the entire day in a hotel negotiating with John Niland. We signed him, and the next day we drafted him.

"So it had become obvious that the system that had made the league was gone, and, more sooner than later, just a few teams would own everybody."

Schramm said, "I went to Pete and said, 'We've gotta do something and I have got an idea. I can pull off the merger, but I'll be the only person involved from our league [the NFL], and the only person I'll talk to is you. And I'll pick one other man from the other league, and he'll have to make the same promise.' And Pete agreed."

From the very day that the upstart AFL was organized in 1960, the NFL establishment had launched active efforts to smother the life out of the infant rival league. In an owners' meeting, George Halas of the Bears offered what he deemed a delightful suggestion. Halas's idea was to place an NFL expansion franchise in Dallas. At that time the AFL Texans were regarded as the linchpin operation of the new league. It was Halas's hope that competition would kill the Texans and that the American Football League would die with them. After three seasons the Texans did indeed leave Dallas for Kansas City (for a time owner Lamar Hunt wanted to call the team the Kansas City Texans), but the American Football League remained afloat.

Naturally, the person that Tex Schramm selected to negotiate the AFL's interests in the merger was none other than Lamar Hunt. "We met initially at Love Field [the Dallas airport] in the lobby beneath the statue of the Texas Ranger [inscribed "One Riot—One Ranger"], and then we went outside and talked in my car. Later, all of the meetings were at Lamar Hunt's house, and after a few weeks the deal was done," Schramm said.

"When the negotiations came to an end, the plan called for the Jets to move out of New York and for Oakland to move away from the Bay Area. This had been agreed to and approved by both leagues. But at the last minute we were afraid of legal complications, so we changed the deal to money."

According to Schramm, that involved indemnity payments from the AFL to the San Francisco 49ers for $8 million and the New York Giants for $10 million, paid out over eighteen years. Also, the Giants would receive an extra first-round draft choice that would be used to bring in a marquee quarterback capable of competing with the Jets' Joe Namath.

The plan also called for the creation of what is now known as the Super Bowl. "At first the franchise structure was to remain as it was in 1966," revealed Schramm. "But then Al Davis out in Oakland made an impassioned plea. I'll never forget this, he said, 'What am I going to say when I wake up in the morning, my kids look at the newspaper and they say, "Daddy, why have we [the AFL] only got eight teams and they [the NFL] have twelve teams?" What'll I tell my kids?' So it was agreed to send three existing NFL franchises over to the AFL. We asked for volunteers and there were no takers. So we offered $3 million, and Cleveland, Baltimore, and Pittsburgh agreed to make the switch. And that," concluded Schramm, "is how the great NFL-AFL merger took place."

One might wonder how one individual like Tex Schramm, the general manager of a franchise located on the horizontal prairie of North Texas, light-years from the media centers in New York and L.A., could throw around that kind of influence in the political structure within the National Football League. But Tex Schramm was never just another GM, just as he was never just another sportswriter after he graduated with his journalism degree from the University of Texas in Austin.

It has been written that in order for someone to be called Tex, he first must move away from Texas. In Schramm's case, the name on his birth certificate reads "Texas E. Schramm, Junior." "Tex told me that, as a kid, he was hyperactive, although they didn't call it that at the time," said Frank Luksa, a Dallas sportswriter who covered the Cowboys almost from the beginning days of the franchise. "Never could sit still, certainly never long enough to read a book. The only way that he finished college was that his wife, Marty, would read the course material to him out loud."

By his senior year at UT, Schramm was the sports editor. Not of the college paper, the *Daily Texan,* but of the big-city paper, the *Austin Statesman.* Schramm's father had been a business associate of Dan Reeves (not to be confused with the football coach), a well-heeled wheel horse in L.A. who bought the Cleveland Rams and moved the team to the coast in the late 1940s. Schramm, who had personal ambitions that did not coincide with the salary of a sportswriter, secured a job as the PR director of the Los Angeles Rams. By the mid-1950s Schramm essentially was running the team. He understood what most NFL executives did not at that time: Professional football, using television as its power source, was poised to become a tremendous growth industry in the entertainment world. While Schramm was working for Dan Reeves, pro football and television had been dating, but they had not yet gone to bed. "Up until then pro football had failed to capture the public imagination," Schramm said. "It was just catching on when the Bears beat the Redskins 73–0 in the 1940 championship game. But the war came along, and people lost interest again."

Even throughout the 1950s, on-the-field fighting was as prevalent in pro football as it was in the National Hockey League. Promoters assumed that this was what the public wanted. "Most of the teams maintained some kind of haphazard TV arrangement," Schramm said. "George Preston Marshall, owner of the Redskins, had one of the better setups, a network that covered the entire southern United States. It wasn't by chance that the Redskins were the last team in the league to integrate. They also had this huge band, dressed in Indian costumes, and before every game they would march up and down the field playing 'Dixie,' if you can imagine that."

In 1957, Tex Schramm took a job as an associate producer with CBS Sports and moved to New York. Schramm says that he made the move partly because Dan Reeves was drinking heavily, and life at the Rams' headquarters often seemed too hectic. Before abandoning L.A.,

Schramm handpicked another ex-journalist, Pete Rozelle, to replace him as the Rams' general manager.

At CBS, which owned the TV rights to the NFL telecasts, Schramm quickly became an innovator. It was Schramm who convinced the network to buy the rights to the 1960 Winter Olympics at Squaw Valley, California, and it was Schramm who convinced Walter Cronkite to work as an anchorman for a sporting event. The U.S. ice hockey team upset the Soviets for the gold medal, and CBS celebrated a ratings coup.

When NFL commissioner Bert Bell died suddenly in 1959, Schramm convinced the league to think ahead. With the league now experiencing unprecedented popular appeal, the last thing it needed was some stodgy coot from the old school running the show. Think young, Schramm told the league. Bring in some bright kid. Somebody like Pete Rozelle.

Things were happening fast in Tex's life. When the NFL hastily acted on George Halas's idea to place an expansion franchise in Dallas in 1960, Tex sensed a once-in-a-lifetime opportunity. The person who agreed to finance the franchise, Clint Murchison, Jr., was a billionaire back when a billion was a lot of cabbage. Murchison let it be known to Schramm that he had no interest in actively participating in the operations of the team. Tex gazed into the future, and what he perceived was power and influence. He packed his bags.

Dallas, Texas, had become the ideal grazing land for persons of Tex Schramm's tastes and temperament. Since the end of World War II, Dallas had been the center of the largest metropolitan area in the entire world that did not have access to a seaway.

Why? There was no heavy industry in Dallas. No manufacturing at all, to speak of. Dallas County and Tarrant County (Fort Worth) were the only counties in Texas that had never produced an oil well. The landscape offered no particular appeal. You could find bigger trees on the moon. The city was bisected by a muddy little stream called the Trinity River, with water that looked like gingerbread batter. In the summer the heat reached levels that melted people's fingernails. About three hundred years ago, the Spanish explorers actually tried to ride camels through the region, and they all died of heat exhaustion.

So why this boomtown amid all this apparent nothingness? The answer: When Jesus chased all of the money changers out of the temple, they all moved to Dallas—international headquarters of opportunists, hucksters, and people who like to play cards.

Dallas is insurance, banks, investment houses, advertising and PR, civil law, fashion retail, and every other known activity that does not require hard work. In a TV show called *Dallas,* on which supposedly prototypical Texans were portrayed, actor Larry Hagman, as J. R. Ewing, pranced around each week in a cowboy hat and boots. In reality, nobody of consequence in the mercantile realm of Big D would be caught dead in a getup like that. Dallas is the realm of the coin. Several counties away, off to the south and the east, in the 1930s, some promoters discovered an oil pool approximately the size of the Caspian Sea. When a Japanese naval officer named Isoroku Yamamoto toured North America and beheld the magnitude of the East Texas oil field, he returned home and discouraged military leaders from attempting conflict with the United States. He realized that the Japanese war machine would eventually run out of gas and that the United States would not.

The men who reaped ungodly fortunes from that oil patch came to Dallas to bank and invest the money. Two such individuals were the fathers of Clint Murchison and Lamar Hunt. As the story goes, once upon a time there was a Texan so rich that he bought a little boy so that his dog would have someone to play with. That would not have been completely out of the question in Dallas. Not all of the rich Texans lived in Dallas. But they would fly in from someplace like Midland, drop fifty grand at Neiman Marcus on shoes and perfume, and fly back out again.

Not surprisingly, the homecoming queens from one out of every two high schools within a seven-hundred-mile radius would soon find the way to Dallas, the kind of young women who always keep their noses to the rhinestone. Finding a woman in Dallas who is actually from Dallas is not easy.

In January 1960, one more pretty face arrived in town. Alicia Landry could have been a movie star. That's what everybody said. When Vince Lombardi, Jr., was growing up in New York, he had a hopeless crush on the wife of the defensive coordinator who coached the Giants along with his father, before he moved to Green Bay. "I thought that she was"—and here Lombardi pauses for a moment to select the appropriate word—"neat."

It would be inaccurate to suggest that Clint Murchison would have hired Tom Landry whether he had known how to coach or not. But everybody agreed that Tom—a former football star at UT who was flying a B-17 in combat missions over Europe at age nineteen—and Alicia made a handsome couple.

With Tex building the business operation, Tom constructing the football portion of it, and Clint writing the checks, a prudent betting man could only presume that the franchise was here to stay. Even with those assets in place, the Dallas Cowboys of the early years struggled mightily. While Halas and the others had been quick to establish the team, Papa Bear would also see to it that the new team would pose no threat in the win column.

The new franchise did not participate in the league draft prior to its first season. The entire roster started out composed of castoffs and orthopedic disasters from the other twelve teams. Typical was halfback L. G. (Long Gone) Dupre, who had been a starter for the Colts in their heralded overtime championship win over the New York Giants. What was long gone by now was Dupre's ability to cut upfield for a first down.

Landry's quarterback, Eddie LeBaron, looked more like a jockey than an NFL passer. The 1960 Cowboys played and lost the first eleven games on the schedule. In the twelfth game, the season finale at Yankee Stadium, they managed a 31–31 tie.

During the off-season, however, Landry quickly determined that the talent deficit between his team and the rest of the league was so significant that no quick fix would happen soon. The team did draft the cornerstone of its defense, Bob Lilly from TCU, after that ridiculous campaign, and the Cowboys upset the Steelers with a whirlwind finish in the 1961 season opener. After that it was business as usual.

For the second straight year, Dallas's top draft choice came from Texas Christian University in Fort Worth. At six seven, Sonny Gibbs, unlike Eddie LeBaron, at least looked like an NFL quarterback. It was Gibbs, on media day at TCU, who told reporters of his desire to graduate from college. "I want to get that pigskin, or sheepskin, or whatever the fuck you call it," he said. Sonny Gibbs did not turn out to be Tom Landry's kind of guy. The only contributor in the entire draft was defensive end George Andrie, selected sixth. After two seasons the Dallas Cowboys were stuck in reverse.

The on-the-field difficulty was amplified by the Cowboys' uniforms. White helmets, white pants that drooped in the butt, stars on the shoulders. The team looked like a bunch of dorks. The Cowboys were running a dead heat with the Denver Broncos, who played in socks with vertical stripes, for the tackiest uniforms in professional sports.

"I designed those uniforms," conceded Tex Schramm, "and they were a . . . bad try." Then he quickly took credit for drawing up the new look, the sleek silver and blue that premiered with the opening of the regular season in 1964 and became the trademark for the team that finally became one of the sparkle franchises in North America.

"The team was shitty, but Tex maintained great damage control," said sportswriter Frank Luksa of the early years. "He understood the media and how to manage them better than any executive in the history of sports. That's why he insisted to Rozelle that Dallas play in the NFL East. He wanted to go against the Giants and Redskins twice a year because that's where the media were.

"He would fly the Dallas reporters to the road games at the Cowboys' expense, just to expand the coverage. We had total access, always, to the players and the staff." In those early years, Southwest Conference football ruled the sports pages, and high school football served as a second religion for much of the population. The Cowboys, in fact, were fighting the Garland Owls and the Arlington Heights Yellow Jackets for headlines in the Dallas and Fort Worth papers.

As a goodwill gesture, Tex saw to it that key writers were invited to Clint Murchison's private island off Florida for a week of fun and fishing. On the road, the media were wined, dined, and wined some more. On one memorable occasion, an overserved photographer for a Dallas newspaper invited himself to join the table of Tom and Alicia Landry at Bookbinder's restaurant in Philadelphia and proceeded to pass out, face first, into a bowl of minestrone. Henceforth the Soup Nose Award was presented annually to the member of the Cowboys media corps who made the biggest ass of himself on the road.

For coach Tom Landry, it could not be said that the early years of the franchise were especially rewarding.

CHAPTER 2

One of the prime benefits of working as a columnist for the *Fort Worth Press,* other than the spectacular salary that eventually allowed me to become a major shareholder in Whitewater Savings and Loan, was the opportunity to meet and interview a fair number of major celebrities. The late 1960s proved to be a particularly active time for that stuff, when I shared my insights with everybody from the Flying Nun to Big Lyndon himself. I spent an entire afternoon sitting in a house trailer in Colorado Springs, drinking scotch with Lucille Ball, who said, "People can say what they want to about Desi Arnaz, but when it comes to business sense, he's the smartest son of a bitch who ever walked into Hollywood."

But the one encounter that sticks foremost in my mind happened in 1968 when I sat down at my assigned seat in the press box at the Cotton Bowl and noticed that the person at my immediate left was Vince Lombardi. Green Bay had come to Dallas to play the Cowboys, and by then Lombardi had retired as the coach but was still working as the Packers' general manager and thus was relegated upstairs. If anybody doubted that the image of the man's forceful presence happened to be something that was enlarged by the media, I can report that, at close range, the Lombardi personality offered all of the dynamic qualities that the newspapers described.

As many books have been written (or so it seems) about Vince Lombardi and the Green Bay Packers as about Abraham Lincoln and the Civil War. People recall that in that season, 1968, living in self-imposed exile left Lombardi far from his cherished terrain along the Packer sidelines, and Lombardi became withdrawn, sullen, depressed.

Lombardi seemed anything but like a saddened and disenfranchised man during that Packers-Cowboys game. Although the season had advanced to a point where it was clear that the Packers were headed into a steep decline ("Seven games into the year and they still stink," Lombardi muttered when the Pack fell behind 10–0), they managed to upset the Cowboys, and half of downtown Dallas could have been lit up on the energy that Lombardi seemed to radiate as the game progressed. On one play, when the Packers ran their power sweep—the trademark of Lombardi football jurisdiction—halfback Elijah Pitts took the football from Bart Starr and had not run two steps when Vince jumped to his feet and shouted, "He's gone!" Lombardi sat down, quickly and sheepishly, realizing that he had violated the "no cheering in the press box" edict. But Pitts *was* gone, by God, on a touchdown run of about fifty or sixty yards. In the proximity of greatness like that, I almost felt impelled to ask Lombardi for his autograph. In the ranks of the sportswriter fraternity, that's a hanging offense. But at halftime I rode the elevator downstairs, bought a beer (they didn't serve any in the press box) and delivered it to the coach. Even though he didn't want it, it seemed like the right thing to do. Lombardi appeared absorbed with the events on the Cotton Bowl floor during the half. When a float carrying some young women rolled onto the field in a typical Dallas tit-and-ass show, Lombardi exclaimed, "What the hell's that?" and grabbed his binoculars. Then he grinned and said, "No harm in looking."

When the game was over and I was leaving the Packers' dressing room after conducting the standard interviews, Lombardi saw me and actually smiled and waved. If you'd have put a mustache and a cowboy hat on Vince when he smiled, you'd have had a spitting image of Teddy Roosevelt. Lombardi had less than two years to live, but there was an allure about the man that left an indelible impression—a do-the-right-thing kind of person. He made me feel almost ashamed that, twenty minutes before the game, I'd been out in the Cotton Bowl parking lot scalping my comp tickets for thirty bucks.

Almost three decades later, I was on the telephone with Vince Lombardi, Jr. The coach's son lived in the Seattle area, where he had moved to work as an executive for the Seahawks football team. Now he traveled the country as a professional motivational speaker. I asked Lombardi about the television ad campaign for a shoe company that used a comedian to portray his father.

Lombardi Junior said that a friend of his who writes books, a fellow named David Halberstam, had called him recently, all upset. Halberstam thought the commercials had crossed the parody line and entered the land of sacrilege. "I told David that I actually thought the spots were reasonably entertaining and that Jerry Stiller had done a really proficient job in portraying my father. I approved the spots. And my family *was* compensated for that promotion, too. Not a princely sum—but enough," he confirmed.

The fact that Lombardi, or at least the memory of a figure from what now certainly qualifies as the distant past, would be selected as a focal point of a major and multimillion-dollar marketing push, seems remarkable. You damn sure don't see any comic actors playing LBJ to hawk, say, Goodyear Tires. And while I probably won't be around to collect, I am willing to cast a small wager that thirty years hence, there will not be any Jimmy Johnson impersonators selling Bud Lite.

Willie Davis, the Hall of Fame defensive tackle for the Packers, has said, "To me, Vince Lombardi never left, never died." Apparently, Willie is right.

SOMEBODY ONCE POINTED out that modern America has evolved into the only society in the history of the earth that takes money more seriously than death. If that indeed has become the case, then imagine a community like Green Bay, where they take football more seriously than money and death is a joke. At the Lyndahl Funeral Home, people can get planted in green-and-gold caskets.

The most unusual enduring entry in the history of big league professional sports in the United States started in 1921 when Curly Lambeau, a frustrated ex-jock, staged a meeting in the composing room of the *Green Bay Press-Gazette* and organized a team. Curly had played in the same backfield with George Gipp at Notre Dame, and he missed the grandeur of playing before a crowd. Besides, Prohibition had become the law of the land, and Lambeau thought the folks in Green Bay might need a new recreational distraction.

After assembling his team, Lambeau made a sales call at the Indian Packing Company in Green Bay. Nowhere is it recorded that Lambeau told them that he wanted to go out and "win a few for the Gipper up there in heaven." But Curly walked out with a check that would buy the football team's uniforms—on the stipulation of the sponsor that the team would be known as the Packers. Green Bay Packers. Nice ring, nice strong consonant sounds.

Curly had put up $50 of his own money to purchase an entry fee in what was known as the American Professional Football Association, and his Packers went unbeaten that year, 1921—up until the last game, which they lost, 6–0. One must dig deeply into the dusty files to learn that the Pack's first ever loss (nowhere is it inscribed in Lambeau Field) came at the hands of a team that called itself the Beloit Fairies.

Fans passed the hat at Packers games that season. Lambeau collected enough to fund the team again when it joined something called the National Football League. Professional football of that era ranked with the two-headed pygmies and the fat lady in a carnival tent show in terms of public esteem, a situation that persisted to some extent into the 1950s. While pioneer franchises in venues like Pottsville, Hammond, Racine, and Duluth passed away quickly of natural causes, the people of Green Bay forged an early bond with their Packers. Lambeau refinanced his team in 1923 with the funds from a dance and rally at the Elks Club. People showed up for that event rather than listen to the Jack Dempsey–Louis Firpo heavyweight fight on the radio the same night.

By then, Curly owned a real gate attraction, a running star named John McNally, who played under the stage name of Johnny Blood. When McNally and a companion came to Green Bay, McNally had suggested that they use aliases. As they drove past a movie house, McNally noticed that the silent film epic *Blood and Sand* was playing. "That's it," McNally told his friend. "You be Sand and I'll be Blood."

The Lambeau-Blood partnership became a grand alliance. Lambeau, the player-owner-coach, offered Blood a hefty wage of $100 a game on the stipulation that Blood arrive in time for the kickoff and $110 if he agreed to remain sober the night before the game. "I'll take the hundred," Blood agreed. A kindred spirit with Blood in certain aspects, Lambeau devoted more and more of his off-season hours to frolics with the pretty people in Hollywood and New York. Johnny Blood liked to recite Shakespeare, and ran for sheriff in Green Bay on a campaign that promised the restoration of "honest wrestling." Both were avid outdoorsmen, forever on the quest of the trophy skirt.

They were the best of teams. They were the worst of teams. In 1929, 1930, and 1931, the Green Bay Packers won the National Football League championship. After big wins on the road, Packers fans would gather after midnight to greet the team train, lining the tracks and carrying torches. Whenever Curly's finances became thin, he could always rely on the Packer backers to bail him out. The ultimate bailout happened in 1950, when the fans bought the team. About 1,900 investors bought stock at $25 a share, the stipulation being that nobody could own more than twenty shares. If the team were ever sold, a stipulation in the corporate charter dictated that profits would be forwarded to the Sullivan-Wallen American Legion post in Green Bay.

In the cold days of early February 1959, the board made a decision that drastically and forever altered the future of the franchise and the league. After the Packers had completed a 1–10–1 season in 1958, embarrassing the stockholders and shaming the town, it was agreed that Coach Scooter McLean had to be replaced.

Tony Canadeo, a Packers fullback in the days when Curly Lambeau was still coaching, had become a person of influence on the Packers' executive committee. Paul Brown, coach of the almighty Cleveland Browns, issued a hot tip to Canadeo. If the Packers were truly intent upon retooling the team, Brown told Canadeo, the one man who could expedite the task could be found in New York, where he worked as an assistant coach with the Giants. He ran the offense. Canadeo had heard of Vince Lombardi, but only as a guard on a famous line that somebody had named "the Seven Blocks of Granite" at Fordham College.

A possible hang-up loomed: Jim Lee Howell was due to retire soon as the Giants' head coach, and Lombardi was rumored as his likely replacement. Another potential drawback was the actuality that Lombardi and his wife, Marie, were a couple devoted to city life. A question lingered as to whether this duo might be willing to move off to a town that billed itself as "the toilet paper capital of the world."

After one meeting with the board, the members from Green Bay were immediately convinced that Vince was their boy. They were delighted with his eagerness to plunge into the head-coaching ranks of the NFL. He signed a five-year contract.

Lee Remmel, who was helping to cover the Packers at the time for the *Green Bay Press-Gazette,* remembers his first exposure to Vince Lombardi. "They held a press conference to announce his hiring at a downtown Green Bay hotel. I didn't know who he was. Lombardi was nationally obscure, and I was surprised at how confident he was of his ability to succeed. He said, 'You are going to be proud of this Green Bay team because *I* will be proud of this team.'

"And he was right."

Lombardi's background was a little peculiar for an NFL head coach, then or now. Vince had devoted years to coaching at Saint Cecilia High School in Englewood, New Jersey. High school coaches seldom, if ever, become head coaches in the NFL. Lombardi received the opportunity that changed his life when Colonel Earl "Red" Blaik hired Vince as an assistant at West Point.

If Blaik's Army teams were not the best teams in the land, they were close to it. Blaik himself told an oft-repeated story concerning Lombardi and his temper. First week on the job, Vince was attempting to correct the work habits of one of his linemen, and the coach was doing it Lombardi style. Just as he seemed poised to peel the kid's skull, Blaik sprinted across the practice field. "*Vince! Vince!*" he screamed. "We don't coach that way at West Point!"

Perhaps that incident at the academy led to Lombardi's willingness to accept the head coach post at Green Bay. Now he could coach any damn way he pleased.

An offensive tackle laboring for the Packers, Forrest Gregg, was like Lee Remmel. He'd never heard of Vince Lombardi. "I was living in and working in Dallas in the off-season, and the papers didn't cover the NFL like they do now. But I saw a little item in the sports section that said that Lombardi had been hired as head coach of the Packers. I had a friend, Tiny Goss (about six-foot-seven and 290 pounds) who I had played with at SMU and he'd gone on to play with the Giants for a couple of years. I called him and asked him if he knew anything about Lombardi. He said, 'Yeah. I know him. He's a real bastard.' So naturally, before I reported to training camp, I was curious about who I would encounter."

Lombardi, on the other hand, held no curiosity about Forrest Gregg. He knew what he had. When Lombardi took charge, he devoted his first weeks to the dismal chore of studying game films of the Packers' 1–10–1 campaign. Then Lombardi reported to the board of directors and announced, "Gentlemen, there is only one professional football player in the whole organization. It's that number 75 . . . Gregg."

Of course, Gregg never knew about that evaluation. It was just as well. Just because Forrest Gregg might be the one player that Lombardi had somehow come to respect in no way meant that the coach would cut him any slack on the practice field. The previous season, some of the veterans had conned Coach McLean into the notion that training camp should move at a humane and leisurely pace. The NFL season was a long one, so why not allow these seasoned pros to play their way into shape as the year progressed? "Come on, Scooter," was the theme that Forrest Gregg remembered in 1958. "Let's blow off the scrimmage and go have a beer."

Forrest Gregg and defensive back John Symank had driven from Texas to join Lombardi's first training camp in August 1959. "We stopped in Milwaukee and called Dave Hanner [a tackle], who had arrived in camp early," Gregg said. "I asked Dave how things were going and I was curious about the new coach and Hanner said, 'Whoo-eee.' And I said, 'What do you mean—whoo-eee?' And Dave said, 'Man, get ready. He's gonna kill us.' We'd planned to stay over in Milwaukee that night but decided then it might be a better idea to get on up there to camp.

"When we checked in that night, I told one of the equipment boys that since it was late, not to wake me for breakfast. But early the next morning, the kid came into my room and said, 'Coach Lombardi wants to see you in the cafeteria.'

"So I went down there and he introduced himself. Full head of curly hair. Big smile. Very cordial. He said the bus was leaving for practice and encouraged me to be on it."

Gregg distinctly remembers his first on-the-field experience involving the new coach. "The workout was tough, and my tongue was hanging out. Then, from across the field, I heard someone screaming. It was Lombardi. Max McGee had run a pass pattern and made the mistake of walking back to the huddle. Lombardi was chasing Max to the huddle, really chipping away at him. Wherever I had played before—high school, college, or pro—the coaches were never afraid to tie into the linemen, but laid off the skill-position guys. I remember thinking, 'At least this Lombardi guy is going to spread it around. This might be all right after all.' "

The extent of the change of training camp lifestyle under Lombardi was almost melodramatic. Right away, Packers players were exposed to a conditioning routine that Lombardi called the grass drill: The squad assembles on the practice field and runs in place. On command, the players flop on their bellies, then hop up again, knees churning. Then, wham, drop backward, then up again. Leonard Shechter, a writer, described the activity in a piece that appeared in *Esquire.* The man doing all the yelling is Vince Lombardi.

"C'mon, lift those legs. Lift 'em. Higher. Higher. Front!" and the players flop on their bellies and as soon as they do, the coach shouts, "Up!" Then it's "Move those damn legs! This is the worst looking thing I ever saw. Move your legs. Keep 'em moving. What's wrong, Davis? You told me you were in shape. Move those legs, dammit! What the hell's the matter with you guys?! You gotta lotta dog in you! You're dogs, I tell you. A bunch of dogs! Let's *move.* For the love of Christ, you're all fat. Ten bucks a day for every pound you don't lose. Ten bucks a day! *Lift those legs!*"

After about twenty minutes (sometimes longer) of grass drill, the bloodletting would begin in earnest. Full-bore scrimmages, twice a day. God, did those players miss Scooter McLean! If they felt hopeless and miserable in that will-shattering camp of 1959, Lombardi shared the outlook. Or at least that's what he claimed. "After the first day of practice, I walked into the trainer's room and I wanted to cry," Lombardi said. " 'What is this?' I yelled. 'A hospital emergency ward? Let's get this straight. When you're hurt, you have every right to be here. But this is disgraceful. I have no patience with the small hurts that are bothering most of you. You are going to have to live with small hurts and play with small hurts if you are going to play for me!' "

Here, Lombardi demonstrated that he was simply a chip off the old Block of Granite. Vince's father, Harry, lived his life according to the beat of a few spartan theme songs, and one of his favorites was the one that went, "Pain is in the mind." After a tough game at Fordham that left Vince's face looking like the garage floor after the St. Valentine's Day Massacre, a doctor sewed thirty stitches inside his mouth. "That night, my mind hurt a lot," Vince was fond of recalling. Now, late in the afternoon, with the foam around their lips hardening into a white glue, the new Green Bay Packers had Harry Lombardi, partially, to thank for their plight.

By the time that the regular season began, it remained uncertain as to whether the Packers were highly conditioned and motivated or simply stir-crazy, but they rattled off three consecutive wins. "We felt that we were a select bunch of people," said Ray Nitschke. Those first three wins were followed by a five-game losing streak. Then the Packers regained their earlier form and chased the almighty Baltimore

Colts across the finish line for the NFL's Western Conference championship.

Willie Davis, asked to recall the early days of the Lombardi reign of tyranny, said, "I am not sure now what it was like. But we learned early that under Lombardi, winning was the easy way out. That was sort of our unofficial motto. You had to win for this man or you were in real trouble." Davis probably did not realize it at the time, but he had it soft. He played on the defensive side. The players who received the full force of the Lombardi Doctrine were his offensive linemen. Lombardi had taught physics back at St. Cecilia High School, and according to Vince's self-discovered natural laws of football sciences, the fulcrum of the team had to be its offensive line.

"The offensive line must function not as the keys to a typewriter but as one man. Timing and rhythm, it's a subtle thing. Take out one of the parts and you look like a bunch of rookies, destroying the best plays ever devised." That's chiseled into a stone tablet somewhere on Mount Sinai. Lombardi went to exceptional lengths to certify that his offensive linemen were the best-conditioned players on the team—thus less susceptible to injury. Loss of an offensive lineman, Lombardi thought, screwed up the intricate timing that was so necessary to advancing the ball in the NFL.

In a team meeting, the coach assembled his oxen. "You know you'll get banged up, and you hope it ain't serious. The offensive lineman must be dedicated to perfection and recognize that perfection can be achieved only through the drudgery of practice. There are no shortcuts to success in football, and the individual who tries to find them will lose his way." Forrest Gregg heard Lombardi make that speech during the first week of training camp in 1959. He suspected that he might hear it again and again through the years and, boy, was he right. "An offensive lineman seldom finds his name in headlines. I know. I was one myself," Vince liked to remind the troops. "The band seldom plays for him. But when he does his job . . . he knows it." And when he didn't, Forrest Gregg confirmed, Vince was always there to remind him.

Lombardi realized that for his power sweep to work properly, his offensive line had to be brainwashed. That sweep wasn't merely the priority play in Vince's offensive scheme. The power sweep, in Lombardi's estimation, pealed across the heavens like a symphony. The coach had learned all about it in college, playing for Fordham against

Pitt, when he was almost trampled by Jock Sutherland's single-wing attack.

"There's nothing spectacular about it. It's just a ground-gainer," Lombardi said. But after a season or so of working for Lombardi, the players sensed that the coach thought there was something almost erotic about the sweep when they worked it right. At least, Lombardi owned up to the rush he would feel on the sideline when "you hear those linebackers and defensive backs yell, 'sweep!' and you can see their eyes almost pop out when they see those guards turning upfield and coming after them. Maybe it's my number one play because all eleven men play as one to make it succeed and that's what 'team' means."

That sweep, though Lombardi portrayed it as a simple tool, like a crowbar, actually included some intricate subplots in its execution for it to function at its diabolic best. The crux of the play involved the tight end. Lombardi used two players at that position during his nine-year tour with the Packers. First Ron Kramer had labored there and later, when the coach sensed that Kramer might be edging beyond his prime, Marv Fleming took the job.

The coach's message to the tight end regarding the power sweep went like this: "Position yourself six to nine feet outside the offensive tackle . . . isolate the end or linebacker . . . depending upon the defensive alignment and never, I repeat, *never* . . . allow that man inside penetration." Failure to comply would result in a quick ticket back to a job within the more conventional elements of the American workforce. Those ends got notified of that on a daily basis.

Paul Hornung won a Heisman Trophy playing for a Notre Dame team that posted wins in only two of the ten games on the Fighting Irish schedule in 1956—quite a feat. But the Green Bay Packers' power sweep made him famous. "Paul doesn't have great speed, but he's a quick and intelligent runner who uses his blockers to gain every possible yard out of every play," Vince said.

That power sweep, with some variations that came on when Hornung became handy with a halfback-option pass play, carried Green Bay into the 1960 championship game against Philadelphia, quarterbacked by Norm Van Brocklin. Ted Dean made a five-yard TD on a gooey playing surface at Franklin Field that enabled the Eagles to win the game, 17–13. Green Bay almost scored late, but the NFL's last sixty-minute man, Chuck Bednarik (aka Concrete Charlie) tackled Jim Taylor on the last play of the great lineman's career.

Packers players staged a wake in the locker room afterward. Lombardi wasn't sympathetic. "The biggest tragedy of this loss was that you guys didn't recognize that you were good enough to win," he told the team. But by 1961, the Packers and their sweep surged through the NFL schedule like General George Patton's tank and infantry corps advancing through a Girl Scout camp. The championship game against Lombardi's former employers, the Giants, became nothing more than another routine search-and-destroy mission, with the Packers winning at Lambeau Field, 37–0. What an ass-kicking. Over in Minnesota, which is ice hockey country, devotees of the sport like to think of themselves as Puckheads. Now, in Wisconsin, it was even more fashionable to be a Packerhead.

The 1962 season worked out essentially as a replica of '61. The championship game, once again, featured the Packers and the Giants, this time in dreadful weather conditions at Yankee Stadium. With the game blacked out on television in New York, a radio newsman commented on the bumper-to-bumper traffic moving toward Philadelphia, where TV coverage would be available. "Imagine going to Philadelphia on a Sunday," the radio man bawled. "What's happening to the human race?"

TV broadcaster Ray Scott wondered the same thing. "They had me and Chris Schenkel perched up on some platform, a photo deck, up on the damn roof along the right field line, to call the game," Scott said. "It was nine degrees, the wind was blowing forty miles an hour, and I was miserable. By the fourth quarter, we were so cold, it was almost impossible to describe the game because our jaws couldn't work anymore. All that came out of my mouth was sounds like 'nnnpph and gguuhhh.' "

New York columnist Red Smith wrote of the game in the now defunct *New York Herald Tribune:* "Polar gales clawed topsoil off the barren playground and whipped it in tan whirlwinds about the great concrete chasm of Yankee Stadium. One minute, fifty seconds remained in the struggle for the championship of the National League, but no hope at all remained for New York. Allie Sherman's men had no arms to combat and no armor to fend off the finest team in the professional game. The defending champions from little Green Bay,

Wisconsin, established themselves once more as despots of the mercenary world."

Vince Lombardi, Jr., remembers some occasions when his mother would yell at the commander of the mercenary despots because he had forgotten to carry out the garbage. "Like anybody else, he had his frailties," the son recalled. "But the characterization of the hard and demanding disciplinarian with the Packers was essentially what he was, and he dealt with me the same way that he dealt with those players.

"It was tough, although I think I might have made it tougher on myself than I had to," Lombardi Junior says, not exactly relishing the memories of playing high school football in Green Bay when his father was coaching another team in the same town.

As the years began to roll past, Forrest Gregg continued to wait for Vince Lombardi to ease the labor-intensive atmosphere that prevailed in Green Bay. Gregg would learn that such yearnings were like hoping that Stalin might someday take up badminton. Lombardi, after he quit coaching, chose to single out Gregg as "quite simply, the finest football player I ever saw."

"But when I reported for preseason training camp at St. Norbert's College, I was treated no differently than any free agent walk-on. I would once again have to prove that I belonged and earn a spot in the starting lineup," Gregg said. The Vince Lombardi of 1961 was the same Vince Lombardi who would greet the team in '67. The grass drill routine remained as ruthless as it always had been. Incredibly, most of the faces in the starting lineup were the same, too. Linebackers Bill Quinlan and Dan Curry had been replaced by Lee Roy Caffey and Dave Robinson. Jesse Whittenton, Hank Gremminger, and John Symank were gone from the secondary, replaced there by Bob Jeter, Herb Adderley, and Tom Brown. Ron Kostelnik was playing one defensive tackle spot instead of Dave Hanner, who was now an assistant coach.

Jim Ringo was not playing center in Green Bay anymore. When Ringo sent an agent representative to Lombardi to negotiate a new contract, the GM-coach took approximately 100 seconds to complete a trade that sent Ringo packing to Philadelphia. Hornung and Taylor were gone by '67, replaced by high-dollar newcomers Donny Anderson and Jim Grabowski. "Vince said that he hated it, having to pay that kind of money to rookies during the old AFL-NFL bidding war," said Tony Canadeo, still the Packers' president. "But he said we had to spend the money to keep those kids from going to the other league. Vince took care of the team's money better than he did his own."

A core group, however, remained on the team. Gregg, Fuzzy Thurston, Bart Starr, Bob Skronski, Willie Davis, Ray Nitschke, Willie Wood, Boyd Dowler, Max McGee, Henry Jordan, Jerry Kramer. They'd all come back again to endure the grass drill, the repetition, the torture, and the grind so that they might win one more, one final championship.

In Green Bay, the town that in essence was the home of the world's greatest high school football team, Vince Lombardi endured as God. One Green Bay man, a roofing contractor named Howie Blindaur, actually mustered the temerity to have a lien slapped on God's house. Because of some dispute, Lombardi had refused to pay Blindaur for work done at the coach's house. Blindaur, being one of the umpteen little stockholders in the Packers, was, in his own way, Vince's boss.

So Vince and Howie went at it jaw to jaw, and after a twenty-minute shouting session, Howie got his check. To this day, though, he's never cashed it.

After Lombardi quit coaching, one of the players who felt he'd yielded a little too much flesh to the coach's bullwhip, announced, "This season will show the public, the nation, and football who *really* won all those championships." So it did. After Lombardi left, the Packers fell on their ass and pretty much stayed there for the next twenty-five years.

CHAPTER 3

Programming executives at NBC stood in mutual agreement when the network's new fall lineup for 1966 had been finalized. One new program stood out among the other prime time entries as an almost certain candidate to flop. This program, *Star Trek,* would be based on the adventures of space voyagers who dared to boldly go where no man had gone before. When Cowboys scouting director Gil Brandt heard that, he thought that the show might be about him.

Brandt, with the endorsement of Coach Tom Landry, had embarked on some bush-beating explorations that shattered precedents for National Football League scouts. With a thin and aging talent pool that left Dallas noncompetitive on the NFL battleground, Landry and Brandt agreed that creative, if not extreme, steps would be required to locate new and better sources of personnel. In short, Landry thought that the Dallas Cowboys desperately lacked good athletes. So Brandt embarked on a nationwide search for people who were known as "Moose" when they were still in grade school. While the remainder of the pro football establishment watched and tittered, Brandt began combing some out-of-the-way colonies where electricity was considered a novelty. He located and signed tight end Pettis Norman and defensive tackle Jethro Pugh from Johnson C. Smith College and Elizabeth City State, respectively—two schools that infrequently appeared on Notre Dame's schedule.

Brandt, an ex-baby photographer from Wisconsin, was also of the opinion that professional football, basically, was a sport for cavemen and easily mastered by individuals with limited experience, or no experience at all, in the arts and sciences of the gridiron. Thus, Cornell Green, a basketball player at Utah State, was allowed an audition at cornerback. Before Green's first workout, he inserted his thigh pads backward into his football pants. Bob Hayes, who had played some football at Florida A&M but was more popularly known as the World's Fastest Human for his skills as a sprinter, was drafted to run post patterns. Mike Gaechter was given the opportunity to play defensive back on the basis of his running faster than Mel Renfro on a sprint relay team at the University of Oregon.

A quarterback at South Carolina, Dan Reeves, was deemed by pro scouts as having too weak an arm to succeed as a pro passer, probably too small to function as a pro running back, and too slow to make it as a pro receiver. "So what the hell," Gil Brandt figured. "Let's give him a contract and see what else he can't do." The late Colin Ridgway received a contract because, in a tie game late in the fourth quarter, a coach never knows when he might need an Australian high jumper.

Tom Landry had been especially pleased with the outcome of the Cornell Green experiment. Green—brother of major league baseball player Pumpsie Green—developed as the exact remedy the Cowboys needed to narrow the personnel chasm between this team and the contenders. Green immediately demonstrated both size and agility and wound up playing at an all-pro level for a dozen seasons. "Go get some more of those basketball players," Landry told Brandt. The basketball player's ability to accelerate quickly and to change directions translated nicely into the work requirements of a cornerback. So the scout concentrated his hoops search around the Big Ten, which in the early '60s was playing a physical game not unlike that of the NBA.

And that is where Gil Brandt located Pete Gent, a six-five forward at Michigan State, where Gent had attended classes with the likes of James Hoffa, Jr., and future Michigan governor Jamie Blanchard. (Some years later, Pete Gent would compose a novel titled *North Dallas 40* that, in essence, did for the image of professional football what *Lady Chatterley's Lover* did for the image of horticulture.) But at first the Pete Gent experience was very typical of how the Cowboys were assembling the NFL's most rapidly improving franchise.

As Gent was completing his tenure at East Lansing, his plan was to become an advertising account executive, and he had a job at Foote, Cone, and Belding, a big-time agency in Chicago. "To have a past reputation as an athlete would be considered a plus at a job like that, but I wasn't crazy about the prospect of playing professional basketball," Gent said. "The NBA then was not like it is now. The schedule was horrible, the money was nonexistent and the travel accommodations were inferior to those of most college teams. I remember coming across some NBA teams sleeping in an airport lobby, waiting to catch a commercial flight. Those guys had it tough, and I thought I didn't want to do it.

"I was drafted by the Detroit Pistons, and then they traded that pick to the Baltimore Bullets for Terry Dischinger. The Baltimore GM called me and offered $8,500 . . . for an eighty-five-game season plus the exhibition schedule. Then, out of the blue, I got a call from Gil Brandt, wanting to know if I might be interested in playing for the Cowboys.

"By now, other NFL teams were looking at basketball players. The Cleveland Browns had drafted John Havlicek to play linebacker. Brandt's offer was this: They would give me $500 to sign, another $500 if I would remain in training camp for twenty-eight calendar days, and $11,000 if I made the team. So I called the guy in Baltimore back and told them I was considering this offer from the Cowboys, thinking the Bullets might up their offer. Instead, the guy said, 'Well, okay. If you change your mind, give us a call.'

"So I became a Cowboy in 1964. They wanted me to become a defensive back, like Cornell Green, but even before the veterans arrived, I knew I wasn't doing well and felt that I was heading for a sandwich and a road map. But they had a lot of rookie defensive backs in camp and not many receivers, so in a morning practice, I filled in on the offensive side.

"In a scrimmage, I caught ten or eleven straight balls and after the practice an assistant coach, Red Hickey [former head coach of the 49ers, who introduced the shotgun offense to professional football] came to me and said, 'If you just listen to everything I tell you, I think you can make this team.' It was close. When it came down to the final spot on the forty-man roster, it was between me and the big quarterback, Sonny Gibbs, who was on borrowed time after his first year."

Tom Landry opted to go with the Pete Gent project, even though the coach and the prospective flanker were leery of one another. "I don't think Tom was ever too happy with me personally. All the players had to take something called the Minnesota Multiphasic psychological profile test," Gent said. "You have to have a kind of criminal personality to play the game, and I guess I didn't completely fit in."

Landry's dubious suspicions of Pete Gent were no more pronounced than Gent's misgivings about a job in professional football. "Basketball is a contact sport. Football is a collision sport and in those days, in the mid-sixties, I believe the game was even more violent than it is now," he said. Back then, "they still allowed chop blocking and crack-back blocking, where we had total license to assassinate somebody. I saw some terrible wrecks out there. And everybody wore those suspension helmets, where your head, inside the plastic, was encased in this little canvas web. The quarterbacks were getting concussions like crazy."

While Gent attempted to acclimate himself to this new job opportunity in what amounted to a demolition derby on cleats, the off-the-field aspect of coping with Dallas—the carnival midway of Southwestern American finance—would prove harrowing as well.

"Dallas was where everybody came to make it big," Gent said. "You ran into a lot of interesting people and a lot of sharp operators, and if you played for the Dallas Cowboys, you had to be careful. Once you got your name in the paper, you quickly encountered plenty of men and women who were trying to get their hands in your pockets."

Still, the day-to-day panorama in this Babylon-on-the-prairie was no more frightening to Gent than the corporate jousting he encountered in his off-season job back at the ad agency in Chicago. "They liked the name recognition that I was getting as an NFL player, albeit an obscure one," he said. "But the company was a bottom-heavy pyramid. They had a lot of creative and hustling guys on the bottom who did all the work and a few guys at the top who were making all the money. So I thought, 'Do I really want to do this?' In Dallas I was living in a furnished apartment that rented for $185 a month that was within walking distance of the practice field. On eleven grand, I was living damn well."

Gent also noticed that eighty-five percent of the inner-city population of Dallas seemed to be made up of young flight attendants. The remaining fifteen percent were employed as models at the Apparel Mart. A typical comment in a Dallas bistro of that era: "Susie got all her good looks from her father. He's a plastic surgeon."

"After my first year, I lived at an apartment called the Four Seasons. The ownership had to let the manager go when they found out that he was letting a bunch of the Braniff stewardesses live there rent-free."

Free enterprise. In the Dust Bowl years, the so-called Okies migrated to California, where they were disappointed in the reception that they received from the fruit growers. In the post-Sputnik years, the Okies packed up again, this time for Dallas, where, they had heard, venture capital was growing wild in the creek beds. Sometimes life could be precarious. Dealing with the wrong crowd could lead to an early departure, via what was known locally as "an overdose of plastic explosive."

But with persistence, judgment, and luck, the benefits could be limitless. In 1966, a stockbroker named Robert Allen "Monk" White made a courtesy call on "an eccentric little fellow with an electronics company. His name was Ross Perot, and he had some growth charts for his business that ran all the way up the wall and halfway across the ceiling."

In the Dallas of the 1960s it was said that "you qualify as Old Money if you know who your parents are," and now it became stylish to send the children away to Ivy League colleges, where they would be taught to say "that's interesting" instead of "no shit?" The atmosphere remained fervently conservative . . . conservative to the extreme. One Dallas-based airline executive actually named his son States Rights. In presidential elections, it was not unusual in Dallas for voters to insert the name "Hoover" as a write-in candidate. They meant J. Edgar, not Herbert.

WHEN PETE GENT reported to the Cowboys' preseason training camp in Thousand Oaks, California, before the 1967 campaign, he had a big problem. Even though he had already flunked five separate physicals, the draft board back in Paw Paw, Michigan, had classified him as 1-A.

"When it was learned that Lyndon intended to escalate the war in Vietnam, the Cowboys, like most other teams, were able to exert some influence and get their players in National Guard units, where they'd serve their military obligations and still be able to play ball," Gent said.

The pro football players, in truth, were no different from many draft-eligible Americans. Not many of the combat-age population base overwhelmingly embraced the U.S. military cause. If somebody like, say, Vince Lombardi had been preaching the mission from the Oval Office, the overseas commitment might have been more widely embraced. But LBJ proved an ineffective pitchman for Western involvement in Vietnam. This Texan in the White House, who began every TV speech with the salutation "Mah fella Umericans," was coming across like some tired old junior high school vice principal lecturing some kids that he'd caught smoking in the schoolyard.

By August, the news on the opposite side of the world was going from bad to grim. In the course of three days a mortar shell killed four U.S. Marines, the Viet Cong kidnapped 143 civilians in Saigon, and a bus jammed with women and children was blown up. Lyndon Johnson said he needed another $4 billion for the war effort. "While the war is hardly beyond the means of the world's wealthiest nation, many Americans are beginning to begrudge such vast expenditures as inappropriate to the results," wrote a *Time* essayist.

Certain alternatives to a trip to Southeast Asia were available that did not require fleeing to Canada. Student deferments offered the easiest solution, although that was often temporary. Admission to a graduate program could prolong the evasive process. So, too, could the precarious tactic of extending one's undergraduate tenure five and even six years without flunking out. One aspiring artist in the Dallas area actually went to the extreme of having a friend chop off one toe with an ax in order to attain a 4-F classification.

That was the route that kept many of the pro football players out of the rice fields. With their wrecked knees and damaged backs, pro athletes like Gent were routinely turned down by the medics. One Cowboys linebacker had a typical story: "When I took my physical, I had a ruptured kidney and actually passed blood into my urine sample. So I got a temporary deferment. When I came back the next year, my leg was in a cast from my ankle to my hip. So this time I was officially 4-F."

But in 1967, because of some snafu in the paperwork, Pete Gent, with damaged ligaments in one knee that looked like moth-eaten yarn, was due for induction the coming fall. "So I went to Gil and told him about my problem," Gent said. "Since it looked like the Cowboys might be short one receiver, they came up with a quick solution. They decided to bring in Lance Rentzel."

Dallas was able to get the talented flanker from the Vikings for a reasonable price—a couple of draft choices. "Lance had some personal problems that the Vikings were aware of, and the coach, Norm Van Brocklin, wanted to get him out of town," said Gent.

Even though Pete Gent finally resolved his misunderstanding

with the draft board back in Michigan—"General Louis Hersey, head of the whole Selective Service operation, actually wrote me a letter of apology"—the ex–basketball player lost his job to the very talented Rentzel.

Lance did not conform to the average demographic of the pro football player in many, many aspects. First of all, he had grown up as a rich kid—his father was a business associate of Clint Murchison's in one high-dollar venture—in Oklahoma City, where he attended a private school called Cassidy. He went on to star at the University of Oklahoma, where he and a couple of other ahead-of-their-time Sooner teammates were the first college players to lose eligibility because of their dealings with a sports agent.

By the time that Lance Rentzel checked into the Dallas training camp, he was married to actress-dancer Joey Heatherton. Lance's mother called him "Wonder Baby" and Joey called him "Dimples." Despite all that, Rentzel quickly became a popular player on his new team.

Landry had felt that if the Cowboys hoped to return to the NFL championship game, a player like Rentzel, who ran precise patterns and was a threat to catch the deep ball, would naturally serve as a key acquisition. Frank Clarke, who had started the title game against the Packers after the '66 season, had lost a step. Landry also was worried that NFL secondaries would locate more effective methods of negating the threat of Bob Hayes with double-zone coverages. In fact, going into the 1967 season, Landry ordained a motif that gave Bullet Bob a diminished role in the Cowboys' attack, and the offense suffered because of it throughout most of the season.

Rentzel, described in one Dallas paper as "a breezy, confident fellow," said that he understood his role. "I think I can offer a threat at flanker and take some of the pressure off Bob Hayes." The new receiver, in early practices, demonstrated superior technique, although the Dallas offense appeared lethargic in early practices.

The highlight of what had been an uneventful preseason effort by the Cowboys had been slated in Houston. Dallas would test its resources in a first ever post-merger confrontation against the AFL. The game was scheduled at Rice Stadium, seating capacity 72,000, and for Tex

Schramm's sake, this game, even though it was a meaningless exhibition, loomed as one that the Cowboys could not afford to lose.

Fortunately for Dallas, the Oilers were attempting to bounce back from a colossally disappointing season in 1966. But still, Tex Schramm had been known to issue comments like, "The problem with the AFL games on television is that the commercials are not long enough." After such derision of the AFL as one slot below Roller Derby when it came to prestige in the sports world, the embarrassment of a Cowboys loss to the Oilers was something that might manifest itself well into the regular season.

As the Cowboys boarded their charter at Love Field for the forty-minute flight to Houston, Schramm got Don Meredith's attention, hissing, "Kill! Kill!" But the game was a joke; everybody knew it, and the idea that Dallas might actually be fired up to play Houston seemed ridiculous. "When we play teams like Green Bay," said Cowboys defensive end George Andrie, "I know that I will be playing across from Bob Skronski, I know what to expect and that helps me prepare for the game. This Houston guy, I've never even heard of."

The ticket-buying fans in Houston took on the same "So what?" attitude as George Andrie. If anybody presumed that Oilers backers would turn out en masse to level abuse on "the villains from the big mansion on the hill," they were misinformed. Only 52,000 paid to see the game, and of those, about half were rooting for the Cowboys. Dallas won, 30–17, giving up some points late. Meredith took a hit from Houston's gigantic Ernie Ladd and promptly turned the quarterbacking chores over to Craig Morton. With Dallas poised to make one more touchdown at the end of the game and Tex Schramm muttering, "Center it . . . center it," Morton opted to allow the clock to run out.

Afterward Tom Landry, who had actually seemed to be stifling yawns on the sideline, took a dig at the AFL officials: "I'll be glad to get back into the NFL. The officials [in their AFL shirts] looked strange in their red stripes. This was a weird setting. I hadn't seen so many flags since V-J Day," said Landry, who, despite his reputation, would occasionally make the effort to appear glib to the media.

ONE WEEK LATER Landry was probably wishing for a return engagement in "weird" Houston. In Dallas's final exhibition tune-up, against Baltimore, Johnny Unitas torched the Cowboys secondary. The Colts won

33–7 and *Dallas Times Herald* writer Steve Perkins, ordinarily an unashamed Cowboys apologist in public print, warned the fans to "get ready for a long and miserable season." What Dallas required, Perkins wrote, was "a Packer-like level of consistency. The Landry system is not conducive to free-style mayhem."

Opening the regular season at Cleveland loomed as a dismal task. In seven previous tries, Dallas had *never* won at Municipal Stadium . . . never really even come close. Even though Jim Brown had finally retired, Dallas chronically had taken the field in an intimidated posture before the enormous, thundering throngs of 80,000-plus fans in Cleveland. Before flying off the banks of Lake Erie, some Cowboys players seemed to have conceded the loss. "Cleveland is a good team, but double tough at home. I've never played a good game there," declared Mike Gaechter.

Dallas fullback Don Perkins, a product of the University of New Mexico who for some reason spoke with skills of elocution that would shame Richard Burton, declared, "We have always moved the ball in Cleveland, but all day we have had the feeling that the Browns are going to win the game. I don't know if they really feel that way or not—that 'Well, here come the Cowboys again'—but they have you thinking that, they do."

Early on, it appeared that Don Perkins was talking not as a defeatist but as a realist. Jim Brown might be gone, but Cleveland could still offer a near replica in the form of Leroy Kelly. While 81,039 football-crazed Cleveland fans raised a deafening din, Kelly put the Browns on top with a five-yard run in the first quarter. The fortresslike stadium, a cavernous double-deck horseshoe, had a daunting effect. This joint seemed haunted. Coach Don Shula could discourse at length about that. His 1964 Baltimore Colts, a team that won a division title from the Lombardi Packers and clearly the best team in football that season, turned to jelly in the championship game at Cleveland and lost 27–0.

But after falling behind, the Cowboys, seemingly to their own amazement, assumed command of the game and the Browns never presented a counterattack until the contest was essentially finished. While Don Meredith was pitching touchdown passes to Bob Hayes and Dan Reeves, the Cowboys' pass rush harassed Browns quarterback Frank Ryan into three interceptions. Cornell Green, who had not been expected to play because of a bad ankle, set up a touchdown with an interception. Chuck Howley returned another one 28 yards for another score, and Dallas beat the Browns 21–14.

Steve Perkins, the Dallas sportswriter who one week earlier had attempted to prepare Cowboy loyalists for the worst, quickly changed his mind. Perkins noted that the Browns' quarterback, Ryan, owned a doctorate in physics and probably knew of the MFT formula (*M* for mass, *F* for force, *T* for time) as the basics in the law of inertia. On this occasion, Perkins added that Ryan also had learned that "M is for murder, F is for football, and T is for trouble."

Defensive end Willie Townes acknowledged, "We were really chopping heads today." Even Landry, rarely known to offer glowing reviews, at least until he had viewed the films, was gushing: "I've never seen a front four play as good a game as they did today." While the win over Cleveland became just one more game lost among the annals of the hundreds that Dallas would play, this might have been one of the most significant wins in the history of the franchise. The Cowboys, until their trip to Cleveland, had developed a bad habit of choking on the road. After finally beating the Browns in that vast and eerie ballpark of theirs, the Cowboys felt as if they had just escaped from death row.

Reporters wanted Don Meredith to upgrade the "good" rating for the overall team performance to "great." Meredith shook his head. "Not great," he said. "Adequate. But stick around and I'll show you 'great' before it's over."

As Landry launched his eighth season as a head coach, one key factor emerged that indicated his regime might finally be approaching a dominant status. In 1960 the Cowboys built their team from an expansion pool that allowed NFL teams to protect twenty-five players . . . so, in effect, Dallas probably did not own a player who could start for any other team in the league. On opening day of the 1967 regular season, starting lineups around the league listed sixteen players who had been let go by the Cowboys.

In Dallas the next Sunday, over 66,000 full-voiced customers streamed into the Cotton Bowl to watch the Cowboys play the New York Giants. Stuck in a traffic jam near the stadium and afraid she might miss the kickoff, Don Meredith's wife, named Chigger, got out of her car, flipped the keys to a cop, and said, "Here, you take it," then ran inside the arena.

The Giants that the Cowboys were facing were no longer the

team of Y. A. Tittle, Kyle Rote, Frank Gifford, Sam Huff, et al., who had challenged and frequently overcome the Cleveland Browns as the dominant force in the NFL East. By now the Giants had stumbled into a melancholy condition of disrepair, and fans in New York were actually becoming more interested in the Jets and Joe Namath. With coach Allie Sherman worried about his job status, the Giants had brought quarterback Fran Tarkenton in from the Vikings to resuscitate the offense. Tarkenton, elusive and hotly competitive, qualified as a good hire. But his supporting cast was lacking.

Against Dallas, though, Tarkenton utilized the Giants' version of Bob Hayes. Tarkenton threw a 52-yard touchdown pass to Homer Jones, and New York actually led in the first quarter, 10–0. But if Don Meredith's wife was willing to have her car towed away in order to see a football game, she had picked a good afternoon to do it. Meredith declared open season on the Giants' secondary and threw four touchdown passes.

The first one was a 52-yarder to Bob Hayes, one of the few track stars whose sprinting talents could be effectively transformed to the football field. According to *Sports Illustrated,* "Hayes streaked through the New York defense like the Santa Fe Super Chief rolling past some blue barns."

Then Meredith pitched a shorter touchdown to Dan Reeves and a third one, a 16-yarder, to Pete Gent, and the Cowboys led 21–10 at the half. Landry would insert Gent into the lineup to give Hayes or Rentzel a breather after they had run deep patterns.

But in the third quarter, a play occurred that essentially propelled Pete Gent into the world of literature. Gent, who caught four passes in the game, grabbed one on a curl pattern and was speared in the back by the helmet of the Giants' free safety.

"At first I thought I might be paralyzed," Gent recalled. "The trainers came out and asked, 'What's the matter?' and I said, 'I can't move my legs.' And they said, 'Yeah, yeah. Of course you can move your legs.' I said, 'I think I broke my back,' and they said, 'Nah. Nah. You didn't break your back.'

"Well, what had happened," Gent said, "was that three little short ribs had been knocked right off my spine. Anyway, the trainers picked me up underneath my arms and dragged me off the field and then just dropped me over the sideline, at about the 20-yard line. I had to crawl, literally, on my hands and knees up the tunnel and into the dressing room."

The Cowboys' medical staff was not known for its reluctance to utilize invasive treatment options in those days, but saw nothing in Gent's condition that a knife might cure. Dallas put Pete Gent on waivers, but three teams claimed his rights, so he stayed on the Cowboys' roster for the rest of the season. Now listed as damaged goods on the Cowboys' inventory sheet, Gent's playing career was all but finished.

"Once you start getting hurt, one injury seems to follow another," he said. "At this point, I could see how good Tom Landry was building that team. And it was like getting to a train station too late. The train was taking off, and I could see that I was not going to get on the last car. And that Cowboys train, it looked as if it was going to go forever. I never did see them stopping."

And a novelist was born.

CHAPTER 4

WHILE THE SECOND HALF of the American twentieth century will be historically recognized for a multitude of oddities, one of the most peculiar might be the emergence of something known as the media analyst. The job requirement simply calls for professionals in this field to enumerate areas and situations that have been harmed or even ruined by television. They tell us that television killed boxing, television killed minor league baseball, television killed drive-in movies and in its fashion led to the demeaning of art and literature.

On the other hand, television served as the mechanism that generated and developed two American postwar icons, Lucille Ball and Vince Lombardi—particularly the latter. The small screen became the ideal showplace for Lombardi's super-tuned, ultra-conditioned, high-performance Green Bay Packers. In an era when mediocrity was becoming acceptable in the consumer marketplace and the advent of technology was convincing some Americans that happiness might be found in shortcuts, the Packers of the 1960s helped to reinforce the otherwise declining ideal of excellence through herculean effort.

While Lombardi and his football team could only supply the visual effects, another individual was supposedly required to articulate the message. Pennsylvanian Ray Scott, with his succinctly stentorian description of what virtually became the annual Packer Conquest, performed as the flawless, impeccable conduit for Lombardi's team and its inimitable precision. Scott's distinct, hype-free play-by-play accounts of the games offered the fundamental texture for the Packers football aesthetic. Ray Scott, almost as much as Lombardi, contributed the flavor that made the Pack such a national fascination. John Madden, some say, would be twice as effective on the air if he said half as much. But most announcers, past and present, just were not born with Scott's knack for the economy of word use.

CBS had actually put Ray Scott in place in Green Bay one year before Lombardi's arrival. When Lombardi came to Wisconsin prior to the 1959 season, both the coach and the broadcaster at once sensed the initiation of a productive symbiotic relationship. And like Lombardi, some peculiarities of destiny had been at work to bring Scott to Green Bay.

Scott believes that two coincidental events provided the magnet that attracted him to the Packers' broadcast booth. With a career that dates back to the virtual Iron Age of on-the-air sports reporting, Scott began calling high school games for a 250-watt station, WJAC (the call letters stood for Johnstown Auto Club) in western Pennsylvania. "The best high school football in the United States was played around there at the time, and that is where most of the major colleges came to get their players," said Scott, who went to Connellsville High, the same school that produced Heisman Trophy great Johnny Lujack.

After the war, Scott took a job at a Pittsburgh radio station, calling college games for Carnegie Tech and Pitt. What Scott accomplished during those years, more than polishing his technique behind the microphone, was that he acquired an understanding of the way sponsor financing of sports broadcasts actually worked. In 1953, Scott convinced Westinghouse Consumer Products to sponsor the first coast-to-coast telecasts of NFL games, and then he persuaded the old DuMont Network to carry the games.

"I only did that for the one season, in 1953. The next year, we couldn't get together on the compensation," Scott said. Shortly after that, a chance encounter on a sidewalk in downtown Pittsburgh generated a significant alteration in his approach to his craft.

"A friend, a retired high school football coach from that area, Pop Wenreich, stopped me on the sidewalk and said, 'Ray, I think I know you well enough to say this: Please don't insult my intelligence!' And I said, 'What in the hell are you talking about?' And the coach told me that he had seen my TV work on those pro games in 1953, and he offered a critique. 'I can *see* that the quarterback is fading back to pass, for God's sake! And if he completes the pass, I can see that, too! All I want to know is who caught it, on what yard line and creating what situation. Don't insult the viewer.' And frankly," Ray Scott said, "that one encounter became the reason that I started calling the games the way I did."

The second event that landed Scott his eventual ticket to Green Bay involved the considerable and yet bizarre assistance of sports radio personality Bill Stern, whose fabled broadcasting career, in Scott's estimation, was just that—a fable. Scott could not deny that Bill Stern generated a flair for dramatics and a kaleidoscopic narrative that made him famous. "But Stern was terrible," Scott asserted. "Always completely inaccurate. But . . . since his career was confined mostly to radio, not many people knew that. I actually produced the first football telecast that Bill Stern ever worked, the 1951 Maryland-Navy game. Twelve times the ball moved on penalty and he never mentioned it. He was *terrible.*"

Terrible, however, for a reason, and Ray Scott can be eternally thankful for that reason, since it provided the ultimate career boost. "In 1955, I was still doing Pitt games on the radio, and when the Panthers were invited to the Sugar Bowl to play Georgia Tech, Gulf Oil, which sponsored the Pitt games and also owned sponsorship rights to the Sugar Bowl, recommended to ABC that I handle the television play-by-play," Scott said. "ABC's response was: 'Who in the hell is Ray Scott? We need a big name for this telecast.' So finally it was agreed: I would announce the second and fourth quarters, and the so-called big name would call the first and third quarters. Naturally, the big name turned out to be—who else?—Bill Stern."

Scott said that he learned years later, after reading Bill Stern's autobiography, *A Taste of Ashes,* that "he had been a drug addict for nineteen years and, on the day of that Sugar Bowl game, he had convinced the house doctor in his hotel to give him a dose of whatever it was he was hooked on. And he had a bad reaction to the drug.

"So . . . when Bill showed up to do the broadcast, he was in a fog. He had the wrong records and the wrong teams, and two minutes into the game, the producer tells me, 'You've got to take over.' I told the producer, 'You have to tell him something.' I don't know what the producer said, but Stern looked at me and mumbled or muttered, on the air, 'Ray . . . you know this Pitt team. I'll be back later.' Well, he never came back.

"Bill Stern was like Howard Cosell," Scott said. "He was a prick, quite frankly. He was always feuding with the media and insulting the writers, just like Cosell did. So after the game, when the sportswriters covering the Sugar Bowl heard what happened—that Stern had been taken off—many of them came after me. They wanted to quote me, saying that Stern was drunk. Well, he wasn't drunk. Bill Stern didn't drink. So I refused to talk to the writers. In fact, I went back to the hotel, bought a bottle of whiskey, went back up to my room, and drank it all.

"The next day, the news director of the radio station where I did my nightly sports show back in Pittsburgh asked me what happened, and again I said, 'I don't know. I don't *know* why he showed up in a fog.' The news director went on the air and repeated that, and the next morning the advertising director from Gulf Oil phoned me and said, 'You can lie to that partner of yours all you want, but I know a drunk when I hear one.' It took me forty-five minutes to convince the guy otherwise. But the notoriety that arose from the Sugar Bowl fiasco was one of the reasons that CBS hired me to handle the regional telecasts for the Packers."

Scott thought the logical choice for that job would have been Earl Gillespie, the radio voice of the Milwaukee Braves, who was well known throughout the marketing base for the Packers. Ad agency–network politics stood in the way of that. Hamm's Brewery had purchased a one-third sponsorship of the Packers telecasts. It did not want to be associated with Gillespie, a name closely allied with the rival Miller people, who advertised on Braves games.

So CBS presented Ray Scott with a ticket to the Badger State, and "because the Packers weren't very good back then . . . their 1958 team under coach Scooter McLean had been a 1–10–1 disaster," they also promised Scott that "if this works out," he would be assigned to a larger region after three years. Now a veteran broadcaster, Scott traveled to Green Bay with a thorough understanding of the actual value of a promise from a television network executive. Scott never moved to Green Bay, electing to commute to all the games from Pittsburgh.

"And," he said, "after three years I wound up as the broadcaster for the glamour team of the NFL, if not all of American sports." Green Bay's blastoff from the depths of NFL darkness was not unexpected to Ray Scott. "Word throughout the pro football business was that the Giants had two assistants—Lombardi and Tom Landry—who were going to be hugely successful as head coaches, and there was never any doubt about that," Scott said. "And one meeting with Lombardi, and you knew right away that the Green Bay thing was going to turn around in a hurry."

Scott and Lombardi immediately sensed that one man's talents would serve to enhance the others. One of Humphrey Bogart's more famous movie lines—"I think this is the start of a beautiful friendship"—comes to mind, but more important, both recognized the potential of a useful and important professional relationship.

"Marie Lombardi told me that other than her husband, I was the strongest-willed person she had ever met. Vince and I had our moments at times, but in general we always remained on cordial terms," Scott said. "From the start of his first season in 1959, after every home game, Vince would invite me over to his house . . . win or lose. He would have a little party down in the game room, and then we would all go to dinner.

"I was always full of questions about what had happened during the game that day . . . 'Why did you do this?' and 'Why did you do that?' Looking back, he always had a reason and a motive for everything he ever did."

BEFORE THE OPENING of the 1967 season, Ray Scott realized that the coach was approaching that year's campaign with unprecedented passion—even for Vince Lombardi. "He made it clear, at least to me, that the prospect of winning what would be his second Super Bowl was significantly more important to him than winning the first one," Scott says. "Why? Because now, for the first time, his star backs were no longer on the team, and this was going to be his ultimate coaching challenge."

Jim Taylor's departure became a bitter affair for both the fullback and the general manager, Lombardi. True, Taylor's best years were now lost in the past. Taylor's greatest game, in Lombardi's estimation, was the championship game that followed the 1962 season. Sam Huff of the New York Giants admitted that he performed every guerrilla tactic available in the NFL manual of arms against Taylor that day. After each play, Huff would punch his elbow into the area of Taylor's larynx, or gouge his eyes or grind his cleats into Taylor's groin. But Sam Huff never stopped Taylor—on a day when the fullback was seriously sick with hepatitis.

Lombardi had *never* won without Jim Taylor on the field to fire out and lead the blocking charge on his power sweep. In Lombardi's first season, while Taylor was out with serious burns after he dropped a pot of hot grease on his bare feet in a kitchen accident, the Pack had lost five straight games. Lombardi the sentimentalist had hoped to see Jim Taylor complete his career in the green and gold. The idea of this man playing out his option to join the expansion New Orleans Saints became something that Vince the GM took personally.

The loss of Paul Hornung had been seen differently—the fallen hero having been hauled away on his shield. The golden boy's chronic neck injury had been diagnosed by orthopedic specialists as something that might put him in a wheelchair if he persisted in participating in the choreography of collision known as pro football. "This might not be widely known, but after the 1966 season Paul toured the whole country trying to find one doctor who would tell him that it was okay to play football again," said Ray Scott. "And he never found one who would tell him that."

IN THE STATE-OF-THE-TEAM message that the coach delivered to his players on the opening morning of training camp at St. Norbert's College in 1967, he addressed the absence of the two players who served as the signatures of the entire Lombardi reign. Lombardi emphasized how much Paul Hornung had contributed to what the Green Bay Packers had become and confessed that Hornung was going to be missed. "That other fellow," Lombardi added, matter-of-factly, referring to Taylor, "—he can be replaced."

In Jim Grabowski, Lombardi felt he had signed the player who would become the Packers' fullback of the coming decade. That was why he had given Grabowski the combination to the Packers' wall safe and that was why Jim Taylor had chosen to leave. As an additional safeguard, Lombardi contracted the services of Ben Wilson, a veteran fullback of four seasons with the Rams.

Throughout the training camp, Lombardi's characteristic bellowing reached unprecedented decibel levels as he drove the players into hitherto uncharted regions of human endurance. The preseason aspect of what the coach was designing as a third straight championship campaign fell neatly into place. After beating the College All-Stars at Soldier Field, the Pack cruised to five easy wins in exhibition games, including one against the Dallas Cowboys, in the fearful Texas August heat of the Cotton Bowl.

The five wins were routine. More important was the play of veteran running back Elijah Pitts and his companion piece, second-year bonus boy Donny Anderson. Their performance in practice and in the preseason games convinced Lombardi that the void left by the injury-forced retirement of Paul Hornung might be filled. Now Lombardi, despite the chasm created by the absence of Hornung and Taylor, established an interchangeable, one-two combo at both running positions. Anderson and Grabowski, the high-octane, work-in-progress additions to the Packers' star system, were teamed with the reliable and experienced Pitts and Wilson.

Imagine the hopeless grind that the thirty-eight rookies (Lombardi always referred to these players as Tentative First-Year Men) had to endure, only to face inescapable dismissal notices at the end of their ordeal. All but a handful had been doomed from the start, and they had to have known it. With a deep veteran roster returning from a championship season, only one newcomer, quarterback Don Horn, was guaranteed a roster slot. The Pack's first-round draft choice from San Diego State, after all, was entering a prolonged study program. Lombardi looked to Horn as the eventual successor to Bart Starr.

Another first-round pick, Bob Hyland, from Boston College, also seemed likely to make the team, and he did. Hyland offered enough versatility to perform at both center and guard, and Lombardi valued depth in the offensive line as essential to winning.

After the final cuts were announced, John Rowser, a defensive back from Michigan, made the roster as a special teams player. Travis Williams, a halfback and third-round pick from Arizona State, made the team and was clearly the star of the entire crop of players in the rookie auditions. Lombardi boomed out rare praise both to Williams and to the media on the player's behalf.

Travis Williams came to camp and demonstrated the kind of breakaway speed that had been missing from other Packers teams. Lombardi thought he had a different kind of weapon available now, and in some key moments during the upcoming regular season Travis Williams would justify Lombardi's praise.

Two other members of the Pack's rookie squad, quarterback Kent Nix and defensive back Mike Bass (the Green Bay coaches erred in letting him go) found work on other NFL rosters. As for the remaining thirty entries on the roll call of the Tentative First-Year Men—names like Dick Weeks of Texas Western and Les Murdock of Florida State and Bob Ziolkowski of Iowa and Dwight Hood of Baylor and Richard Tate of Utah and on and on and on—after the passage of a reasonable number of years, they could tell coworkers and offspring, and with some element of truth, of having been a part of the Green Bay Packers' famed Ice Bowl team.

BY 1967, OFFENSIVE tackle Forrest Gregg had already accumulated credentials satisfactory for the NFL Hall of Fame, not to mention enough championship rings to open his own pawnshop. Eleven years earlier Gregg could not have suspected that this would be the outcome.

When he earned All-American credentials as a versatile lineman at Southern Methodist University in 1955, playing both offense and defense, Gregg began receiving brochures from NFL teams. "If I was going to play pro ball, I hoped it would be with the Rams or the Colts. My ex-teammate at SMU, Ray Berry, was playing at Baltimore, and that looked like a team on its way up. I got a letter from Green Bay, wondering if I might be interested in playing there. I never wrote them back," said Gregg.

Weeks later, he walked through the athletic offices on the SMU campus and was flagged down by the sports information director. "He said he had some good news for me . . . I had been selected in the second round of the NFL draft . . . by the Green Bay Packers. So I went and looked in an atlas to find out where Green Bay was. I thought it was in Minnesota."

But Gregg *did* sign with Green Bay. "I was supposed to play in the College All-Star that August, and they invited me and three or four other draft picks up for a sort of orientation thing. The Packers were still playing in the old City Stadium, and I remember being quite surprised. It was just one step up from Wildcat Stadium, where I had played in high school in Sulphur Springs, Texas. The equipment was beat up, not new stuff like we had in college. I remember my first impression: This is not good.

"But I made the team and was getting paid for it—$7,500 for my first season. That season—1956—I lived in a cheap motel with most of the players outside of town. Housing was tough to find in Green Bay. They didn't have any apartments. Around town the people were great, but all I heard was 'Lambeau.' The people remembered his old teams, and when they talked about them I envisioned the players as being ten feet tall," Gregg said.

On the field as a professional rookie, Gregg did not encounter any players of that stature. "But NFL was different from college. The players were bigger. Faster. Meaner. Uglier. I remember playing across from Gene 'Big Daddy' Lipscombe at Baltimore, and they didn't call him that for nothing. I tried to hold him on every play. My line coach, Lou Rymkus, told me that was the only way a lineman could survive in the pros. Finally, Big Daddy, between plays, came to me and said, 'Hey, Forrest, I've got a deal for you. If you quit holding me, then I won't kill you.' Not many NFL players were earning fortunes, but they took their football seriously."

As a decade's worth of football went by, and Gregg remembers the years passing quickly after Lombardi's arrival, circumstances greatly improved. Like the rest of the Packers who had endured the course of Lombardi's tenure, Gregg enjoyed nationwide regard as a God of the Gridiron. "I was looking forward to winning a championship again in 1967. Taylor and Hornung were gone. That was taken away from us. But Elijah [Pitts] had matured into a terrific professional running back," Gregg said, "and I was confident we could do it again."

The Pack looked well fortified for the championship run as preparations began for the season opener against Coach Joe Schmidt's Detroit Lions at Lambeau Field. In the last of the preseason games Green Bay had flattened the Giants, 31–14. Bart Starr, who missed three of the preseason games with painfully bruised ribs, had come back and was ready. Typical of Starr, while evaluating his showing against the Giants, he said, "The big thing is timing. Our blockers gave me time to do the job. If the quarterback is rushed, he can't find his receivers. I had the time, the receivers ran good routes and got open, and I was lucky enough to hit them." Starr never deviated from the script.

Another promising feature of the preseason rub-out of the Giants had been the work of a second-year defensive end, Jim Weatherwax. At six seven and 260 pounds, Weatherwax, subbing for the banged-up Lionel Aldridge, showed good instincts, and Lombardi was intrigued.

George Halas—not Papa Bear himself but his nephew, working

as a Bears scout—assessed the Packers and said, "Poor Vince. He has so many players, he doesn't know which ones to play."

It appeared that with the season set to begin and the Pack deep, experienced, and eager to three-peat, Lombardi's biggest worries might be more societal than football-related. The coach had become concerned over the Vietnam War protests and the concomitant misbehavior that those demonstrations might spawn. Five years as an assistant coach at West Point only served to heighten Lombardi's die-hard zeal for discipline. The hippie movement might have been under way in San Francisco, but Lombardi insisted that his players keep their hair cut in a style favored by U.S. Marine fighter pilots.

"Before one of those preseason games at County Stadium, I showed up at my father's room at the Pfister Hotel," recalled Vince Junior. "I'd let my sideburns grow some, not bushy but down parallel to my earlobes, which was stylish at the time. By 1967 I was married and had two or three kids. I don't think I had seen my father for a couple of months, and the first thing he said was, 'Get rid of those sideburns!' So I went back to my room and shaved them off."

Vince Junior noted that the coach, by the 1967 season, had added long hair to his list of absolute taboos for all Packers personnel. "He told the players that long hair would cause boils under their helmets," said the coach's son.

The regular-season curtain was finally ready to rise—with the orchestra in tune and the understudies having memorized their lines just in case—and the entire state of Wisconsin had become choked with anticipation. The choking sensation intensified rapidly when the game began. Packers loyalists carried a carefully honed grudge against the Detroit visitors. The Lions were the outfit that, on Thanksgiving Day 1962, had routed what might have been Lombardi's greatest team, 26–14, imposing an ignominious blotch on an otherwise splendid transcript. Furthermore, Lions tackle Alex Karras authored some disrespectful remarks after that game, an act that Packers fans regarded as tantamount to telling jokes at a funeral.

Now the damned Lions were at it again, showing Green Bay no respect. From the press box, Ray Scott described as precisely as possible four Bart Starr passes that were intercepted by Detroit. With Lombardi running the Pack, the number of Green Bay interceptions and fumbles approximated the pregnancy rate among the nuns on the campus of St. Norbert's College where the team trained.

For the entire 1966 season, out of 251 passes, Starr had seen only three picked off. But in the first quarter against the Lions, Starr pitched three interceptions in a row. Lions rookie Lem Barney snared one and ran it back 24 yards for an easy score. To amplify the angst at Lambeau, the hated Karras had been running over and around Jerry Kramer, almost at will. The important time element that Starr had prioritized after the final preseason game now caused the quarterback considerable misery. Over the course of the afternoon, the Detroit rush knocked Starr down seven times before he could pass, and four times Alex Karras was the person who knocked, pulled, or jerked the quarterback to the turf. Karras, an off-the-field celebrity who KO'd a horse in a highlight scene in the motion picture *Blazing Saddles*, later confided that Jerry Kramer had flunked his self-styled "knuckles test." Said Karras, "If his knuckles are white, he intends to block forward and the play is a run. If his knuckles are pink, the play is probably a pass." At the half, Detroit led, 17–0, and in the stands at Lambeau Field, the knuckles of the crowd of 50,000-plus remained white.

Lombardi and the rest of the staff maintained their composure in a halftime effort to rescue the team. The Pack returned to the field refreshed and gradually regained command of the football game. Winning at the NFL level often can be refined down to the smallest detail in the close games.

Before the final squad cut a week earlier, an "on the bubble" candidate, rookie John Rowser, barely made the squad. Now, in the third quarter, it was John Rowser who would lay a "chain reaction" block that leveled four Detroit Lions defenders and allowed Donny Anderson to escape on a 43-yard punt return. That play set up an Elijah Pitts touchdown run, and the Packers now trailed by only ten points. The afternoon brightened some more when Mel Farr, the Lions' best runner, was hauled off the field hurt.

Starr, still under duress from Karras, began locating an assortment of receivers, who in turn started running for good yardage after the catch. In the fourth quarter, Starr connected with Carroll Dale for 51 yards, and after a 23-yard holding penalty against the Pack, the quarterback located Grabowski in the flat and the fullback wasn't apprehended until he had fled 53 yards. Elijah Pitts scored again from short yardage and the Packers trailed now 17–14.

With the hour growing late, and Green Bay pinned at its own nine-yard line, Starr, his tortured right rib cage now feeling rather aflame after a long day's worth of hammering from the Lions, found himself chased out of the pocket once again by Alex Karras. Starr flicked a desperate short pass to his safety valve, Pitts, who negotiated a sudden zigzag maneuver, located precious running room, and sprinted all the way to the Lions' 13-yard line. Here, the Packers offense was stymied, and Don Chandler kicked a field goal that tied the game with 1:32 to play.

Green Bay forced a Detroit punt and a late pass, Starr to Boyd Dowler, that left the Packers in range for a 45-yard field goal try by Chandler that would have won the game. On the sideline, assistant coach Dave "Hawg" Hanner yelled, "Kicking team! Kicking team!" But before Chandler could attempt his kick, referee Norm Schachter pointed out that the game was already over. Vince Lombardi, acting steamed for the first time on a trying afternoon, flung a lineup card high into the air and stalked off the field, suggesting to reporters that they ask "him" (referee Schachter) how time could have run out. "I can't understand it. There were eight seconds left when that play started, and those were the quickest eight seconds I ever saw in my life!" Vince yelled.

The fast finish might have robbed the Packers of a miracle ending. Vince Lombardi would admit afterward that he was relieved to capture at least the tie. Miracles are for churches, not football games.

Of more pressing significance were Bart Starr's shocking quartet of first-half interceptions. Tommy McCormick, Green Bay's new offensive backfield coach, donned rose-colored glasses. "We gave the ball away five times in the first half [Green Bay also lost a fumble]. When you do that even twice in this league, you usually lose. Bart had one of those days a quarterback will have, and still we didn't lose. He had a lot of help on a couple of those interceptions. He got stuck good just as he was throwing."

Starr, naturally, seemed contrite about the effort. "My passing was just bad, that's all," he said—even though he finished the game with 321 yards worth of completions.

Nobody knew what to expect from Vince Lombardi and his postgame temperament. The tie had been the Pack's first since a deadlock against the Rams in the team's last nontitle season in 1964. The coach remained, on this occasion, on the mild side. "That's the most hustle I've seen out of those guys [the Lions] in three or four years. And that

Alex Karras was just sensational. We were fortunate," Vince decided, "to come away with a tie."

Joe Schmidt, the Detroit coach, chose to side with Lombardi on that issue. While beleaguered Bart Starr spent his day avoiding the Lions' defense like the Frankenstein monster fleeing a torch-bearing mob of villagers, Schmidt's guy, Milt Plum, had gone unmolested by the Packers' rush. "We should have won," Schmidt said. "We took it to them better than they did to us. But a 17-point lead had melted and everyone knew what might have been was not."

"That Green Bay. They really have to work to lose a game, don't they?" Karras chimed in.

Now with the season under way and, along with it, the drive for a third straight championship, Vince Lombardi might have a new slogan: Winning isn't everything and when you don't, a tie beats the hell out of a loss.

But did he really believe that?

CHAPTER 5

As the Dallas Cowboys continued the construction phase of what would become a championship regime, it seemed that more and more often scouting director Gil Brandt was doubling as casting director for Ted Mack's *Original Amateur Hour.* Brandt seemed relentless in his enthusiasm for drafting hurdlers and high jumpers and power forwards as well as football players from college towns that did not appear on most road maps.

So Lee Roy Jordan, Dallas's first-round draft pick after the 1962 season, arrived as something out of the ordinary. Jordan was not signed because of his background in Greco-Roman wrestling. Nor was Jordan the product of the Cave Spring College of Radio and TV Repair.

Jordan's credentials as a football player, and nothing else, were secured and sealed when the University of Alabama dispatched a talent scout to watch a small-town high school game in the delta area just north of where the Sipsey and Alabama Rivers pour into Mobile Bay.

As often happens when the colleges venture this deep into the sticks in search of talent, the scout who came to see one player became enamored with another. Such was the case with Lee Roy Jordan, who had grown up as one of seven children on a farm, where the family raised everything from cattle to peanuts, near the town of Excel (population 345 if the census includes the suburbs). Jordan remembers that he enjoyed the "physical things" of farm work.

"I still had a year to go in high school, was the biggest kid on the team playing fullback and linebacker, and had a somewhat better game than the guy they [the 'Bama scouts] were coming to see," Jordan recalled. Afterward, Alabama assistant coach Jerry Claiborne, who later became head coach at Maryland and Kentucky, told Jordan, "The next time through, I'll be here to see you." The year was 1958 and "Bear" Bryant, whose real first name was Paul and not Legendary, as most people in Alabama might presume, had settled into his first year on the job as head coach of the Crimson Tide. Country singer Little Jimmy Dickens produced a big hit in which he sang about a kid who got his education "out behind the barn." Lee Roy could relate to that. By his junior year in high school, Jordan was already married. So, when a personage such as Bryant invites the quintessential country boy to join a big-time college football program, the farm lad rarely declines. After Jordan completed his senior season, Bryant sent another assistant, Gene Stallings, to make sure that Lee Roy would be Tuscaloosa bound.

While Stallings went ahead to enjoy a long and successful tenure as a coach, both college and pro, he would experience few days better than the one when Lee Roy Jordan signed his letter of intent that bound him to the Tide. By Jordan's junior season in college, he stood out as the hood ornament on a defense-oriented Alabama team that won the national championship. While that team's roster included a sophomore quarterback named Joe Namath, Bear Bryant—after his eventual retirement—listed Jordan as his all-time favorite player. That might have been partially due to the fact that the season after Jordan left, Namath got loaded one night and drove the streets of Tuscaloosa yelling, "Bear Bryant! Fuck you!" For that effort, Broadway Joe got kicked off the team and missed the Sugar Bowl game.

'Bama and Jordan had been deprived of back-to-back national titles when Georgia Tech upset the Tide, 7–6, in 1962. But Jordan, as the captain of the team, finished his career at the Orange Bowl, where he participated in the pregame coin toss in the grandstand. "John F. Kennedy flipped the coin," Jordan said. "He was surrounded by Secret Service agents and his family. I called the flip correctly and he gave me the silver dollar to keep as a souvenir. I had it framed." Jordan played the game of his college career that afternoon, as Alabama shut down Oklahoma and Joe Don Looney, 17–0. By then Jordan knew he was shortly to become solvent, since he had already been selected as the first-round draft choice of both the Cowboys and the Boston Patriots of the American Football League. He always knew that he would sign with Dallas. While the financial offers were similar, Jordan felt that the bromide "You can take the boy out of the country but you can't take the country out of the boy" had probably been written for him. "I knew that I probably wouldn't adapt that well to New England life, and Dallas was a southern city more than a southwestern city in those years," Jordan said. "Of course, in Dallas there were more things to do than in Excel, or Mobile, or any other place I'd ever seen, for that matter."

Jordan took the Cowboys' contract offer and showed it to—who else?—the man he called his second father, Bear Bryant. "The contract called for a $25,000 signing bonus, and Coach Bryant said I didn't need that kind of money in one lump and told me to spread it out.

"So I signed for a $5,000 bonus, plus a car and a no-cut deal that called for $17,500 the first year, $18,500 the next year, and $19,500 the year after that. I remember Coach Bryant saying, 'That's a helluva lotta money, Lee Roy,' and, at the time, it was. Obviously, compared to modern-day NFL money, it wasn't, and people have told me I came along twenty or so years too early. Maybe. But I prefer my era, when the team concept was much more in place and nobody felt like they needed to put on special on-the-field exhibitions to enable them to get another endorsement contract."

If Lee Roy Jordan remained satisfied with his rookie compensation, Tom Landry was delighted with the acquisition of the middle linebacker that he desperately required to activate a defense that might finally allow the Cowboys to become competitive. As the New York Giants' defensive coach, Landry had used Sam Huff as his flagship. In Jordan, Landry felt that he now had a linebacker more mobile than Huff, yet endowed with the same predatory instincts.

Not only was Jordan destined to become one of the key elements in the cast that became known as the Dallas Doomsday Defense, but he kept Gil Brandt's entire draft for that year from vanishing in flames. Other names on the Cowboys' draft list—Auburn linebacker Jim Price, Ole Miss guard Whaley Hall, Kansas guard Marv Clothier, Iowa halfback Bill Perkins, and Boston College linebacker Lou Cioci—were jettisoned back into the private sector by the end of training camp.

The NFL analyst from *Sports Illustrated* at the time, Tex Maule, fostered the suspicion that Landry had been concocting something lethal in his basement defensive laboratory, and, astonishingly, picked the Cowboys to win their division before the 1963 season. "Dallas Defense Can Win in the East" was how the magazine headlined its cover story. Tex Maule's assessment proved premature: The Cowboys lost their first four games and staggered to a 4–10 record.

"The Cowboys weren't winning when I signed and were still very much in an evolutionary process, although the core of a winner was already on the roster," said Jordan, who had become accustomed to playing for a team that lost one game every two seasons. "But you could see that with Don Meredith, Don Perkins, Frank Clarke, Bob Lilly, Dave Edwards, Cornell Green, Chuck Howley, and one or two others that things were headed in the right direction."

Like every other player on the Cowboys roster at the time, Jordan promptly discovered that the notion of adjusting to life on a 4–10 team stood as rather simple compared to learning to cope with the arcane world of Tom Landry football. Most professional football players respond to a straightforward communication technique in which the coach shouts out observations like: "Hot-dammit, Jimmy! You couldn't scatter shit with a rake!" Certainly, at Alabama, Jordan could scarcely recall an instance in which Bear Bryant or his assistants did not quickly articulate such constructive criticism.

Now Cowboys rookies were confronted by a man whose opening address to the newcomers in training camp included a preamble stating that he (the coach) had devoted his life to Jesus Christ. The new players customarily exchanged nervous glances at that disclosure. But the players were quickly assured that belief in God was not a prerequisite to sticking with the team; however, a devout devotion to the coach and his football theory was strongly encouraged.

"Tom was a quiet, mild-mannered type of motivator," Jordan said. "Had he been a stronger person in voice and demanded more of us, we might have won some games we didn't win. He didn't push us to our maximum level in practice like, say, at Alabama. He never pushed us to our limit."

Football players on the Green Bay Packers roster of the 1960s probably could not say the same about their professional experience. What Jordan and the Cowboys on the defensive side of the ball were exposed to was a graduate-level course in tactics, masterminded by Tom Landry, that offered the ultimate in complex sophistication. Eventually, the Landry Method would be popularly known as the Flex. It involved concepts alien to the proactive instincts of most defensive players, and a rare mental discipline was required in order for a player to function within the structure.

For a college linebacker, particularly on Bear Bryant's Crimson Tide, the fundamental job requirement involved pursuit of the ball and "on every play, going to the spot where you thought the ball carrier was going to make his break," Jordan said. The design of the Landry approach employed a different theory, based on containment. "Instead of pursuing the ball, every player had a gap-oriented responsibility and, if everybody did his job, then the ball carrier would have no place to go. You couldn't leave your responsibility to go help someone else because there was always the possibility that the back would come back through where you had come from.

"It was all designed to control the great runner, like Jim Brown. Tom Landry designed it for that and for twenty years, largely, it worked brilliantly."

Still, even players like Lee Roy Jordan, equipped with a keen football mind and tempered by nicely refined defensive instincts that enabled him to sense where the ball was going, required a slow indoctrination into the Landry Method.

At Green Bay, Vince Lombardi did not mind making public the structure of his "three-year plan" with high draft choices. In his first year, the player was expected to sit, be quiet, unlearn childish collegiate habits, and conform to the professional way of life. In the second year, the on-the-field aspect of the learning experience was accelerated and, if the player was not making a substantial contribution to the won-lost effort by the middle of his third season, he was soon to enjoy the sensation of liberation that came with unconditional release.

Landry would never publicize the fact, but he operated with the same program. In times of frustration, Landry would make a speech in which he told the team that "some of you are professionals, others are amateurs drawing pay." At no time was Lee Roy Jordan regarded in the latter category.

Jordan served a two-year apprenticeship under Jerry Tubbs, who doubled as middle linebacker and assistant coach. After those two full seasons, Landry felt that Jordan had taken in enough of an understanding of the strange nuances of the Flex to entrust him with the middle linebacker's role on a full-time basis.

From a safe distance, life as a starter on an intriguing pro sports franchise might seem desirable. In reality, the challenge of working under the standards of an ultimate football epicure like Landry, who yielded praise grudgingly, if at all, often proved the opposite. Then the chore of functioning as a Dallas Cowboy had become complicated by a completely non-sports-related catastrophe that took place near the completion of Lee Roy Jordan's rookie season.

After JFK was assassinated on Elm Street in Dallas on a Friday afternoon, National Football League commissioner Pete Rozelle quickly presented a directive that the full schedule of games would go on the following Sunday as scheduled. While the rest of the country shut down, Rozelle noted that it would have been the president's wish that the games continue.

So, at the precise moment when Jack Ruby was shooting Lee Harvey Oswald in the stomach on live TV late Sunday morning in the basement of Dallas police headquarters, the starting lineup for the Dallas Cowboys was being introduced to a cascade of boos at Cleveland's Municipal Stadium. "I wasn't in Cleveland that day," says Jordan. "I was on injured reserve for one game with a punctured kidney.

"But for the rest of the season, and for the next few seasons, the Cowboys got the same reception on the road, no matter where we played, usually. It was like *we* were responsible for the killing, and it was horrible. In Philly and D.C. and New York, it seemed like everybody hated us. They were very vocal in their abuse of the people who murdered JFK."

By 1967, the Ice Bowl season, that problem had largely gone away. Jackie Kennedy was dating somebody named Lord Harlech, and so, in the minds of the public, the mourning must be over. The Cowboys now had earned, if not the respect, then the curiosity of a sports nation as the team that almost toppled the unbeatable Packers in the 1966 championship game. Now fans were eager to see what Landry and his team might generate for an encore.

In Dallas, after the Cowboys had ventured into Cleveland to beat the Browns and then had followed that up with a systematic hammering of the New York Giants, a rapidly expanding fan base presumed that the remainder of the 1967 regular season would serve as nothing other than a window-dressing formality prior to the much awaited rematch against Lombardi and the Pack.

A Cotton Bowl crowd of over 75,000, which was capacity, came flooding into Fair Park to watch the Cowboys play their third regular-season game, against the Los Angeles Rams. At least an hour before game time, the ranking swans of the Dallas social set congregated inside a circus tent pitched on the west access steps to the stadium. The sold-out, or nearly sold-out, Cotton Bowl had become a regular home-game event for the Cowboys. With a possible championship beckoning, the success of the team now could be measured by the positioning of the Lions Club band. In the early years, when persons reporting downtown for jury duty outnumbered the spectators in the Cotton Bowl, the band enjoyed a view from the fifty-yard line in the east stands. As paying customers began to arrive in more abundant quantities, Tex Schramm moved the band farther from the choice seats. By 1967, it performed from behind the goal line and, eventually, the band played its music from bleacher seats stuck in the south-end-zone tunnel that led to the dressing rooms.

But inside the party tent, season-ticket holders could and did slam down ample portions of hard liquor, since the Cowboy Club enjoyed official private club status with the Texas Alcoholic Beverage Commission. On Sundays in Dallas, the Cowboy Club was clearly *the* place to be seen. The gathering in the tent consisted largely of the thirty-five to forty-five set that was inhaling deeply of the full-scale entrepreneurial Dallas boom scene. While the autumn of 1967 might be remembered as the time when burning one's draft card became stylish in certain pockets of the Left Coast, the *New York Times* nonfiction best-seller list included titles like *Anyone Can Make a Million* and *Happiness Is a Stock That Doubles in a Year.*

While the Republicans pondered their roster of candidates for the presidential run coming up in 1968, New York mayor John Lindsay announced that the identity of the person at the top of the ticket didn't matter "because at this point, Mickey Mouse could beat Lyndon Johnson." Lindsay could well have made that conclusion from a poll of the perhaps 1,500 upscale show ponies inside the Cowboy Club tent, where persons of the liberal persuasion were not among the plurality.

On this particular Sunday, with the Rams in town, conversation in that tent did not concern politics. Most of the men in there wore Gant shirts, Weejun loafers, and a smile that said, "Everything is completely under control. And after today . . . we'll be 3-and-0."

On the field of the Cotton Bowl, as both teams warmed up, Lee Roy Jordan wasn't as certain, and neither was Tom Landry. Cowboys practice sessions for the Rams game had not been crisp. Jordan realized that the Dallas defense remained vulnerable at the cornerback spot opposite Cornell Green. In the championship game of the season before, Bart Starr had picked on the other corner, Warren Livingston, at will. Livingston had been jettisoned in favor of a new face who was not faring much better. Mike Johnson, adequate as an offensive left halfback in a University of Kansas backfield that included Gale Sayers at right half, now struggled as an NFL cornerback.

The top quarterbacks in the league, the Starrs and the Sonny Jurgensens and the Johnny Unitases, customarily enjoyed a feast day when they located a weak spot like that in the opposing secondary. Roman Gabriel of the Rams also qualified as such a quarterback.

Late in the week, Landry's preparations for the Rams had been complicated by word that a Rams scout, Norm Pullum, had been detected in the vicinity of the Cowboys' practice facility near North Central Expressway. Landry suspected that a spy had infiltrated his camp. He filed an official protest with the league office. When word of that hit the public print, everybody was laughing except Landry. (Interestingly, when Pullum was spotted poking around a Packers practice later that year, *nobody* laughed.)

"I don't know how much they saw or how they interpreted what they *did* see," Landry said, "but other teams don't use a lot of different formations like *we* do."

When the Rams hit town on Saturday before the Sunday game, their coach, George Allen, just beginning his reign as Landry's everlasting nemesis, took complete advantage of what now had enlarged into a slapstick flap. He presented countercharges that a suspicious character in a tree, watching a Rams practice, had been identified as a Cowboys scout, Bucko Kilroy. "I told one of my assistants to throw a rock at him, but he was too far away," Allen deadpanned. Bucko Kilroy, at the time, weighed more than three hundred pounds. "I wasn't going to mention it until all of this came up," continued Allen, maestro of the mind game and unchallenged virtuoso of the offbeat motivational tool. Few men in the business of coaching professional football were endowed with the kind of imagination to exploit the likes of a Bucko Kilroy to rev up his team's competitive juices. The spy controversy served as the ideal distraction. With the slightest lapse of focus on the part of the Cowboys, the edge in a close game would be shifted to the Rams.

Allen, the former Bears defensive coordinator, had assumed the head coaching job in Los Angeles after a bitter departure from George Halas. At first, Halas refused to allow Allen to break away from his contract in Chicago. Now in Los Angeles, Allen became devoted to the idea that he, not Lombardi and not Landry, would prevail as the winning coach in Super Bowl II.

By 1967, the NFL game had metamorphosed into a competition in which the team with the best front defensive four, and not the best quarterback, might be the one to capture the championship. Dallas held a strong hand in this aspect of the game. The quartet known as Willie (Townes), Lilly (Bob), Jethro (Pugh), and George (Andrie) had become more consistent in producing harmonies that dominated a game. Lombardi's defensive front also came with nice credentials. Ron Kostelnik and Lionel Aldridge brought job skills that meshed well with those of the other two, future Hall of Fame players Willie Davis and Henry Jordan. The front four often would resort to guile and finesse techniques to function at maximum level.

"Our defense basically revolves around the concept of playing keys," explained Henry Jordan. "We move with them all the time. On a trap play, for example, Aldridge's opposing tackle will fake a pass block by going for our middle linebacker. Now, I have moved with my key, the offensive guard, and I am trapped by him. Then Aldridge will move with his key when he sees him going for the middle linebacker. If Lionel had simply crashed straight ahead, he would have been trapped by the guard, who has pulled and come across. But instead he has moved into the hole by following the tackle, and thus he fouled up the trap."

But in the brutal and heartless realm of hand-to-hand trench combat, nobody could hope to match the firepower of the Rams' Fearsome Foursome. Each member of the group brought his personalized trademark of destruction to the stadium on Sunday. At six five and 260 pounds, end Deacon Jones could run the hundred-yard dash in ten seconds flat, making him a terrifying specimen in his day.

Opposite Deacon Jones on the other end, Lamar Lundy matched Jones's 260 pounds but stood one inch taller. Ominous and frightening in his physical presence, Lundy played a minor role in the motion picture version of *In Cold Blood.* Lundy's role? The two murderers, hitchhiking, are offered a ride by a highway motorist, played by the

Rams defensive end. The murderers freak at Lundy's threatening countenance and decline the lift.

Inside, at tackle, Roger Brown, with his 295 pounds of guided muscle, pointed out that his style was dictated by the opposing team. "They hate me and are trying to cut off my career. So I'm going to hurt them first."

Merlin Olsen wound up immortalizing himself as a television broadcast star, by starring in commercials for a floral-delivery outfit, among other endeavors. Before that, in his playing prime, Olsen agreed that an activity like blindsiding a quarterback into partial consciousness was, if not addictive, at least "exciting. I like to bloody them up a little."

Olsen has never attempted to deny a story that reportedly happened during a halftime, when a Rams coach admonished, "Merlin, that guard you're playing across from is outthinking you." As the story goes, Olsen replied, "That's okay, Coach. By the end of the game, he'll be as stupid as I am."

On a Sunday afternoon in the Cotton Bowl, Olsen and company played at the pinnacle of their Fearsome Foursome reputation—especially Olsen, who, to his happiness, found himself stationed head on with Jim Boeke, the least forceful player in the Cowboys' offensive line. As a public figure, Boeke might be remembered for three things. Boeke was the player who jumped offside with the Cowboys positioned at the Packers' goal line in the title game that followed the 1966 season, just as Dallas seemed poised to throw the contest into overtime. Also, Boeke was fairly well known in West Coast circles for his off-season employment as Ricky Nelson's bodyguard. And in a modern-day circumstance, some fans might occasionally recognize Boeke's name in the credits of the hit ABC sitcom *Coach,* on which he gets an occasional speaking role. But what Boeke might mention as the day he best remembers is the one when Olsen and company beat his brains out.

The Rams captured the lead in the first quarter when Gabriel himself scored from the three-yard line. Dan Reeves had apparently tied the game for Dallas in the second quarter with a one-yard dive, but Harold Deters's extra-point try was blocked.

After the half, Les Josephson made a 27-yard touchdown after Maxie Baughan, a linebacker, recovered a fumble. Then Lance Rentzel leaped high for a Meredith pass and tipped the ball into the eager hands of Ed Meaders, who clutched the interception and danced 30 yards for a giveaway touchdown. The Cowboys were through for the afternoon. Dick Bass capped the day with a 21-yard run, and the Rams not only breezed to a 35–13 win, they kicked down the Dallas facade and ruptured the fairy-tale dream of the Cowboys' fans. The only genuine excitement came in the second half when an end-zone fan snatched a policeman's service revolver and began waving his trophy around while other spectators crawled beneath their seats.

Afterward, in the Cowboys' dressing room, Tex Schramm wore the expression of a man who had come home to discover his front porch stolen. If the Rams had indeed employed the services of a spy, their agent had done his job marvelously well. Tom Landry labeled "all phases" of the Cowboys' showing against the Rams as "miserable."

This was one game when Lee Roy Jordan was happy to be playing for Tom Landry instead of Bear Bryant, who probably would have mandated a three-hour scrimmage in the parking lot after such a stinkout. "I hate to see the films. It's gonna be embarrassin'. The films don't lie. You can't fool them," Jordan remembered saying.

"I couldn't contain their wide plays and nobody was coming up. We had no pursuit. We tackled bad," he added and placed himself among the teams' leading offenders. "Two or three times, I had a ball carrier nailed and let him get away. I had my arms around Dick Bass and he ran for a touchdown."

Offensive guard Jim Boeke, after his awful pounding by the Rams' front four, could probably hear the distant strains of bagpipe music. The week before, in their 38–24 tap dance over the New York Giants, the Cowboys had rolled up 414 yards of total offense.

Against the Rams, the yardage numbers plunged to 272, and many of those came in garbage time after the Rams had sewed the game up in the third quarter. The Dallas ground game collected 51 yards against Olsen, Brown, Lundy, Jones, and company. Referring to the offense, Don Meredith, as usual, was pragmatic. "We didn't play an alert game," he said. "But I don't guess the defense is too proud of itself, either."

So dominant were the Rams that, even though the game was simply one of the fourteen regular-season encounters, the fans and media now realized the trip back to the championship game would amount to a game-by-game, blood-and-guts ordeal. All of this hardly came as a revelation to Tom Landry. It merely confirmed that his

Dallas team was not yet a finished product and that some sleight of hand coupled with plain luck would be necessary for the Cowboys to hold up their end of the rematch appointment with Green Bay.

Vince Lombardi himself was not overjoyed when he heard the result of the Rams-Cowboys game. Dead set on returning to a third straight championship, Lombardi held every confidence that his team could once again handle Dallas. Those Rams, with slick and unpredictable George Allen at the controls, now loomed as something more ominous.

CHAPTER 6

In the early autumn of 1967, Fenway Park served as the core of the ever broadening American sports galaxy. The Red Sox, Twins, White Sox, and Tigers had raced neck and neck through a prolonged and thrilling stretch run before Boston finally prevailed and won the American League pennant.

On the morning of the seventh game of the World Series against the St. Louis Cardinals, the carillon of Boston's Park Street Church pealed out the melody of "The Impossible Dream," and Cardinal Cushing bestowed a blessing on the Red Sox. Despite the call for celestial intervention, Bob Gibson stood on the mound for St. Louis in the seventh game. Gibson, as usual, was throwing gas and the Red Sox became the Dead Sox. Afterward, Gibson said that he had reached a point in his life where the win-at-all-cost ethic had become so intense that he refused to let his seven-year-old daughter beat him at tic-tac-toe.

Packers halfback Donny Anderson watched the seventh game of the World Series with keen interest. Had it not been for a decision that he had made at the crossroads of his life six years earlier, he might have been on the field that afternoon at Fenway Park. Instead, Anderson found himself laboring for Vince Lombardi and attempting to fill the cleats of the now retired Paul Hornung.

Donny Anderson had grown up in the remoteness of the Great American Outback, a town called Stinnett in the upper reaches of the Texas Panhandle. "That's ten miles north of Borger, or sixty miles north of Amarillo, however you prefer it," Anderson says. Few regions of the lower forty-eight American states are as remote as the treeless stretches that run along a stream called the Canadian River. When it comes to a test of faith, the winter months can be just as trying throughout the Panhandle as the infernal summertime. And this territory tends to produce people who are as plain and tough and sometimes as strange as the landscape itself. Although it is theorized that lithium salts in the groundwater supply help to tranquilize the population, the breathtaking emptiness of this commonwealth-of-the-wind can produce behavior of the sort detailed in psychiatric texts.

In a town near Stinnett, according to Panhandle folklore, a woman promised her nephew that she would buy him a shotgun for his sixteenth birthday. All the boy had to accomplish in return was to memorize the Old Testament. The kid accomplished the feat in six months, and, when the aunt gave him the gun, he loaded the thing and promptly blew her head off with it. The locals all joked that if the aunt had insisted on the kid's memorizing the whole Bible, she might have lasted out the year.

Fortunately for Donny Anderson, his exceptional athletic skills provided a healthier kind of outdoor outlet. His passion was baseball. In high school, Anderson, a natural left-hander, had been hitting baseballs such great distances that a pro scout bought a road map, located Stinnett with a magnifying glass, and came to watch him play.

"The Red Sox offered me a contract right out of high school, and I was tempted," said Anderson. But he played another sport in high school, too, and college football coaches were always on the hunt for somebody like Anderson, who was known to be large, strong, and, as they say in West Texas, "swuft." Baseball. Football. In the end, all that really mattered to Donny Anderson was that somebody was offering him a free one-way ticket out of Stinnett. "The money the Red Sox offered me was not that significant," Anderson said, so he decided to accept a football scholarship to Texas Tech.

Not only was Texas Tech located down in Lubbock, which had been the hometown of Buddy Holly, but also the coach, J. T. King, told Anderson "that I could play baseball there and basketball too, if I wanted to." Naturally, on his arrival, King told his halfback that he should probably forget baseball. And Anderson did. While Tech football teams were resoundingly mediocre, Anderson—playing in an era when Southwest Conference sports were limited to the exclusive participation of white boys—consistently demonstrated rare breakaway speed for a player of his size.

Vince Lombardi watched a film of a 95-yard run that Anderson made against TCU, noted that the halfback was also punting the ball for a 44-yard average, and decided that Donny would look great in green and gold. Anderson had the sort of personal background that won the approval of Lombardi as well. The Green Bay Packers' roster was loaded with players who had grown up in the hard towns of the Rust Belt, or along Outhouse Row in the deep South, or in little dipshit prairie hamlets like Stinnett, Texas. If the player had been exposed to physical hardship as a kid—and the likelihood of that was high in the uncompromising backwoods locales—then that was all the better; the player had already learned to hate and therefore might more readily tolerate Vince Lombardi.

What Vince did not like were the bronzed gods that came out of schools like UCLA, and, when Donny Anderson signed with the Packers, defensive halfback Willie Wood was the only Californian on the whole squad. And Willie Wood did not show up at the Packers' training camp carrying a surfboard. Wood, not drafted as a quarterback at USC, had sent Lombardi a postcard, begging for a tryout. So for the cost of a postage stamp, Wood would become one of six free agents to land in the NFL Hall of Fame. Lombardi described the defensive back as "pound for pound, the hardest tackler I ever saw."

Fortunately for Anderson, his route to Green Bay had been less challenging. The AFL-NFL merger still would not happen for another year. Now enjoying the status of a first-round pick by both Green Bay and the Houston Oilers of the AFL, Anderson realized for certain that ranch life in Stinnett was behind him for good and forever.

Now Anderson faced a decision more perplexing than the football-baseball choice he had faced four years earlier. "The Green Bay Packers were the kings of the sport at that time. I was still a big baseball fan back then, a baseball nut, really, and to me the Packers were like the New York Yankees," Anderson said. "Plus, the National Football League was established, and Houston and the AFL had not yet achieved that level of prominence. The Packers had a proven coach and a proven offensive line, and it made more sense to go in that direction."

There was one hang-up. The Oilers, over the long run, had a more lucrative contract pitch. "Well, I didn't have any problem playing and living in Houston. Plus, my father worked for Phillips Petroleum, and Bud Adams, who owned the Oilers, also owned sixty-six percent of Phillips Petroleum," Anderson pointed out. "So Bud Adams came at me with a contract offer that included some interesting fringe benefits, such as the ownership of some filling stations, that the Packers could not match. All they had was cash. So it was a little bit of a problem."

Still, the Packers' offer to Anderson, the contract that he eventually did sign, probably was the largest sum paid out to a player over the course of the AFL-NFL bidding war for rookies that lasted five years. "I don't know if my contract was the biggest. They told me that it was. All I know is that when Jim Grabowski and I both signed with the Packers, they called us the quote, unquote million-dollar-bonus boys."

So Anderson embarked to training camp with the Packers in the summer of 1966, fully anticipating the enmity of a locker room full of Hall of Fame football players who, some of them, would be earning perhaps one-fourth what Anderson was being paid. If not apprehensive, Anderson remained curious about the reception that awaited the "million-dollar-bonus boy" from the likes of a Jim Taylor or a Henry Jordan. "I expected them to envy the unproven entity. God knows, I realized that it didn't make sense," Anderson recalled. "You should pay the proven people the big money and not pay the rookies anything. But it didn't work that way. What I found out immediately was that Vince had told the team that if they wanted to continue to win, then the team had to pay for players like Grabowski and me and that was that. So we were accepted right away. With one exception. Ray Nitschke was a little bit . . . uh . . . well, let's just leave it at that. That was just Ray being Ray."

Anderson had been at work in the Packers' training camp about ten minutes when he realized something. Whatever his teammates thought about the state of his finances was of little consequence. What mattered now was the ordeal of everyday survival in Vince Lombardi's Neighborhood. "The practice-field atmosphere was unbelievably intense," the rookie halfback quickly learned, "and it became apparent right away why the Packers had been winning all of those championships. All of the stress was placed on developing the mental toughness and the refinement of a thought process that did not allow room for mistakes. The Green Bay Packers simply didn't make mistakes, and when you don't make mistakes, that separates you from a lot of other teams.

"Vince felt that any time the Packers were in a close game in the fourth quarter, we would win it because we would execute and do it properly and win. Of course, this was coupled with the conditioning business, the stuff where he talked about fatigue makes cowards of us all. Vince had a jillion quotes just like that. But the notion was simple enough. He felt that if you weren't in the right kind of shape, then you'd lie down and quit when the game was on the line, no matter how mentally tough you thought you were."

Anderson learned something about what to expect from his rookie season. What Lombardi wanted from Anderson, as Paul Hornung's stand-in, was for him to stay on the bench, keep his eyes open, and speak only when he needed to ask an intelligent question.

"In 1966, in our second regular-season game, I learned what it really meant to function as a Lombardi Packer. We were playing at Cleveland, we were losing 20–14 with 2:14 to play, and we didn't have the ball. I was just a rookie on the sideline and I turned to Fuzzy Thurston—he was kind of my mentor—and I said, 'This doesn't look too good.' And Fuzzy said, 'Nah. Here's what's getting ready to happen. The defense will hold them, we're going to get the ball back and go on down and score. Then we'll kick the extra point, go take a shower, get on the airplane, and go back to Green Bay.'

"What happened next was that Cleveland punted, we got the ball and drove sixty yards to score. Bart Starr threw a little screen pass to Jim Taylor, who ran it in for a touchdown. Don Chandler kicked the extra point, and the next thing I knew, we were all on that plane going back home, drinking a few beers and laughing. For the young guys, you became a believer pretty quick, because you could *see* it. The test of greatness comes when you believe you're going to do it. You train your mind to think that way. The Packers had won and won and won under Lombardi. Just the same as the reverse situation. If you're batting and facing some pitcher and you're zero-for-thirty against the guy, then there's an excellent chance that you're getting ready to be zero-for-thirty-one."

Throughout Donny Anderson's rookie season, that postgame setting would become a weekly event, although the Packers rarely needed to score in the final two minutes to seal the issue. It was frequently mentioned during the Joe DiMaggio era that nothing in life could compare with being young and a Yankee. Anderson discovered that being a single man on the cheerful side of thirty and playing for the Green Bay Packers also would serve to provide some of life's simple pleasures. Or, as they like to say in Green Bay, "It beats the hell out of getting kicked in the teeth with a frozen boot."

Townspeople remained cordial, and while nobody ever mistook Green Bay for Monte Carlo, the town offered some places to socialize. Monday nights became particularly eventful. "We played on Sunday, so Monday became our Saturday," Anderson recalled, and locations like Speed's, the Tropic, the Zuider Zee, the Left Guard (which was Fuzzy Thurston's joint), and the Left End (of which Max McGee owned a part) became nightly haunts.

"Vince had a couple of rules about that kind of behavior," Anderson said. "We could hang out wherever we wanted to, as long as we wanted to, as long as we sat at a table and didn't actually sit at the bar and drink. If we did and he found out, the result would probably be a fine."

The bar thing was one of Lombardi's many idiosyncracies. He figured that in the eyes of the public, a Green Bay Packer seated at a table in a tavern was enjoying a cocktail. A Packer seated on a barstool was getting soused. Lombardi once chased several of his players out of an airport lounge as they watched two other NFL teams play on TV. Even though the players were not drinking, they were standing at the bar.

Donny Anderson discovered quite a few things about Vince Lombardi during that elysian season of 1966. "Vince used two separate philosophies with all the players. He analyzed every man on the roster to dictate which philosophy to set in place. For some Vince would use the carrot as the bait—the carrot being a new salary, a new contract, a new car.

"With others, instead of the carrot, Vince would use the whip, and he was always popping it. This involved continuing exposure to corrective criticism, which basically was a form of country boy ass-chewing. But either way, Vince Lombardi had made his personal commitment. A commitment to family, a commitment to God, and a commitment to the Green Bay Packers, and if you did the same thing, you became a helluva good football player—*or* Vince would tear you down until you couldn't do it anymore.

"And," Anderson continued, "there were some guys who could not play for Vince because he put so much pressure on them. The practices were intense. The games were intense, and you had to learn how to perform under terrific pressure."

After the Green Bay Packers had beaten the Cowboys, 34–27, in the NFL championship game, and the team traveled to Santa Barbara for two weeks to prepare for the battle against the Kansas City Chiefs, it is Anderson's recollection that the coach deviated from this carrot-or-whip routine. For the final week of practice in particular, Vince tossed away the carrot and the players were driven like peasants working on a Soviet barley farm.

"Let's just say that after winning in Dallas, Lombardi didn't let us drift too far," Anderson said. "He told us that none of us were any good and that if it hadn't been for him, none of us would have ever become world champions and he wanted us to know that. That's how he motivated us for Super Bowl I, even though they didn't call the game that back then. He got us so mad, he knew that we would prepare better."

Afterward, the browbeaten Pack might have wondered if it was worth it. At least one player thought it was. Linebacker Lee Roy Caffey used his winner's share of the championship-game bonus money to buy a small farm back in Texas and then sold his entire watermelon crop to a grocery store back in Green Bay. If the Pack could repeat in Super Bowl II, then Caffey said he could afford a moonshine distillery.

In September 1967, when the Green Bay Packers embarked on Vince Lombardi's grand and final crusade, the marching song for most of the United States was a ditty titled "Light My Fire." The fire that Vince Lombardi was trying to light and the one the Doors were singing about were not exactly the same. Said Jim Morrison: "I'm interested in anything about revolt, disorder, chaos, and especially activity that has no meaning. It seems to be the road to freedom." Not surprisingly, the Doors were never invited to sing "The Star-Spangled Banner" at any Green Bay Packers games at Lambeau Field.

On the world fashion front that same fall, the rage was brown. According to Pierre Cardin, "Brown has class. It lends an air of distinction." And the editor of the French edition of *Vogue* cooed, "Brown is so warm, so wonderful against a tanned skin." Like the Doors, the arbiters of taste in the fashion world would have been hard-pressed to locate a safe haven in Green Bay in 1967. Then, as now, the ensemble tended to call for green shoes and a gold handbag, or vice versa.

Down in Milwaukee, the parents of a Marine officer were talking about their son's fiancée from D.C., describing the twenty-three-year-old woman as "quick-witted under the hat, bubbling and sharp." Mr. and Mrs. Robb were talking about Lynda Bird Johnson after meeting her in the White House. "The greatest thing that Mrs. Robb and I got out of all this was to know that these young people are truly in love," said Mr. Robb. The father of the groom-to-be, a Republican, withheld comments on his impressions of Lynda Bird's old man.

Upstate in the Green Bay region, nobody cared about any of that. After the Packers' hair-raising comeback against the Detroit Lions, which earned the 17–17 deadlock, fans were obsessed with the topic of how Green Bay would respond to the next challenge. That involved pro football's ultimate grudge match, the Packers against the hated Chicago Bears, the hated George Halas, the hated Dick Butkas and the not necessarily hated but greatly feared Gale Sayers.

After Bart Starr's alarming four-interception showing (when he had thrown only three in the whole previous season) against the Lions in the first half, the fans—not to mention the coaching staff—needed reassurance that this was merely a Bart Starr aberration. At least, nothing like that would happen again. They were right. Instead of throwing four interceptions against the Bears, Starr threw five.

Furthermore, Jim Grabowski, the other "million-dollar bonus boy" now working as Jim Taylor's full-time replacement at fullback, fumbled three times against Butkas and company, and the Bears recovered all three. Eight turnovers!

The punch line was that the Green Bay defense limited Halas and the Bears to a total of four first downs and nineteen yards passing as the Packers, despite the most outlandish giveaway display in the entire history of the Lombardi tenure, somehow won the game, 13–10.

DONNY ANDERSON, NOW in his second year and being called on to earn some of that million-dollar bonus, demonstrated the kind of initiative that Lombardi demanded. In the second quarter Anderson, back to punt, caught the Bears in a state of temporary brainlock, saw an opening, and ran downfield for forty yards. That burst of inspiration set up Grabowski's two-yard touchdown dive and left George Halas sputtering. "One of our men totally failed on his assignment on that play," Halas said. "Someone was supposed to come in from that side and he didn't, that's all." That lapse cost the Bears the game. Halas remained careful not to identify that "someone," although his name undoubtedly would appear on the waiver wire the next Tuesday.

Vince Lombardi, whose team never made mistakes, could not have been any happier than Halas. After Starr threw interceptions on the Pack's opening two possessions of the first quarter, Grabowski fumbled on the first two drives of the second quarter. Later in the second quarter, Starr threw a pass that Boyd Dowler juggled. Then, as Dowler fell down, the football actually bounced off his Packer helmet and into the hands of Chicago safety Richie Pettibone. That was one of three interceptions for Pettibone that afternoon, one short of the NFL record. Starr's five picks also left him one shy of a listing in the Green Bay record book.

Somehow, Green Bay led 10–0 at the half, mostly because the Bears were playing somebody named Larry Rakestraw at quarterback. But with the Pack tossing the football around like a hot rock, the Bears could have tasted some success with Liberace playing quarterback. So when Butkas recovered another Grabowski fumble at the Packers' 40-yard line in the fourth quarter, the inevitable finally came to pass. Sayers disappeared into the Green Bay end zone from 13 yards away, and with three minutes to play, the score stood at 10–10.

Finally, though, Starr and the Packers mounted a drive during which they did not shoot themselves in the foot, throw up, or fall into the orchestra pit. Just as Starr had done in the fourth-quarter drive that had tied the Lions, he again tossed a dump-off pass to Elijah Pitts to launch the march. After Green Bay crossed midfield and Grabowski plowed into the Chicago midsection, butted Butkas in the teeth, and rumbled ahead for nine yards, placekicker Don Chandler bent over on the sideline, pulled up a clump of grass and tossed it into the air. The kicker didn't like what he saw. The wind, out of the northwest, was blowing hard.

When assistant coach Dave Hanner yelled, "Kicking team!" with the game on the line for the second time in as many weeks, Bart Starr would put the ball down 45 yards from the goalpost. With the wind blowing partially in his face but also from a direction that might blow the ball off to the left, Don Chandler was not crazy about his odds when he loped onto the field. The kicker also noted the ominous presence of Gale Sayers stationed at the goal line. If the kick came up short, the lethal Sayers would attempt to run it back. After Chandler kicked the football, he said, "I knew it was straight enough. The wind was swirling, like coming from two directions at once. I watched Gale Sayers, and when he didn't react I knew then that it was long enough, too."

As the ball cleared the upright, only 63 seconds remained on the clock, and with the Bears' passing offense nonexistent all day, Halas and Chicago were now doomed. When Green Bay won its championships in 1961 and 1962, players like Hornung and Jerry Kramer had handled the placekicking chores. Lombardi's decision to bring in Don Chandler, the ex-Giant kicking specialist, now appeared inspired.

But Vince Lombardi was not feeling especially inspired when the game ended, nor was he elated, relieved or anything other than gravely concerned and moderately horrified over the eight-turnover burlesque. After two games, home games at Lambeau Field at that, the Pack had surrendered thirteen giveaways. Lombardi must have felt tempted to place a call back to Fordham and hire an exorcist.

"We're having a hell of a time, apparently, but it's a tribute that they can still come back," Lombardi said. The coach addressed the awkward questions of the reporters with a civil tongue. In earlier years, somebody would have been fitting Lombardi with a straitjacket after a showing like that.

"Starr is not going to throw interceptions. You don't change that way. Not in one year. Maybe this is the year when things happen to us. We've had nine good years, but everybody gets bad bounces and we've had ours in the last two weeks."

Lombardi paused. The man had never been known to dwell on "ifs" and was certainly not prone to speculate on the great unknown that some people refer to as the future. But now Lombardi felt obligated to offer a prophecy: "One of these days these things are going to stop. It might be next year, this year, this week, in two weeks. But someday we are going to put it all together and stop making these mistakes, and this might become a great team."

THE FOLLOWING WEEK, as the scene shifted to Milwaukee and County Stadium, the Packers elevated their record to 2–0–1 with a 23–0 win. But somebody would have to dispatch a search party to locate the great team that Vince had envisioned. Those guys were still missing in action. The shutout win had come at the expense of the awful second-year Atlanta Falcons.

The day before the Falcons game, in Madrid, Master Sergeant Donald Redmond of Seattle somehow managed to fall into a bullring. While Redmond's wife and six of his nine children looked on, the enraged bull gored the man to death. But other than Sergeant Redmond, few individuals on the planet were experiencing a more difficult time than Bart Starr. In pregame introductions, some fans, mindful of Starr's 4.5 interception rate of the previous two games, booed the quarterback. In the second quarter, with the score 0–0 and the Packers' offense gasping and sputtering, the only genuine football player on the entire Atlanta roster, linebacker Tommy Nobis, blitzed and rammed Bart Starr, who wrenched his right shoulder badly on the play.

So it was out with Starr and in with the veteran backup, Zeke Bratkowski. Right away Bratkowski pitched touchdown strikes of 5 and 50 yards to Carroll Dale. "I am fortunate to have a team that can adjust to me," Bratkowski said afterward. Meanwhile, the Packers' defense labored mightily to restore some measure of dignity to what seemed to be developing into a flawed season. Henry Jordan tackled Atlanta's Junior Coffey with such savage determination that he ripped the thigh pad from the fullback's pants. "Pride? You've heard us talk about pride?" snapped Jordan when the game was over.

Starr, his face reflecting the agony of his injured shoulder, the frustration of having been hammered off the field by the Atlanta Falcons, and whatever sensation that he experienced when he heard the boos, sat in front of his locker and swallowed a pain pill. An ice bag was taped to his shoulder, and he didn't feel like answering the prying inquiries of the morbidly curious sportswriters.

"I really don't care to say anything," Starr announced. "Please don't construe this as being rude. I just don't want to say anything."

"Who knocked you out of the game?" asked a reporter who already knew the answer to the question. Reporters like to do that from time to time, just for the hell of it.

"I don't know who hit me," answered Starr.

Lombardi was not in a chatty mood after the contest and was certainly not eager to discourse on the topic of the pregame boos directed at his proud quarterback. Green Bay Packers are not used to receiving that type of reception from the home crowd. "Boos? I didn't hear any boos.

All I heard was cheers," announced Lombardi. "If there were any boos, they must have come from the press box."

Lombardi was perplexed. By the end of training camp, he knew that his ability to stimulate his veteran stars was reaching the point of diminishing returns. The Starrs and the Kramers and the Nitschkes and the rest had heard those speeches one time too many. Now the coach was wondering if those retirement plans that he had been mulling over might actually have taken form one year too late.

CHAPTER 7

California's recently elected governor was becoming conspicuous in locations well beyond Sacramento. He needed some national exposure. In the fall months of 1967, Ronald Reagan appeared at speaking engagements in ten states. A presidential election was set for the following year, the Republican ticket seemed wide open, and at least a dozen contenders were applying for the job. While Richard Nixon was intent on a political comeback in 1968 and seriously telling his campaign handlers that he wanted Vince Lombardi as his running mate, the pundits were guessing the more likely ticket would involve Nelson Rockefeller and Reagan.

So Reagan began telling Americans what he thought they wanted to hear. He began each and every speech with the following remarks: "In California, we have some people called hippies. For those of you who don't know what a hippie is, he's a fellow who has hair like Tarzan, walks like Jane, and smells like Cheetah." Reagan never made it to Texas that year, but if he had, his definition of the hippie would have needed further explanation. The hippie movement would establish itself on Mars before experiencing much progress in the Texas of 1967.

Texas had meticulously cultivated its special quality of eccentricity for generations. Texas remained a nation of its own, and there was no room here for freaks wearing beads. Dallas County district attorney Henry Wade labored passionately to guarantee that citizens of his fair town would never be exposed to the ravages of the Age of Aquarius.

While the Dallas of the sixties was largely characterized as an anything-goes kind of society, that "anything" had better not include a little marijuana. The Texas Penal Code authorized life terms, if necessary, for persons found in possession of even trace amounts of marijuana. Henry Wade deemed it necessary. If, say, some bellhop got caught with a joint in his sock, he might be off to the state penitentiary in Huntsville, where the throw-away-the-key approach was popularly enforced.

One such individual was a Dallas resident named Leotis Johnson, who "offended the state" by giving one marijuana cigarette to an individual who turned out to be a cop. A Dallas jury handed Johnson a prison term that exceeded one hundred years. The civil libertarians of Dallas, all five of them, rallied to Johnson's defense. When Texas governor Preston Smith passed through town, he was greeted with demonstrators who chanted, "Free Leotis! Free Leotis!" Smith turned to his press aide and asked, "Why are they hollering about *frijoles* [Mexican beans]?"

So persons afflicted with latent hippie urges learned to stay underground. Interestingly, one of the most recognizable celebrities in Dallas in 1967 existed in the private and lonely life of the closet hippie. Although Henry Wade didn't know it, coach Tom Landry suspected it. Cowboys quarterback Don Meredith had been known to exhibit tendencies that defied the "hang 'em high" mentality that often prevailed in the state.

Don Meredith did not wear his hair like Tarzan. He did not dress like the original Sonny Bono. He never marched in a peace demonstration. He never slept with Janis Joplin, and if he ever smoked pot, he certainly hadn't done it in a public park. Don Meredith was another kind of hippie, his own self-styled brand. What made Meredith a hippie largely concerned his thoughts regarding authority. Again, he never threw rocks at a SWAT team or made any "Burn, baby, burn" speeches. Meredith didn't hate or resent authority. In his world, authority simply did not exist. The result was that Meredith and Tom Landry, the ultimate man of structure, never meshed at the psychological level. A coach-quarterback relationship in which both men think as one—thought to be essential to consistent winning patterns in the NFL—just never happened between Meredith and Landry.

IN 1964, WHEN the Cowboys still suffered the weekly Sunday pangs of the NFL learning process, the team was boarding a plane to Philadelphia, where Dallas was destined to get beat. Don Meredith sat at the gate at Love Field, tapping his hands on an attaché case as if playing a bongo drum (the closet hippie at work here). As Landry walked past to board the plane, Meredith said, "Hey, Tom. Are you sure you want to go through with this?"

But the team started winning anyway, because Landry developed brilliant offensive schemes and Meredith—fearless and talented—made things work at game time. On Landry's weekly television program, the coach would sit with a movie projector and demonstrate the nuances that made his plays work. For example, Meredith would toss a screen pass to Dan Reeves for 33 yards. Landry would stop the projector, reverse the film, and rerun the play sometimes a half-dozen times to illustrate, say, how a fake handoff to Don Perkins pulled a couple of linebackers out of position and an open lane was created that resulted in a big gain.

In contrast, Vince Lombardi liked plays that worked because somebody like Jim Taylor threw a block that resulted in a linebacker sitting in a dentist's chair for about a week. Because of the power sweep, the American Chiropractic Association should have voted Vince Lombardi Man of the Year. Simply a difference in style. But after the passage of several seasons, Meredith mastered the deceptive dance steps of the star matador, and the Cowboys' finesse offense began rolling up yardage and touchdowns. Tom Landry's offensive playbook, thicker than a James Michener novel, had became famous—or perhaps notorious—around the league for both its length and its complexity. Asked to comment on Landry's remarkable tome of offensive scriptures, it was Don Meredith who said, "It's a pretty good book, but everybody gets killed in the end."

For such a slick operator, both on the football field and in the more stylish Dallas nocturnal retreats like the Cipango Club, where the money men would gather, it was odd that a man like Meredith, with his obvious urbane proclivities, was the product of the rural East Texas soil. But when Meredith completed a spectacular high school football career at Mount Vernon, Texas, he made it clear that he and the country boy scene were forever parting company.

TCU, a national football power when Meredith hit the recruiting circuit, made a hard run. Meredith, in fact, had a big brother who had played there. Abe Martin, the TCU coach and a down-home sort of

Vince Lombardi, waiting for the moment of truth at the Ice Bowl.

Dallas coach Tom Landry, dressed for the occasion.

Broadcasting legend Ray Scott (left) interviews Ray Nitschke.

Forrest Gregg (75) leads the way for Paul Hornung on the famous Lombardi Sweep.

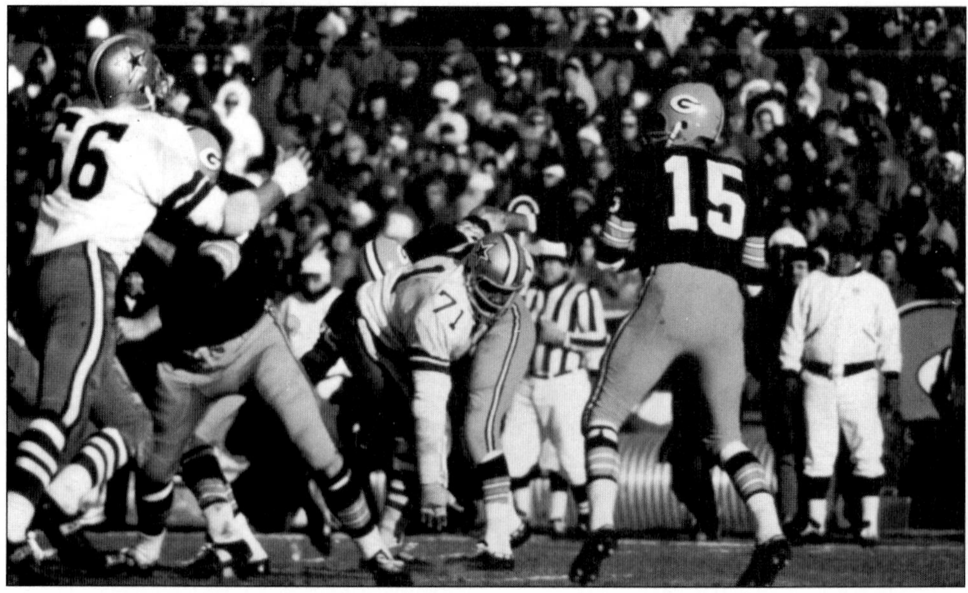

Ice Bowl hero Bart Starr drops to pass while George Andrie (left) and Willie Townes (71) bring defensive pressure.

Starr gives the ball to Ben Wilson.

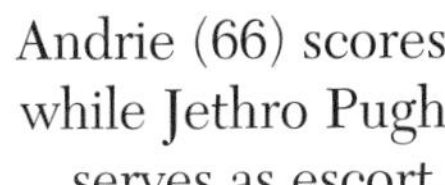

Andrie (66) scores while Jethro Pugh serves as escort.

Don Meredith (17) hands off to fullback Don Perkins.

Don Meredith withstood heavy pounding in the early years of the Cowboys franchise.

Offensive stalwart tackle Forrest Gregg symbolized the Packers' championship ethic.

Starr hands off to Green Bay's Travis "Roadrunner" Williams (23).

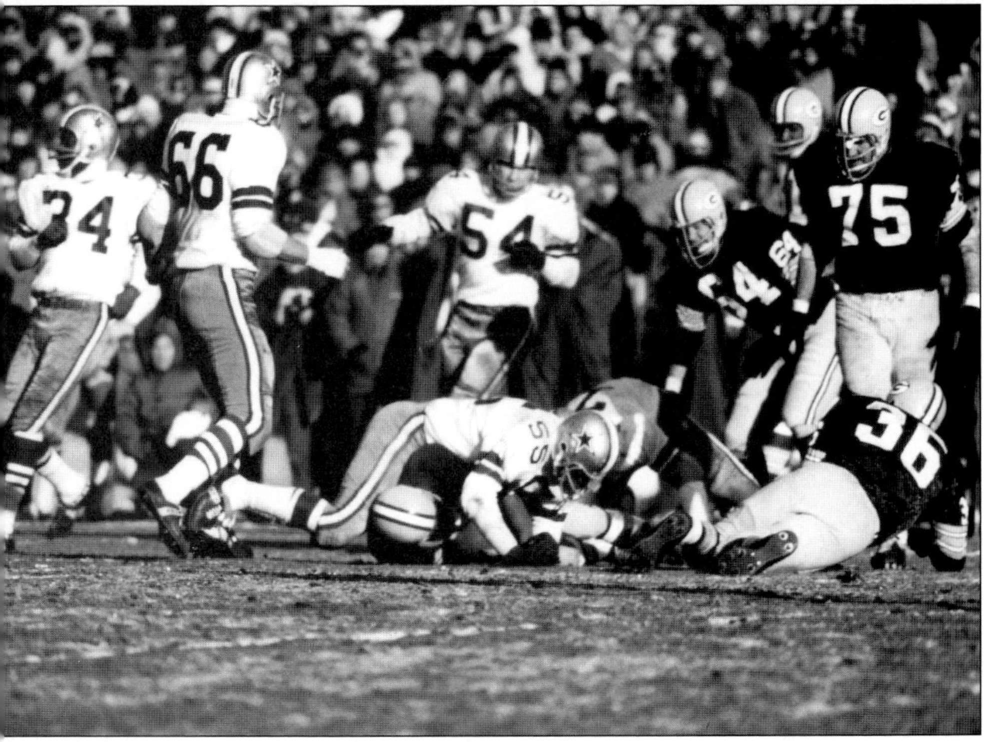

Linebacker Lee Roy Jordan (55) stops a Packer play.

Donny Anderson (left) came through under pressure in the Packers' winning drive at the Ice Bowl.

Chuck Mercein (30), Marv Fleming (81), and the Cowboys' Mike Gaechter (27) struggle on the treacherous turf.

Carroll Dale (84) snags a pass in Green Bay's first scoring drive.

Herb Adderley (26) intercepts a second-quarter pass.

Hall of Famer
Bob Lilly manhandles
the Green Bay line.

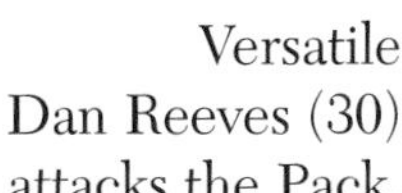

Versatile
Dan Reeves (30)
attacks the Pack.

Green Bay's football devotion—then, as now—appears limitless. The gang at Lambeau Field—the NFL's greatest fans—experience Ice Bowl ecstasy.

Willie Davis (87) gives his coach a weather report.

man, presented his pitch. "Donnie," said Abe, "we're all real low-key around here on this campus. I mean, you can wear overalls to class and spit on the floor if you want to, and nobody will care."

"Hell, Coach, I can do that back in Mount Vernon," Meredith answered. Bear Bryant, when he finally retired, said he never worked harder to recruit a player than he did Don Meredith. But Bear Bryant was coaching at Texas A&M at a time when that school offered an all-male enrollment and a social life akin to that at the Citadel. "Coach Bryant," Meredith told the Bear, "there's not a coach in the world I would rather play for. I'd go anywhere to play for you, except, of course, at some school where girls aren't allowed."

Master of the one-liner, Meredith once said in a radio interview that the most memorable game in his whole playing career actually happened in high school, when he had helped his team rally from a 26-point deficit and win against a hated rival in the East Texas woods. "Wow!" said the radio guy who was conducting the interview. "An experience like that. That must be the greatest feeling a young man can have."

"No," answered Meredith. "The second most." So it was entirely appropriate that Don Meredith would accept a scholarship to SMU, regarded throughout the land as one of academia's leading game preserves for girls. Rich girls. Pretty girls. An unlimited vista of coed scholars. As a freshman, the story goes, Meredith enrolled in a class because he thought the course was named after some Kappa Kappa Gamma named Polly Sigh. With the campus situated in easy proximity to the more active precincts of Dallas nightlife, the throb of an active social whirl endured as an ever present chord in student life. Locally, it was said that SMU stood for Suck Me Unconscious.

Meredith enjoyed a sensational football career at SMU, married one of those coeds who was both rich and pretty, and was drafted by the Los Angeles Rams. But the new Cowboys' franchise retained his rights in exchange for several future draft choices. So Meredith returned to Dallas, sentenced to spend his entire professional football career beneath a microscope, subjected to the perpetual in-depth study and evaluation of Tom Landry and the city in general.

In the fall of 1967, the nation was horrified to learn that Joe DiMaggio was joining the payroll of some off-the-wall baseball owner, Charles O. Finley, out in Oakland. DiMaggio, a national treasure at age fifty-two, fielded questions about his good name being exploited by Finley. "Exploit me?" said DiMaggio. "We are all exploited, in a way, when we take a job." Meredith would not have argued that point with Joltin' Joe.

His evolution as a starting quarterback had been slow in coming. A golden rule in the National Football League in those years was that quarterbacks must endure a five-year term of apprenticeship before being licensed as competent. Landry was an active proponent of such thinking. According to Tex Schramm, Meredith was "the only player on the team who was really making any money." But the highest-paid player experienced abundant bench time. Little Eddie LeBaron did most of the playing.

When Meredith did play, the early returns were erratic and understandably so. While Meredith might not have totally grasped all of the puzzling nuances of the Landry offense, neither had most of the other offensive players. Additionally, Dallas's offensive line was a sieve. Botched blocking assignments frequently left Meredith all alone and vulnerable to blindside shots from weakside defensive ends or red-dogging linebackers or blitzing safeties who delighted in laying cruel and unusual punishment on the quarterback.

The Cowboys' football machine had been too slow to roll in the minds of some fans, who were quick to blame the quarterback. "I can remember the pregame introductions in the Cotton Bowl. They would introduce the offense, and everyone would trot out there with great applause and then they'd say, 'Starting at quarterback . . . number 17 . . . Don Meredith . . . and when Don trotted out he always got the boos," recalled defensive star George Andrie. "And it really used to piss me off. They took it out on Don, I guess, because he'd been around so long in Dallas, because of the SMU thing and all. That possibly didn't affect Don too much, but I think it affected the team. If that had happened to me, I would have gotten out of football or gotten out of town. I would have said, 'Screw Dallas.'

"But Meredith took a pounding game after game, because, in large part, we had some pretty crappy blocking schemes that weren't well enough designed to pick up a good pass rush. In fact, Don used to get the dog shit beat out of him back there, but he played hurt and never bitched, either to the team or to the press. And if you look at the films, whenever he did get time to throw, he was the most accurate passer in the whole damn league."

The man they called Dandy Don presented a stronger off-the-field persona. Meredith's advice to teammates was, "Remember your ABC's: Always Be Cool." After a game at New York, according to Pat Toomay's book, *The Crunch,* the Cowboys' charter plane sat on a runway at LaGuardia for two hours because of bad visibility, while the players got blasted in the rear of the plane. When the jet finally did take off, something that sounded like an explosion emanated from somewhere underneath the plane. Bob Lilly stood up and shouted, "This is it, baby! It's all over!" Linebacker D. D. Lewis, a product of Mississippi State, was seated next to Meredith and saw that the quarterback never looked up from the paperback he was reading. "God-damn! Goddamn!" Lewis shrieked. "Aren't you scared?"

"Uh-uh," Meredith answered. "It's been a good 'un."

His activities on the leisure scene were not bound by the dictates of the Tom Landry playbook. Meredith, who divorced his SMU wife and married Cheryl "Chigger" King from Fort Worth, embodied the free spirit. While most Texans liked to collect guns, Don collected oddballs, or at least unusual people. For example, he was known to socialize with the likes of Dimitri Vail, a portrait artist who bought a pale yellow house in Highland Park because the color of the mansion matched his Cadillac.

Frequently, Meredith would arrive for postgame parties at a dive known as Dewey Groom's Longhorn Ranch, located on the shabby end of the downtown area. In his company often was a songwriter with an as yet nonexistent singing career. Back in the sixties Willie Nelson wore Robert Hall suits, favored the Brylcreem ("a little dab'll do ya' ") look and could have passed for a recent graduate of the undertakers' academy. "But Willie had written some damn good songs by then, and Don liked his stuff," remembered Lee Roy Jordan, also a regular at Dewey Groom's. "You know. 'Hello, Walls' and the song that goes, 'Turn out the lights, the party's over,' that Don used to sing when he was doing the TV thing with Howard Cosell. Those early Willie Nelson songs had a quality of sadness, or loneliness, to them, and there was a side of Meredith, maybe his true side, that strongly identified with that stuff." (Meredith's life did take a tragic turn when his and Chigger's daughter was born with profound congenital defects.)

Of all the Cowboys players, none was a more loyal advocate of the Meredith cause than Lee Roy Jordan. "Meredith was the most entertaining guy I ever met in my life, and he never received credit for the talent that he had," Jordan said. "Of course, he never really did adhere to Tom Landry's outlook, which was a total focus on football and that not having fun was something that goes with the job.

"Don caught most of the blame when things didn't always go right with the Cowboys. Tom was the source of a lot of that. That was Tom's style, and he didn't take *any* of the blame. Go back and look in all the papers after the defense had a bad game or the offense had a bad game, and it was always the individual players who were at fault.

"I don't know how much that bothered Meredith," Jordan added. "Back then, Don's announced intention was never to have a job, and he did a damn fine job of that. Oh, he wound up doing *Monday Night Football* . . . but what's that? One night a week."

Pete Gent remembers Meredith best for "that happy-go-lucky exterior, but behind that was a deep thinker. He had a great memory and would quote poetry and biblical verse, word for word. Don had a great sense of what he was doing and what his job was.

"That sort of flippant attitude," Gent believed, "was designed to help the other guys relax. As opposed to not giving a shit, he cared [about winning] more than anybody."

With the arrival of Bob Hayes, fresh off a three-gold-medal sprint performance at the Tokyo Olympics, Meredith's on-the-field task became easier. Unfairly characterized as the man "with nine-point-three speed and twelve-flat hands," Hayes quickly demonstrated that whenever he stepped onto the field, he was a touchdown waiting to happen. In fact, he was not endowed with 9.3 speed. He had 9.1 speed, as some defensive backs with 9.3 speed found out. So, in order to stop Hayes, NFL defenses were redrawn. Against the Cowboys, more stress was placed on neutralizing the touchdown potential of Bob Hayes than on planting Don Meredith in a shallow grave.

Hayes materialized as Meredith's salvation in 1965. But in a late-season game against the Cleveland Browns, an occasion when the Cowboys attracted their first sellout audience—ever—to the Cotton Bowl, Meredith piloted a great closing drive while the Dallas fans became berserk. Underdog Dallas trailed 24–17, but stood first-and-goal on the Browns' one-yard line. Meredith not only chose to pass on a first down but threw an interception as well. The next day, in the *Dallas Morning News*, sportswriter Gary Cartwright informed his readers: "Yesterday, the Four Horsemen rode again . . . War, Famine, Pestilence, and Meredith."

So Meredith would listen to the Cotton Bowl boos, and they

never really quit until Meredith quit after the 1969 season. When he returned to the Cotton Bowl in the first season of ABC's Monday night NFL telecasts, quarterback Craig Morton became the person who had inherited the boos. With the Cowboys losing badly to St. Louis, the crowd began to chant, "We want Meredith! We want Meredith!"

"Hear that, Don?" said Howard Cosell.

"Yeah, I hear it," Meredith shot back. "They may want me, but I'm not goin' in."

After the Cowboys had beaten the Browns at Cleveland to open the 1967 season, they were eager to sample life on the road. That was particularly the case after the 35–13 home loss to the Rams. At least in that stadium in Washington (one year before the place would be named RFK), the boos they would hear wouldn't be showering down from the Cowboys' own fans.

In 1967, the Redskins had not yet reached the perennial contender status that they would enjoy with the arrival of George Allen. But one of the NFL's hottest rivalries originally began to take shape in the fourth regular-season game on the 1967 slate—Dallas at Washington. Meredith endured an early pounding, mostly through the obsessed play of the 'Skins' middle linebacker, Chris Hanburger. After Meredith banged his throwing hand against the helmet of the blitzing Hanburger, the quarterback feared a broken finger. "I felt a sharp pain and thought, 'Uh-oh. I just won't look at it.' But finally I did and the middle finger was bright red," Meredith recalled. "I tried to wiggle the finger and sure enough, it moved. The red was the paint off Hanburger's helmet."

With Sonny Jurgensen flicking quick passes that bedeviled the Cowboys' rush, the Redskins led at the half, 7–0. Dallas tied the game in the third quarter, Meredith finding Lance Rentzel with a 25-yard TD, and took the lead when Danny Villanueva kicked a field goal.

Jurgensen moved Washington to a late touchdown on a drive that was sustained by a successful fake punt. Charley Taylor caught an eight-yard touchdown pass, and, with a minute left, Washington led, 14–10. Meredith, desperate, hit two frantic passes along the sideline to put the Cowboys in Redskins territory. With time almost gone, Hanburger charged into the Cowboys' backfield again and gored the quarterback in his side just as he delivered a pass that fell incomplete.

Now 18 seconds remained, and Dallas, facing fourth down, was about to fire its last shot from the Washington 36-yard line.

Meredith felt a searing pain from the blast he had just taken from Hanburger, and as the Cowboys broke for the huddle sportswriter Steve Perkins noted, "Meredith appeared groggy and listing to starboard like an America's Cup entry."

As the quarterback retreated for the final pass, halfback Dan Reeves broke toward the flag stuck where the sideline and the goal line intersected. Reeves ran without escort, Meredith noticed, and lofted a pass in that direction with a big arc. Dan Reeves, the former South Carolina quarterback with skills deemed lacking by NFL standards but who had become the most versatile clutch player in team history, thought the pass might have a hang time of about six seconds. But the ball arrived in Reeves's hands instants before Hanburger could arrive to avert disaster.

With an obstructed view from their bench, some Dallas defensive players saw a yellow object float skyward from the other side of the field and thought for a moment that it might be a penalty flag. The object, in fact, was a yellow legal pad that 'Skins coach Otto Graham had flung thirty feet toward the heavens when Reeves, ball in hand, trotted into the Washington end zone.

Defensive lineman Willie Townes rumbled all the way to the end zone and embraced Reeves in the hug of a 290-pound football bear. "I was scared to death," said Reeves. "I tried to say, 'Lemmee go!' and all that came out was 'Awwk!' I could feel my heart fluttering in my throat like a little bird."

Tom Landry met Otto Graham in the center of the field.

"We stole it," said Tom.

"Yep. You did," said Otto.

"Another day at the office," said Meredith.

A reporter asked Landry if he had noticed that Meredith appeared in some physical distress before the TD heave. "No," said Landry. "I'm so used to seeing him that way, I can't tell the difference anymore." But on the flight back to Dallas, the quarterback started thinking otherwise as the pain increased to a surreal intensity. Meredith was sure that he had serious internal wounds.

"That night, back in Dallas, Chigger Meredith called me and said that Don had been taken to Baylor Hospital. He had a collapsed lung," remembered Pete Gent, who rode to the hospital and managed to sneak inside Meredith's room in the intensive care unit. "He talked, but not much. They had him hooked up to a breathing machine, and Don was in absolute agony. I had seen him in incredible pain before, but nothing like this. He had a big hole in his side and blood dripping from his mouth.

"Then," says Gent, "when we studied the films of this game that Meredith had won pretty much single-handed, Tom would watch certain plays and say, 'Don should have done this. Or Don should not have done that.' He took him apart."

If Don Meredith was going to be absent from work and stuck in the repair shop with a busted carburetor, Landry had to be thankful to God and the NFL schedule-maker. Dallas's next two opponents occupied skid row in the standings. First, the Cowboys would play the New Orleans Saints, a team in its first season of competition but already headlong into the process of establishing a reputation as a barf bag of a franchise. That game was set for the Cotton Bowl. After that, the Cowboys would visit Pittsburgh for an appointment with the habitually punch-drunk Steelers.

Perfect timing. Landry now could gain some seasoning for Meredith's backup, Craig Morton. The Cowboys' coaching staff had confidence that game experience was the only ingredient missing before Morton, a coveted prospect from Cal Berkeley, might even compete with Meredith for the starting job. Landry was so impressed with Morton's overall football capacities that he had told his staff that if Morton never made the grade at quarterback, for whatever reason, he would switch him to tight end. Morton appeared strong, durable . . . not like Don Meredith, who was always getting his lungs punctured.

The stockpiling of exceptional ability at the quarterback position was a priority in the Cowboys' building operation. Roger Staubach, the Naval Academy grad then serving a hitch in Vietnam, would be available to press for a job two years down the road.

Morton's starting effort against the Saints turned out to be something that would sooner be filed with the bloopers than the highlights film, which was hardly Morton's fault. The Cotton Bowl playing surface had already been chopped up the day before when Texas beat Oklahoma, 9–7, in the annual college passion play that always highlights the State Fair of Texas in October. Early on Sunday, the North

Texas skies opened, then collapsed, and by kickoff time for the Cowboys-Saints game the field was better suited for alligator poachers than football players. For four quarters, the teams slopped through the quicksand. Morton said that the football felt like "a sponge with lead in it."

Nursing a 7–0 lead, Morton found Hayes wide open behind the Saints' secondary but threw the sponge over the receiver's head. Two plays later, Hayes was open again for a TD. Morton's throw was directly on target, but this time the sponge slipped through the receiver's hands.

As so often happens in games like that, the longer the favored team laughs its way through the motions, the better the chances of the underdog. Down by a mere three points and with the rain pouring, the Saints moved close to the Dallas goal. A touchdown would secure the upset. Bill Kilmer, playing for the Saints in his pre-Redskin days and facing fourth and goal, found a receiver, Vern Burke, open in the Dallas end zone. Kilmer's pass squirted from his hand straight up into the air. The quarterback caught his own ball and attempted to run it in. But linebacker Chuck Howley rammed Kilmer out of bounds and said, "Thanks for the game," after delivering the hit.

Reeves now fumbled the football back to New Orleans. With the goal line five yards away and the game in its final seconds, Kilmer fumbled the center snap and the miserable Saints had, as the saying goes, snatched defeat from the jaws of victory. Few of the Cowboys had anything meaningful to say about the ludicrous win. "I never saw anything so sloppy. I'm talking about the field and not the way we played," said George Andrie. "When it's like that, you forget about how you won or by how much. You take what you got, gratefully, and move on to next week."

THE SETTING FOR the "next week" that Andrie was talking about seemed to offer limitless opportunity. Nobody paid much attention to the Steelers of that era. In 1967, Terry Bradshaw was a freshman at Louisiana Tech and Franco Harris was still in high school. A team called the Pittsburgh Pipers, playing in a new league (the ABA) best known for its red, white, and blue basketball, commanded about as much esteem as the Steelers, who shared Pitt Stadium with the college team. With quarterback Bill Nelson hurt, the Steelers would start their backup passer, Kent Nix, who had been cut by the Packers after training camp. As backup quarterbacks go, Nix was no Craig Morton, supposedly.

The Steelers' only chance, it appeared, involved somehow getting out to an early lead, then relying on a trick defense of stunts and blitzes to frustrate and confuse the Cowboys. Instead, Bob Hayes outran Pittsburgh defensive back Brady Keyes, and Morton hit him with two early and easy touchdown passes of 55 and 37 yards. Pittsburgh, playing under coach Bill Austin—a former Lombardi assistant at Green Bay—seemed done.

Kent Nix, taking a shallow drop and popping away with short slant patterns like he was throwing darts, patiently brought his team back against a complacent Dallas defense. Nix threw one touchdown pass to John Hilton, then ran three yards for another. In the fourth quarter, Nix marched the Steelers on a 91-yard drive and gave the team the lead, 21–17, on an 11-yard pitch to J. R. Wilburn. Only 1:12 remained to play.

Morton threw a pass to Rentzel, who ran 45 yards up the field until Keyes slammed into him at the Steelers' 20. Rentzel fumbled, the ball bounced crazily upfield, and Reeves pounced on it, giving Dallas the ball at the Steelers' six. One running play gained a yard. Then Morton dropped back to pass and quickly evacuated the pocket to avoid a heavy rush. Tight end Pettis Norman, knocked flat as he left the scrimmage line, got up, decided to ad-lib and ran toward what looked like an open spot in the end zone. Morton found Norman for the TD with 0:24 remaining. The Cowboys won only after barely surviving the likes of Kent Nix. The defense, at least, had been impressed with Nix and his quick delivery, and Lilly called him "son of Jurgensen."

FOR THREE STRAIGHT Sundays, the Cowboys stumbled into irrational and unplanned circumstances to win games in the final seconds. For three straight Sundays, the Cowboys won games that they should have lost. For a franchise that had been making a habit of doing things the other way around, this might have seemed like progress.

In the Bible that Tom Landry was used to reading, however, there were no passages that read: "Thou shalt rather be lucky than good." With its 5–1 record, there was something about this team that Landry thought was disturbing.

The following Sunday, playing against what was a half-ass Philadelphia team that season, Craig Morton threw three interceptions. Dallas had used up its allotted supply of fluke finishes. The Eagles upset the Cowboys, 21–14, and Tom Landry wondered why it was taking so long to reinflate Don Meredith's lungs.

CHAPTER 8

It was a different story at Green Bay. With the Green Bay Packers' steamrolling success story at full force and the proud team blazing from battle site to battle site with relentless élan, Vince Lombardi had ascended to a status as American hero, and as 1967 turned into October, Vince Lombardi remained undefeated.

Lombardi's remaining autumn aggravations were the professional gridiron neo-gladiators who were trying to drag his Green Bay Packers down to the plateau occupied by most other mortals. The Detroit Lions, who had almost done just that by tying the Pack in September, were scheduled for the rematch.

This time the Pack, now 2–0–1, entered hostile territory for the first time after playing Detroit and Chicago at Lambeau Field and Atlanta in Milwaukee. Tiger Stadium, in downtown Detroit, was rarely an easy visit for the Pack, even during the Lombardi dynasty. Some of these Detroit fans were direct kin of the assembly-line workers who staged the epic sit-down strike at the General Motors plant at Flint, Michigan, and drove the cops away by firing at them with five-pound automobile door hinges propelled by slingshots made out of inner tubes.

So the Lions' followers came with tough-guy credentials, and this stadium in Detroit had been the site of what was probably Lombardi's most ignominious loss, back in 1962. Now Lombardi faced the additionally challenging prospect of traveling to Detroit without his quarterback, Bart Starr.

With Starr on the shelf for at least three weeks with a wrecked shoulder, the replacement was Zeke Bratkowski. Zeke brought twelve seasons' worth of National Football League experience and savvy with him. That also meant that Bratkowski was no pup at thirty-four years young. Only one player on the Packers' roster, pass catcher Max McGee (thirty-five), had been around longer. Zeke and Max sort of resembled each other, and, thin across the scalp, neither would seek a career modeling in shampoo commercials.

Lombardi valued experience above all else at the quarterback slot, but nobody had to remind the coach that a player of Zeke's age also presented limited mobility and a hard hit might indeed snap one of Bratkowski's tired old bones. And these were the same Lions who had rendered a dreadful pounding unto Bart Starr just a month earlier, with Alex Karras supplying most of the crunch. If Bratkowski became disabled, then Vince's last alternative was San Diego State rookie Don Horn, who had yet to take a regular season snap. Vince knew that if anything happened to Zeke, the Pack might well be undone.

WHILE A CROWD of 55,000 Motor City zealots cheered their guts out, the Lions surged off to a 10–0 lead, just as they had at Lambeau Field when Starr had pitched four interceptions. On the field it was obvious that the Lions had once again arrived at the game ready for a fight. Detroit receiver Pat Studstill and Packers cornerback Herb Adderley exchanged punches after one play. "Me and Herb, we're like two women living in the same apartment. We're always hollering at each other," said Studstill after the game.

This time it would be the Lions' quarterbacks, Milt Plum and Karl Sweetan (the latter like Dennis Rodman a product of South Oak Cliff High School in Dallas), who were offering explanations to the media about some interceptions. One of the key plays happened in the second half, when Green Bay's Dave Robinson deflected a Milt Plum pass toward Ray Nitschke, who intercepted the ball and ran it in for a touchdown. "When I caught the ball, I made an abrupt turn and yanked a muscle in the back of my leg. I wanted to lateral the ball back to Robinson, but he didn't know about my leg and was already upfield and blocking," was how Nitschke described it. "So I hobbled on in."

Nitschke suffered a hamstring pull, the kind of injury that puts modern-era players on the injured-reserve list, sometimes for a prolonged stay. In Nitschke's case, he rubbed some Vicks ointment on the bum leg and finished out the season without further problems. After the Ray Nitschke touchdown, the Lions were no longer a factor.

Sweetan, with a stronger arm than Plum, had entered the game to engineer a comeback with long passes, which only led to another interception, this one by Adderley. "Few people can throw deep against us." That was Lombardi's terse footnote to the game, won by the Packers, 27–17.

The meaningful subplot involved the private war of Alex Karras versus Jerry Kramer—a rematch of the earlier bout which had been won so thoroughly and completely by the defensive tackle. Karras made few, if any, mistakes during that game but committed a big one afterward. He told the wire services and thus the world: "The Green Bay Packers? They're just an average team. They're going to get beat often." After that fiasco, possibly the most disastrous of Jerry Kramer's career and certainly his most trying afternoon since the Pack had achieved championship status, the guard began watching movies . . . hours and hours' worth.

"I watched movies of that game and movies of games from other years that involved Karras," Kramer said, explaining his preparations for this day. "I knew what I had to do and I did it." Kramer, enjoying the afterglow and issuing a mind-game gambit that might come in handy in future years, refused to say what the "it" was that had made him so effective against Karras. Unlike their brutal assault of Bart Starr, the Lions' pass rush knocked Bratkowski down twice during the encore bout at Tiger Stadium but offered little pressure most of the game.

"I'd have to say that it was a lovely day," added Kramer. He mentioned that Karras made a lot of tackles "about ten yards down the field," where he had been knocked or shoved by the Packers' line. "Alex showed great pursuit," Kramer said, twisting the knife a little more.

IN STRATEGY SESSIONS before the Packs' second meeting with the Lions, Lombardi mentioned in a news conference that he truly didn't know the identity of the team Green Bay would meet the following week. Lombardi had made such a comment before, to illustrate the concentration he put on the task at hand as opposed to gazing down the road. Given the upcoming result, Vince might have been better served by taking the Lions for granted and plotting better offensive tactical plans for the Minnesota Vikings.

The Sunday skies over County Stadium in Milwaukee presented a sullen prelude. A dark storm was blowing across Lake Michigan from the east, and the afternoon was ideal for perhaps the witches of *Macbeth.* Days like this sometimes cheered up Lombardi. He liked to call this Packer Weather, but of course, if this was Packer Weather, then it had to be Viking Weather as well.

The Vikings franchise had entered the league on an expansion basis, one year after Dallas, in 1961. The Vikings had been allowed a full draft before their first season and given access to better talent than the early Cowboys had. But unlike Dallas, the Vikes never quite jelled into contender status, and now the coach, the sometimes turbulent Norm Van Brocklin, had been replaced by an import from the Canadian League. And with Fran Tarkenton now employed by the New York Giants, Minnesota was quarterbacked by another CFL refugee—Joe Kapp.

Minnesota came into the game in Milwaukee with an 0–4 record, and that bothered Vince. He sensed a kamikaze effort from Minnesota. What also bothered Vince was that Bart Starr remained on medical leave. True, Bratkowski had been the conductor in two good wins over the Falcons and the Lions. But Minnesota, despite the four losses, seemed to be building a superior defense. A rookie playing end, Alan Page, demonstrated a flair for the pro game. He showed rapidly advancing skills and technique and, as Page got better, so did Minnesota.

On the week of the Vikings game, a nun in Manitowoc, near Green Bay, had addressed the Wisconsin Women's Press Association on the topic of a "woman's right to nag." This nun, with the actual name of Thomas More, declared that the women of Wisconsin and women of the world not only have the right to nag but "the duty to do so and recurrently remind people of what needs to be done." Although nobody ever accused Vince Lombardi of being nun-like, the team noticed that the coach had been "on the nag" all week as he exercised his right and duty to remind his Packers of what needed to be done against the Viking defense.

Still, the Packers offense did finally get killed, and a Green Bay streak of sixteen straight games without a loss—dating back to another meeting with Minnesota the previous November at Lambeau Field—finally came to an end.

The game opened well for the Pack. Bratkowski exploited a busted coverage and hit Carroll Dale with an 86-yard touchdown strike. Then Carl Eller, Jim Marshall, Page, and others proceeded to frustrate the Green Bay attack. The Packer offense started and ended with the success of its running game, and on this inordinately dark afternoon in Milwaukee, Minnesota denied Green Bay the rush.

"They stopped us whenever we had to go, and that's the story," said Jim Grabowski in what was hardly a startling admission. The Packers finished the game with an appalling 42 yards on the ground. Joe Kapp completed an equally appalling two of eleven Viking passes for a feeble 25 yards. With the score tied 7–7 and the game getting late, this time it was the Pack that made the ruinous mistake. Bratkowski, in Green Bay territory, used the play that Bart Starr had used in the drives that salvaged a tie against the Lions and a win over the Bears.

Evidently, the Vikings sensed what was coming—a toss to halfback Elijah Pitts. Minnesota's Earsell Mackbee got to the ball first. After the turnover, Fred Cox kicked a field goal and suddenly County Stadium seemed empty. The crowd of over 49,000, the biggest ever to watch a Packers game in Milwaukee, fell quiet. So did Bratkowski when the game was over, as he stuffed his socks into an equipment bag. "I was trying to throw over the sidelines . . . away from an interception, and he [Mackbee] went over and grabbed it." Bratkowski shrugged. "It looked like he made an excellent play."

The Vikings made plays like that all day. Nine times, the Vikings stopped the Packers on third down. Was it the Vikings' defense, though, or a dysfunctional Packer attack that resulted in the nonproduction? After five games, Green Bay had scored but 87 points, placing the Pack twelfth out of sixteen teams in the NFL's most-watched statistical category. After the Vikings game, the Packers' turnover toll had reached 22 after a total of only 24 for the entire 1966 season. Sure, the Packers had their Gold Dust Twins, Anderson and Grabowski, but it appeared plain that the offense missed the devastating blocking of the now long-departed Paul Hornung and Jim Taylor.

Lombardi seemed down. "Neither offense was worth a damn," he declared. "Somebody is going to beat you, and if anybody is going to do it, it might as well be them," he said, gesturing toward the Vikings' dressing room, over there toward the man who would soon replace Lombardi as the high priest of conquest in the Icelands.

* * *

"IT WAS IMPORTANT that we win today, and it didn't matter if it was the Packers or the Little Sisters of the Poor." The speaker was Bud Grant, the new Vikings coach, who had compiled a 121–66 record with Winnipeg and had won the Grey Cup (Canadian football's version of the Stanley Cup) four times. Grant, described in the papers as "a tall, graying but extremely dashing gentleman," was throwing down a new statement of purpose, insinuating that the Packers might better prepare themselves to be set aside. "The Vikings are not awed by Green Bay, physically or otherwise," Grant said. "Maybe it's because of the geographic closeness. Those Eastern teams who play the Packers once every two or three years wonder, 'What are they going to do to us?' We have a different attitude: What are we going to do to them?"

Who was this Bud Grant character to barge in here and talk like that? Not only that, but also to resort to the extreme measure of circumventing the critical fundamental mistake and defeat the Packers at their own game. Joe Kapp said he approached Grant on the sideline as the clock wound down and the game was deadlocked at seven and demanded, "Can't we *throw* the ball more?"

Grant gave Joe Kapp a dead stare and said, "Nope."

A FRONT-PAGE HEADLINE in the *Green Bay Press-Gazette* read: "4 Killed, 36 Wounded" and, for a change, the dateline was somewhere not in Vietnam. No. These were the casualty reports from the opening day of deer hunting season in Wisconsin.

Some friends of Lombardi had taken the coach on a Wisconsin deer hunt—once. Before the expedition, Packers players, as a practical joke, presented their coach with a gift: a hunting jacket with a red target painted on the back. Deer season was an annual ritual in which the intrepid sportsmen, fortified to the gills with the warming influence of distilled grain products, ventured into the frosty fields and blasted away with high-powered thirty-aught-six rifles at anything that moved, which could turn out to be another hunter. This was a particularly tough weekend in 1967. In search of killer buck, along with the hunters blasted by friendly fire, another eighteen riflemen died of heart attacks.

* * *

AFTER AN AFTERNOON at Memorial Stadium in Baltimore, Vince Lombardi and most of his Packers entourage probably wished that they had been otherwise occupied back in the Wisconsin woods, participating in *that* carnage, though with only a loss and a tie to blemish their record, the Packers actually were on firm footing in their division race.

With the NFL-AFL merger in a transition process in 1967, the NFL, for the first time, had been subdivided from two divisions into four. All that was required of the Pack during the regular season was to finish ahead of Detroit, Minnesota, and Chicago—all with mediocre win-loss marks—to qualify for one of the four playoff slots. The moment of truth would come later, in a preliminary playoff game against whichever team won another division—Los Angeles or Baltimore—and these were superior outfits.

After the shattering loss to the Minnesota Vikings at Milwaukee, the Packers bounced back at Yankee Stadium and hammered the anemic Giants, 48–21, thanks to a revival of the rushing attack. "When we run, everything goes. This is a team that has to run the ball," Lombardi said. The coach was impressed with the elusive qualities of the Giants' quarterback, Fran Tarkenton. "He's an amazing little fellow," the coach said, "and he's not so little, either."

Now Lombardi was eager to find out how his Packers might measure up to a more genuine upper class of competition at Baltimore, with Bart Starr finally back in the lineup. With Don Shula doing the coaching and Johnny Unitas doing the quarterbacking for the Colts, the competition was real.

Two omens—not particularly good ones—passed over the Packers quickly. First, in the game program, Elijah Pitts's first name was misspelled as "Eliza." Then, early in the contest, Lombardi experienced something that did not happen often. He was accosted on the sideline by a drunk. Things like that could happen sometimes in Memorial Stadium, a baseball park where many spectators were situated at field level and within comfortable spit-wad distance of the visiting team's bench. Some of these fans, like the Wisconsin deer trackers, would get fueled on Kentucky antifreeze.

Vince, using a "Can you believe this?" tone, described the scene later. "This guy . . . just walks up to me and starts poking me and following me around. He wanted us all to sit down so the fans behind us could see better." Then he shifted to the "We are not amused" tone favored by British royalty. "The sideline stuff is terrible in this park. They let everybody down there. So this guy is drunk, he's following me around, and the policeman just stands there and looks."

Sadly for the Packers, their kickoff team impersonated the cop—just stood there and looked when the outcome of the contest was still very much at issue. Green Bay scored early, a 31-yard touchdown pass, Starr to Donny Anderson, and Baltimore scored late, Unitas to Alex Hawkins for ten yards, then missed the extra point. Behind 10–6 with 2:16 remaining on the fourth-quarter clock up underneath the National Bohemian beer ad on the Baltimore stadium scoreboard, Lou Michaels tried an onside kick. While the people in the seats behind the Packers bench might not have clearly seen what happened next, Vince Lombardi received an excellent view. "I saw the ball go by and somebody [on the Green Bay special team] should have had it," Lombardi commented, his voice full of wonderment. Under the odd circumstances, Vince's mood with the reporters was surprisingly cordial. Often Lombardi was harder to deal with after a big win. "We knew the onside kick was coming. My God . . . 60,000 people in the stands knew it was coming. Everybody knew it was coming. It turned out fortunate for them and bad for us."

Defensive back Rick Volk recovered Michaels' kick at the Green Bay 34-yard line. "The game was on the line. That's for sure. I saw the ball, and all I had to do was go over and get it," Volk said. That put the Green Bay defense in the negotiating position of a man seated in an electric chair. Johnny Unitas, naturally, threw the switch. On a fourth-down play, Unitas scrambled for seven yards to pick up a first down. On the next play, he threw a touchdown pass to Willie Richardson and the Packers were beaten, 13–10.

Since the Pack was still in command in its division race, that outcome was not of dire consequence. Bleak and serious tidings, however, had issued from the training room. Elijah Pitts limped off the field in the first quarter. The diagnosis was a torn Achilles tendon. "He may be through," said Vince, and Pitts was. So was Jim Grabowski, with a knee injury that not only concluded the season but essentially the career of the "million-dollar-bonus boy" whom Lombardi had handpicked to replace the great Jim Taylor. Lombardi said what he always said when guys got hurt: "How did losing Pitts and Grabowski affect the outcome? I haven't got the slightest idea. They're all professionals. We're supposed to have the people to replace the ones we lose."

Lombardi maintained a cardinal rule in which he never blamed a scoreboard defeat on the absence of a starter. To do so, Lombardi believed, would only serve to impair the confidence of the backup player. But that same Sunday night, after the loss to Baltimore, a fullback in Washington, D.C., who had sensed that his faltering football future was headed on a precarious course, received a telephone call from the executive offices of the Green Bay Packers.

New Trier High School in Winnetka, a north-end suburb of Chicago, has produced an interesting array of graduates who include Rock Hudson, Charlton Heston, Ann-Margret, Bruce Dern, and Ralph Bellamy. Also, a future Chicago Bear, Mike Pyle, came out of New Trier, and it was Pyle who then convinced still another New Trier player, Chuck Mercein, to attend Yale.

"I had a lot of scholarship offers out of high school, including most of the Big Ten schools," said Mercein, a fullback and linebacker. Mercein's father, Tom, had been a radio personality in the Chicago area, "sort of the Don Imus of his time," Mercein said. "But his career was not going well when I completed high school, and Yale offered certain people a grant-in-aid on the basis of scholastic and athletic achievement and financial need. So I received what amounted to a free ride from Yale. The year before, Yale was unbeaten, had won the Lambert Trophy, always played before home crowds of 50,000 or so people, and of course, I would be getting a broad-based, broad-stroked liberal education."

The Yale experience for Mercein had been all that he had hoped and anticipated it would be—with a bonus. "I never had set my sights on pro football, either in high school or in college. I felt blessed just to be able to play the game, and I had contained the goals I had to reachable levels," he says.

But Chuck Mercein had a strong senior season at Yale in 1964 and was informed by the Buffalo Bills that he would be their "focus player" in the coming draft. "So being a Yale product was no hindrance in positioning myself in pro football. They [the Bills]offered me a three-year no-cut contract worth over $100,000, or thereabouts, and I was flattered. I also thought that the Dallas Cowboys would draft me from the NFL. Gil Brandt had been all over me." (Dallas used its first pick on Craig Morton.)

"But I was surprised to receive a call from Bill Ford with the Lions, who wanted to draft me as the seventh overall player in the NFL draft. Ford asked me if I had signed with the other league, and I told him 'no' but also told him that he should know that I had the Bills' offer in my pocket. Ford said the Lions were not willing to match the three-year no-cut portion of the deal, so I told them not to waste their pick on me, which might have been a brash and foolhardy thing to say, and I was wondering if I hadn't screwed up.

"In fact, I probably had. I slid down to the twenty-eighth pick in the NFL draft, but Wellington Mara of the Giants finally called. I told him about the Bills' offer, too, and Mara said, 'We have no problem with that.' So I became a Giant and then scored all ten points—a touchdown, a field goal, and an extra point—for the College All-Stars in their 17–10 loss to the Browns, although Dick Butkas won the MVP."

With New York, Mercein found himself backing up at fullback Tucker Fredrickson, the top player overall in the '64 draft. "But the next year we kind of reversed roles. Tucker, I think, was hurt and I played most of the year, was among the NFL's top ten rushers well into the season, and averaged about five yards a carry." But then, as now, the NFL players received not a salary but hazard pay because of the on-the-field risk factor.

Henry Jordan of the Packers, noting an escalating injury factor throughout the league in 1966, said, "There are no longer any dirty players in the NFL. Now they have guys who are trained to injure you scientifically."

Larry Stallings, a St. Louis Cardinals linebacker, seemed to illustrate that when he hit Mercein from behind, "and I got a ruptured kidney and was pissing blood for a month and missed the last four games of the season."

Still, Mercein felt good about his pro status going into training camp with the 1967 Giants. Unfortunately for Mercein, none of the history or political science courses that he had concentrated on at Yale had taught him much about the realities that face a midlevel talent in the cold-blooded dominion of professional sports. The Ivy League fullback had not yet learned that a feeling of security is often abruptly displaced by a bus ticket or a room with a view at Heartbreak Hotel.

"The fact was that I never communicated too well with Allie Sherman," said Mercein, and during the 1967 preseason the fullback watched whatever element of interchange that he did have with the coach begin to disintegrate. Sherman started to rag Mercein about his Yale background. "On a couple of occasions he looked at me and asked, 'Whataya doing up here?' meaning the NFL. Well, the fact was that Allie Sherman was this little guy from Brooklyn with a southern accent, and I couldn't figure him out, either. As they say at Yale, we didn't get along worth nuthin'."

When the last cuts were announced, the Giants traded to Cleveland to get Larry Costello, an experienced linebacker, and Mercein was cut loose. "But I cleared waivers because of my high salary. There was nothing I could do. I was upset."

Now living in Scarsdale with a wife and one child, Mercein decided to sustain hope that his pro career had not yet vanished and joined a semi-pro team known as the Westchester Bulls—a rather precipitous departure from his existence within the majestic showroom of big-league football. "No, playing for the Westchester Bulls was not a happy time, but it turned out all right because I still didn't have any quit in me and I wanted to stay in good shape, in contact shape for football and remain sharp."

After two weeks, Allie Sherman was on the phone. He needed a kicker. "I didn't want to be a kicker, although I was capable of kicking 48-yard field goals," Mercein said. "Sherman was worried about his job by then, and when he signed me back on as the placekicker, the first thing and really the only thing that he told me was, 'If you miss one, you're gone again.'

"So. It was kind of funny, looking back. I went out to kick an extra point against the Steelers, I think it was. I made the kick, but there was a penalty. The Giants were called for holding, and they moved us back about 15 yards. So now the extra point would be like a 30-yard field goal.

"I missed it, Sherman released me, and I knew then that I wasn't coming back."

By now Otto Graham, the coach of the 1964 College All-Star team that included Mercein, Butkas, Roger Staubach, and Fred Bilitnikoff, had become head coach of the Washington Redskins. Graham offered Mercein a tryout. "It went well, and Otto said that while there was not time to activate me for that Sunday's game, that a contract was waiting and I could sign it Monday morning."

Enter fate. "On Sunday night, Wellington Mara from the Giants called. He said he knew that the Redskins were offering a contract and wondered if I had signed anything, and when I said, 'Not yet,' Mara said he had just received a call from Vince Lombardi and asked me if I might be interested in joining the Packers. With Jim Grabowski lost because of his hurt knee in the Colts game that afternoon, Vince needed a fullback and needed one quick.

"The phone rang again and it was Vince Lombardi. 'Do you want to play for Green Bay?' he asked me," said Mercein, still relishing his memory of the moment. "My heart was pounding a thousand beats a minute. I told Lombardi that I could be on the next plane, and he said, 'That's exactly what I want you to do.'

"Talk about a sudden turn of events," Mercein declared. "The following Tuesday I wasn't sure whether I was attending a football practice session or an induction ceremony for the NFL Hall of Fame. The first guy who walked up to me and introduced himself was Forrest Gregg. The next was Bart Starr, then Herb Adderley. They all said that if there was anything they could help with, to just ask, and they said that they were happy I was on the team."

They might not have realized *how* happy they were that this cast-adrift ex-Yalie had joined their team until the final minute of a memorable football game on New Year's Eve, when the opponent was the Dallas Cowboys and the chill factor was about 75 below.

CHAPTER

9

In New York, in 1967, a play had opened, *The Trial of Lee Harvey Oswald,* at which the audience served as the jury. Columnist Walter Winchell himself went to see it and wrote: "The authors [of the play] in our opinion libel and slander the people of Texas and particularly Dallas. The show is another member of the fast-buck army. Recommended for people who have trouble sleeping."

Down in Dallas, the football team was drawing some less than flattering reviews, too. After a stinko performance at Philadelphia, Coach Tom Landry felt that if the Cowboys were destined to be any kind of factor in their far-fetched quest to win Super Bowl II, his defense would have to accomplish that. Dallas's defensive unit remained a work-in-progress by midseason, 1967, but the main portions of the formula had been blending into a potent mix.

Chuck Howley, secured from the Bears via a trade in 1961, developed an uncanny sense of where the ball was going on almost every play. A hard case from West Virginia, Howley's approach to the game involved a limited display of the social graces. A rookie defensive end recalled an episode in a training-camp scrimmage. Howley yelled out some blitz code—"Bullet!"—that the rookie had never heard of, and after the snap the linebacker left cleat marks on the kid's back. "I don't understand that 'bullet' call—what am I supposed to do?" Pat Toomay asked. "I don't care what the fuck you do," Howley told him. "Just stay out of my way."

At middle linebacker, Lee Roy Jordan's kill-or-be-killed approach became a natural fit for the ebb and flow of the pro game. One of the top running backs in the league, Tim Brown of Philadelphia, found Jordan's approach a problem for both his football and his show business careers. Brown's face was structured to appeal to the tastes of motion picture casting agents, and on the Monday after each game the Eagles back would travel to New York for acting and voice lessons.

Against the Cowboys in the Cotton Bowl, Tim Brown ran out of the backfield on a pass pattern through an area that Lee Roy Jordan regarded as private property—off-limits, no trespassing. Although Brown's role in that play was to act as a decoy, Jordan leveled a forearm beneath the halfback's facemask. Tim Brown left the field, as they say in the National Hockey League, "spittin' Chiclets." Thanks to Jordan, he'd lost his four upper front teeth. In the Eagles' dressing room later, Brown's teammate, halfback Israel Lang, was indignant. "The Cowboys are supposed to be a class outfit. Huh! That Lee Roy Jordan has got about as much class as a goddamn goat." Given the responsibility that Jordan felt was his as a specialized requirement of his job, he probably took that as a major compliment.

Landry's secondary had developed two all-pro candidates, Mel Renfro and Cornell Green, the ex-basketball player. Renfro, indeed, would wind up in the NFL Hall of Fame. And Mike Gaechter, with terrific speed, made it difficult for any quarterback to throw consistently deep against the Cowboys.

On the front line, teams routinely assigned two blockers to Bob Lilly, which rarely accomplished much. By 1965 Bob Lilly was playing in the Pro Bowl, an occasion that he later recalled most vividly. Not so much for the game but for something that happened a day later. Before returning to Dallas, Lilly stopped in Las Vegas to play blackjack and quickly dropped an amount that exceeded his paycheck for the Pro Bowl, plus a little extra. Milton Berle, recognizing Lilly and sensing his plight, said, "Having some trouble, big guy? Here, I'll help you straighten this out." With Berle playing his hands for him, Lilly got back to even.

A Bob Lilly clone, at least in size, played to Lilly's immediate right. As defensive end, George Andrie was not receiving the media attention he probably deserved simply because he played in such proximity to the all-world Lilly. As a consequence, Andrie might have to be satisfied to be remembered as perhaps the most underrated defensive player in Dallas history. Still, he was aware the odds against his playing in the National Football League at all were so long that even Milton Berle might not have helped.

At the dawn of the 1960s, Andrie played in the line at Marquette

University in Milwaukee. Al McGuire coached the Warriors to an NCAA basketball championship. The football team, when Andrie played at Marquette, ranked right up there with nonalcoholic beer on the popularity charts of upper midwesterners. Then, before Andrie's senior season, the school actually canceled the whole football program.

Not great for a fellow's confidence level. "Actually, I was contacted by the Calgary Stampeders from the Canadian League. And Calgary's coach, Bobby Dobbs, had a brother, Glenn Dobbs, who was coaching at the University of Tulsa," Andrie said. "After several confusing phone calls, I agreed to play at Tulsa during my last year of college eligibility. When your school drops the sport it's all right to transfer. I didn't know what the hell was going on, really.

"Football players of that era had no one to advise them. My parents never did advise me. Hell, I don't think they even knew I was going to college. When I got down to Tulsa, I found out that I wasn't even set up to enroll in any classes. They said, 'That's all right. We'll graduate you anyway.' But . . . I had a feeling that all of this might not work out, so I went back to Milwaukee and finished school at Marquette. And that was when I received a telephone call from Gil Brandt with the Dallas Cowboys, asking me if I had any interest in continuing to play football. He sent me this off-season workout program that the Cowboys use."

With the likely exception of Roger Staubach, nobody made better use of the conditioning guide than George Andrie. "I ran. I lifted weights. I got into the best shape of my life. I have never, before or since, been so well prepared for anything as I was before that Cowboys training camp. I had no idea what to expect. I knew absolutely nothing about professional football. Pro football in those days was nothing as far as I was concerned. It wasn't even on TV.

"I even went to the gym and boxed every day. If there were going to be fights, then I wanted to be ready for that crap, too. What I had to overcome most, as it turned out, was the advice I was getting from people in every direction. All of it negative. 'You didn't even play last year.' All that stuff. If I listened, I never would have gone and tried it. That's what I had to overcome and, when I finally did get to camp, I found I was totally prepared, even though I had been divorced from football for almost a year and a half."

In truth, Andrie was not prepared for the sign that greeted all players who arrived at training that listed an agenda of misdemeanors, accompanied by a schedule of fines. If a player had failed to have his ankles taped before a workout and suffered a sprained ankle, he had to pay a hefty fine. A smaller fine was issued for missing curfew, but the amount escalated rapidly for each fifteen minutes the player stayed late. Fines were also levied for being late to meetings or meals. Offenses that fell under the broad definition of gambling drew heavy fines, so it was rare to see players shooting craps or playing roulette games in the dormitory basement.

Once Andrie got past the fines sign and onto the practice field, his personal outlook quickly improved. Other than the Ice Bowl game, when Andrie would recover a Bart Starr fumble and score a touchdown that almost spoiled the ending of the Vince Lombardi dynasty, the day in George Andrie's football career that he best remembers happened in his first morning at training camp. "It was a simple drill. They lined me up across from a big offensive lineman, Ed Nutting, who was from Georgia Tech and projected as a starter. The line coach, Jim Myers, said that all he wanted me to do was go from one point, where I was lined up, to another point, where an imaginary quarterback would be setting up to pass. All I had to do to get there was maneuver my way past, around, or over Ed Nutting. So the coach goes 'Hut . . . hut,' and on the snap count I threw Ed Nutting over on his back and ran over him.

"So Myers, the coach, says, 'Okay, okay, Andrie, let's try it one more time. Come on, Nutting. Let's get it going.' So we tried it again, with the same result. I threw Ed Nutting over on his back. Now don't get me wrong," Andrie said. "I've got nothing against Ed Nutting. He's a great guy. All I know is that after that little session on the workout field, I had opened their eyes, and from then on I had a great camp."

Since Andrie had not the slightest notion of what to expect from life in professional football, he also could not have had any idea of what to make of Coach Tom Landry. While Andrie would earn a doctorate in the study of the fine points of NFL warfare by the time he retired, he was still not sure how to define the Cowboys' coach. "Tom never had much communication with his players," Andrie said. "Maybe that's good in a way, because when there is no communication, then at least there can never be any *mis*communication. Tom told you what you were supposed to do and that was that. When you didn't do it, he never said much . . . just looked at you.

"Landry, I guess, assumed that all his players were self-motivated like me. And most of them probably were. That was my impression. I was like them and they were like me. When you have forty guys, though, not all of them are going to be alike. I guess there were some borderline guys, and if Landry had kicked them in the ass we might have gotten there [to the Super Bowl] sooner."

Another obstacle to the Cowboys' journey to the promised land of the Super Bowl was consistency of performance on both sides of the ball. "I joined the Cowboys in 1962, and by the time we were finally playing against the Packers in those championship games, we were very competitive on the defense, with Lee Roy and Chuck and Bob and Mel and Cornell Green and Jethro Pugh and so on," said Andrie. "But we'd make mistakes, we'd do things, we'd screw up. On one play we'd get a great pass rush, but one of the defensive backs would cover the wrong guy, and against a quarterback like, well, let's say Sonny Jurgensen, bang. That's a touchdown that would cost you a game.

"It was just a few *little* things that we needed to correct. I don't know why it took so long to make those corrections. But it did."

Another recurring nightmare in the adolescent stages of the Dallas football team was that on frequent occasions, when the offense showed up armed and dangerous, the defense went to lunch and took the rest of the afternoon off. The next Sunday, while the defense embarked on a feeding frenzy, the offense looked like something out of an Abbott and Costello movie.

Three games leading into the midpoint of the 1967 season served as the perfect illustration of the syndrome. Against New Orleans, with heavy rain and a muddy field, the Dallas offense had no spark. Against the Steelers the next week the Dallas defense had been slowly picked to pieces by a rookie quarterback, Kent Nix. Somehow, Dallas won both games, but the following week they put the whole package together: The offense looked pathetic, the defense reeked, and the Cowboys lost—to the Eagles.

In Dallas that autumn of 1967, a bombardment reached the high-gear stage. All of the women and quite a few of the men did not realize it, but they had declared war on the ozone layer. While Los Angeles had its smog problems, the air around Dallas was becoming clouded with aerosol hair spray.

The favored coiffure of the American woman matched that of

Mary Tyler Moore as she appeared on *The Dick Van Dyke Show.* Outside the Dallas city limits, in places like Waxahachie and Wills Point, the beehive look remained the vogue. By 1967, the men were abandoning traditional barbershops and heading for the styling salons, where they, too, received heavy doses of the mist. So the go-go folk of Dallas, heads now protected from the elements by congealed, transparent lacquer, also found insulation from the terrible wartime events exploding in Vietnam in the heady distraction provided by the football team.

With the Atlanta Falcons scheduled in the Cotton Bowl, there were high hopes that the Cowboys might be in store for a long-overdue blowout. Yet that's also what the fans had figured might be coming against New Orleans and Pittsburgh. The Cowboys hadn't, in fact, looked like anything resembling championship caliber in over a month. At least Don Meredith, now over his siege with the collapsed lung and resulting pneumonia, was back and listed in Landry's starting lineup. The new Meredith—happy to be back—sounded like the old Meredith. In a pregame prediction, Meredith guaranteed a restoration of the offense and a 35-point showing against the Falcons.

While one sportswriter later reported that against the Falcons, "the Dallas Cowboys weren't exactly whipping a granite wall," Meredith's reappearance in the lineup plainly reignited the offense. He opened the game with a 60-yard touchdown pass to Dan Reeves. On the next possession the Cowboys drove 80 yards in nine plays, the ninth being a seven-yard touchdown pitch to Reeves. After Dallas kicked off, Lee Roy Jordan intercepted a Falcons pass and ran it back 33 yards for another score. By the time it was over, the Cowboys had won, 37–7, and Dan Reeves had scored four touchdowns.

Afterward, Meredith addressed the media in his classic, wisecracking, finger-snappin' Dandy Don style—a sort of combination of Joe Namath and Muhammad Ali. "I told ya'll our offense would score thirty-five points, but I included Lee Roy's touchdown in that mix. I knew that he would run an interception in for a score because he told me he would. But we did score a safety, too, and I hadn't taken that into account. Don't let this get around, but we're going to win the whole thing."

Dan Reeves described his four-TD effort emotionally. The night before the game his first son, Michael Leon, had been born. "If I was running better today, it was because I was so proud of my little boy,"

Reeves declared. Tommy Nobis, the Atlanta linebacker who had maimed Bart Starr three weeks earlier, had a different idea. "You have to gear your defense to stop Bob Hayes," Nobis said. "So when you do that, the other guys, like Reeves, can hurt you, too."

A win over the Atlanta Falcons was not something to be enshrined in the Library of Congress, even if you scored in triple digits. The Cowboys game that day was well remembered for an entirely different reason by those who were in the stands. In the west stands spectators quit watching the game when Bubbles Cash, carrying cotton candy in both hands, strolled down the steps of the aisle perpendicular to the fifty-yard line. Clad in what fashion experts described as an orange microskirt, the well-endowed Miss Cash enjoyed a stadium reception of gasps that turned to cheers. Persons holding those fifty-yard-line season tickets—and those were the same people who played golf at Northwood and Brook Hollow Country Clubs—could not have responded more enthusiastically if Lady Godiva had made a grand entry. Who knows what might have happened if Bubbles had showed up in the end zone. Although the Chamber of Commerce never printed this on its letterhead or in any of its brochures, the official town motto might well read: "Dallas—The City with a Sex Drive" or "Dallas—The City with Tits the Size of Your Head."

When Bubbles created such a sensation in the stands, the media rushed to learn more about her while she posed "bumpily" for newspaper photos. As it turned out, Miss Cash worked as an ecdysiast at a well-known Dallas cultural outlet called the Theatre Lounge. That word, "ecdysiast," is of ancient Greek origin, and it means "someone who dances and disrobes in public while men in the audience make noises like creatures of the barnyard."

Miss Cash, in modern Dallas, could teach Sunday school in the same costume that incited hysteria at the Cowboys game in 1967. Her impact on the community was such that the city's most distinguished newspaper columnist, Blackie Sherrod, allowed Miss Cash into his office for a private audience. Bubbles, it turned out, was like all the rest of the Dallas women . . . they were from someplace else. In Bubbles's case the point of origin was identified as Soddy Daisy, Tennessee. Her Christian name, she said, was Theresa Mia, and after the photos of her Cotton Bowl debut reached the international wire services, she heard from home. The message from Soddy Daisy was, "Let the hems out and behave yourself," Miss Cash confided.

Describing her profession, Bubbles denied that she was either a stripper or an exotic dancer. "I just happen to take my clothes off," she said. Describing her approach to wardrobe selection at events like Wednesday night church services and Sunday afternoon Cowboys games, Miss Cash said, "if you show a lot of top, cover up the bottom. If you show a lot of bottom, then cover up the top. If you want to see both, then come to the Theatre Lounge."

Here, the basic and primal instincts of the sportswriter came into play. Sherrod sought statistics from the person he was interviewing. "I'm nineteen," Bubbles said.

"No . . . I mean . . . ," the tamed journalist stammered.

"Oh, *those* statistics," Bubbles said. "40–23–35."

Blackie Sherrod would later describe what next happened: "A button popped off Miss Cash's blouse. 'Oops. Excuse me,' said she. 'Think nothing of it,' I answered, flicking a cigarette lighter and setting fire to my nose."

The Cowboys' new mascot identified her favorite player as Bob Hayes. "He's such a cute little thing, but he runs and bangs into people like some big old Jethro Pugh," Bubbles said. She also announced her intention to travel to the sites of Cowboys road games. "What happens," Blackie Sherrod wondered, "if the Cowboys wind up in Green Bay for the championship game and the temperature is around zero?"

"That will put me to the test," she said. "But I'll be there."

Tex Schramm, the pro football visionary who, along with Pete Rozelle, hammered out the network television agreements that made the NFL into an entertainment-industry powerhouse, watched the Bubbles Cash craze with fascination. Tex felt another brainstorm coming on. Why not, Tex wondered, locate about fifteen or twenty little dancing replicas of Bubbles Cash—girls who make the Rockettes look like the Pittsburgh Steelers' front four—dress them in skimpy silver-and-blue short shorts with halter tops and white boots, and call them the Dallas Cowboys Cheerleaders? While Dallas would ultimately fall one foot short of playing in the Super Bowl, Tex Schramm will no doubt always remember 1967 as one very special kind of year.

Bubbles Cash, as promised, arrived suitably attired at the next Cowboys game, scheduled, appropriately, in New Orleans. In the Crescent

City, every woman who doesn't answer to Blanche DuBois *will* answer to a name like Bubbles Cash. Therefore, the woman who caused eyeballs to pop at the Cotton Bowl became just another pleasant image in the crowd of over 80,000 at Tulane Stadium.

NFL football held extreme novelty value during its first season in Cajun country, and the fans were as manic and enthusiastic as the Saints team was feeble. Tom Landry, as was his fashion, had been concerned that the crowd might stir the Saints into some kind of frenzy, and he was pleased to see his team play the kind of game that would take the heart out of the home team early. "We had them on the run—really pouring it on them. A lot of their people were getting hurt," was Landry's cool assessment.

Even Dallas fullback Don Perkins, who managed to leave the general impression that the grimier aspects of the pro game did not meet his standards of dignity, noted, "We were supposed to get beat up down here, but I noticed it was their guys who were hobbling off the field."

In the fourth quarter, with New Orleans trying to make the game close, quarterback Gary Cuozzo threw a pass that Cornell Green tried to intercept but tipped and juggled. When Green fell down, he lost control of the football. But the back judge ruled the play an interception and a fumble . . . and that Mel Renfro picked up the ball in the Cowboys' end zone and advanced 28 yards. "From where I was standing," Landry confessed, "I would have thought they would have ruled that an incomplete pass." The Saints' fans felt the same way, and they started getting agitated when Dallas tried a reverse on the next play and Frank Clarke ran 56 yards. Since many of these dilettantes were sipping from flasks containing a delicate but sassy chardonnay, the throng began to express its disapproval. The booing reached such a crescendo that Don Meredith could not shout out the play in the huddle, much less hope that his offense could hear a snap count at the line of scrimmage.

The din would not subside for fifteen minutes, and when the Saints waved their arms in an effort to silence the crowd, the frenzy only increased. When Meredith finally did run a play, he fumbled the snap and the Cowboys were denied another touchdown.

Somebody asked Landry if, when the Saints fans were hyperventilating in the stands, he had considered taking his team off the field. "No," Landry said. "Not, that is, when I'm fourteen points ahead."

* * *

Dallas, now poised to enter the stretch run of the season, appeared to be a cinch to nail down a playoff slot, and soon. Like the Packers, the Cowboys' regular season, barring catastrophe, had been designed to serve as an appetizer for the playoffs. All Dallas needed was to finish ahead of the Eagles, Redskins, and Saints, and the Cowboys would probably have to finish under .500 to lose their division.

With the Redskins coming to Dallas, the Cowboys appeared well positioned to lock the race up early. Instead, the team played a game that reminded Tom Landry of his 1960 crew that went 0–11–1. For a football organization loaded to the gums with some of the acknowledged virtuosos of the game at the skill positions (the ones who throw, catch, kick, and run with the ball), Landry couldn't remember a Cowboys team that had made as many physical pratfalls as Dallas performed against Washington. The passes that weren't overthrown were dropped. Danny Villanueva shanked a punt. Dallas even botched an extra point.

The play that best characterized the personality of the game came when halfback Dan Reeves took a pitchout, stopped, and threw a long downfield pass that appeared to be a 54-yard touchdown strike to Lance Rentzel. Instead, the flanker tapped the ball up, juggled it from hand to hand until Washington's Richie Harris sprinted over to snatch the ball away from Rentzel for an interception. "Just no excuse for it," said Rentzel. By the time the Cowboys woke up from their odd trance, they were trailing Washington 27–6, and two late Dallas touchdowns offered only an anticlimax.

Sonny Jurgensen completed 23 of 33 passes for 264 yards. "He reminded me of myself," laughed 'Skins coach Otto Graham. "No. Seriously. I was never the passer that Sonny is."

Both Tex Schramm and Landry looked dismayed as the team dressed hastily. Everybody seemed in a rush to get the hell out of the Cotton Bowl. "We had a three-game lead with five to play, and we blew it. We couldn't close the sale," Tex Schramm said.

Tom Landry looked over the Cowboys' schedule. The next week a dangerous St. Louis Cardinals team—much better than the Redskins, who had just flattened Dallas—was due in the Cotton Bowl. The week following that, Dallas would play the Colts—in Memorial Stadium, where Don Shula's team had beaten Green Bay. "Now we are going to find out what we are made of because it is going to be tough from now on," Landry told them.

When the Cardinals hit town on Thanksgiving Day, it appeared at first as if Landry and his team would face another excursion through football purgatory. In the game's first minute, St. Louis quarterback Jim Hart connected with his tight end, Jackie Smith, for a 67-yard TD.

"When something like that [a long bomb exploding into the face of the defense before the players have had time to work up a sweat] happens, then you know one of two things might happen," Landry deduced afterward. "Sometimes, you go into a game too tense, and then when they hit you with the big play early, it loosens you up.

"Or . . . you're going to be a big flop for the rest of the game."

Dallas retaliated with a salvo of long-distance touchdowns. Bob Hayes returned a punt 69 yards. Meredith completed a 48-yard pass to Rentzel that set up a touchdown by Perkins. Meredith threw a short pass into the right flat that Hayes turned into a 59-yard touchdown. Meredith connected again with Hayes for 53 yards in the third quarter, and Reeves completed his halfback-option pass to Rentzel for 74 yards. When it was over, Dallas had beaten an excellent St. Louis team, 46–21.

Just when Landry *seemed* ready to write off the season, the Cowboys' offensive choir went out and sang in octaves that the coach had never before heard. He came out of it looking like a world-class psychiatrist—the gridiron was his couch.

CHAPTER 10

Cynicism and American journalism tend to go together like big feet and professional basketball. Look at what one New York–based news magazine, *Time,* wrote about Frank Sinatra's first public appearance as chairman of the American-Italian Anti-Defamation League at a rally at Madison Square Garden. He said the organization "was seeking to remove the stigma of gangsterism from the land that produced Dante, Michelangelo, Columbus, Mussolini and Capone." The article further noted that Sinatra arrived at the rally just in time to miss all of the speeches and sang Italian ballads like "I've Got You Under My Skin" and "Moonlight in Vermont."

Viewed from a certain perspective, it might seem strange to some that the organization would select Old Blue Eyes to front its cause. Actually, if American-Italians needed a spokesman who had won the total approval and admiration of the nation in 1967, they needed to look no farther than Vince Lombardi.

The coach glistened with pride in his heritage. Lombardi maintained nonnegotiable rules that forbade anybody other than Packers football players or team employees on the buses that carried the team from the hotel to road-game stadium sites. One year, Vince noticed a couple of unfamiliar faces among a Packers pregame caravan and began shouting, "No civilians on the bus! No civilians on the bus!" But who turned up on the bus to Candlestick Park for a Packers contest against the 49ers, at the coach's invitation? None other than Joe DiMaggio.

Furthermore, Lee Remmel, sportswriter for the *Green Bay Press-Gazette* and now the head of public relations for the Packers, recalled the days when he covered the team and described Lombardi as "kind of like the Godfather." In this context, Remmel was not necessarily referring to Lombardi's ethnicity. He was merely illustrating that when Lombardi was running the Packers, there was never a question as to the man's total authority, and if anyone needed any favors from the team, they had to go directly through Lombardi.

"On road trips the sportswriters for the *Press-Gazette* routinely traveled on the Packers' chartered plane," Remmel said. "But it was no standing deal. We had to get his permission to ride before every game. Nothing was ever taken for granted."

Modern experts of the psychological sciences have identified a categorical typing for a person who exhibits coach Lombardi's workplace characteristics. So imperially commanding was Lombardi over all facets of the Packers' empire that the word "Caesar" might have been more fitting for the man's job title than "coach." "For instance," remembered Remmel, "none of his assistants [by 1967 the staff consisted of Phil Bengtson, Jerry Burns, Dave Hanner, Tom McCormick, Bob Schnelker, and Ray Wietecha] were ever allowed to talk to the media. Even in training camp, if you needed a comment on any given player, an evaluation of a rookie and what his chances might be of making the team, you had to go to Lombardi. The assistants were not allowed to talk about anything—period."

Lee Remmel devoted his adult life and a fair portion of his childhood to working in print journalism. "I wrote for the grade-school newspaper, and when I was a teenager I had a job as correspondent for a weekly paper in Shawano County, northwest of Green Bay. When I was a junior in high school, I covered two murders in three days and a projected strike by Menominee Indians against the federal government," Remmel says.

He had been working full time in every known news-gathering capacity at the *Press Gazette* for nearly twenty years when Vince Lombardi came to Green Bay. But Remmel was not prepared for the sometimes harrowing ride that came with the daily coverage of a man like Lombardi, who scrutinized every word written in the local press about him and his football team. Lombardi could be quick to anger over coverage that he perceived as negative, yet was reluctant to provide meaningful information regarding the state of his team.

"Although it is standard policy now, there were no Monday news conferences to review the game of the day before," said Remmel.

"The only time I was allowed to speak to the coach was each Tuesday morning, on the phone, from 9 a.m. until 9:05. I had to have my questions prepared, obviously, and he gave me monosyllabic answers. So I had to do a creative writing job to produce a story. It was not like some radio broadcast where all that you need is a sound bite. You need some substance to write a news story, and that was hard to get from him."

Remmel remembered being thrown out of the Packers' dressing room by the coach himself on cut-down day before the start of the regular season in 1967. "I'd never seen him so irascible. He figured that I was in there counting noses, to see who had been cut and who hadn't, and Vince was not prepared to announce the names at that point. The off-seasons were different. Every year I was assigned to interview Lombardi for the Packer Year Book. You still had to have your questions prepared, but he was relaxed and gave great and comprehensive answers to all the questions, and I got some wonderful stuff then. But in the regular season—forget it."

Remmel distinctly recalled two episodes in his relationship with the coach that led to hot words. "One time, I blew up at *him.* But sometimes when his temper cut loose, the person who Lombardi was yelling at might not be the actual source of his wrath. When Lombardi had been an assistant coach at Army, his boss there, Red Blaik, pointed out that Vince had an unusual thermostat."

If the everyday sportswriters who dealt with Vince Lombardi on a local, upper Wisconsin basis had presumed that the coach might take a more serene turn over the passage of years, Vince fooled them. "As the years went by and he continued to win, he became even more—maybe 'arrogant' isn't the right word, but it's pretty close," said Remmel. "He wasn't so much that way in the early years, but the more he won, the more I guess he felt he should be immune from criticism in the media.

"The funny thing is that when he *won,* after the game when talking to the writers Vince could be just unbearable. And when he *lost,* he would show a real humility. I'm sure, though, he had to force himself to be affable after a loss because it bugged the hell out of him to lose."

Vince's behavior after the difficult loss at Baltimore was a typical example. "The Packers had not only lost the game late when Baltimore recovered an onside kick, but lost halfback Elijah Pitts in the first quarter and fullback Jim Grabowski in the second quarter. . . . They were gone for the season," recalled Remmel. "But Lombardi was as talkative and friendly to the media as I had ever seen him. And for the remainder of the season, I think he did the best coaching job of his entire tenure at Green Bay."

While Vince Lombardi reigned, nobody made the mistake of thinking of Packerland as a democracy. But the trains always ran on time. And he was, as he was supposed to be, a winner.

After Green Bay's loss at Baltimore and the prospect of mounting casualties (all-pro guard Fuzzy Thurston joined Pitts and Grabowski on the disabled list), pub conversations from Kenosha to Port Wing rang out with concern.

In Michigan's Upper Peninsula, known to be Packers territory during the Lombardi monarchy, four motorcycle gangs—the Highwaymen, the Vikings, the SSmen, and God's Little Children—staged an all-day beer party on an abandoned farm that wound up in a gun battle. Anxiety over the struggles of the Pack, perhaps, had boiled over into such hostile activity.

Now Cleveland would come traveling into County Stadium, and every devotee of the Packers' cause respected the Browns as a tough and resourceful team. The Pack had beaten Cleveland in the championship game at Lambeau Field just two seasons before but had gotten its nose bloodied in the process. The fallen Elijah Pitts sat in a cold dugout at County Stadium before the game with his surgically repaired appendage in a cast. As he watched the Browns warm up, Pitts shook his head. "Their quarterback, Frank Ryan, wears that number 13. I don't know what to make of that," Pitts mused. "I was the thirteenth player that the Packers picked the year I was drafted, so I regarded that as a lucky number."

Pitts soon learned the meaning of it all. Green Bay's Travis Williams, the rookie rocket that Lombardi had been touting as a concealed weapon since training camp, returned Lou Groza's kickoff 87 yards for a touchdown. Exactly thirteen seconds had elapsed and the Packers led 7–0. On the thirteenth play of the game, the Browns' number 13, Ryan, fumbled, Ray Nitschke recovered, and one of the greatest routs in Green Bay *and* Cleveland history was under way.

Bart Starr threw a 28-yard touchdown pass to Donny Anderson. Starr threw a 14-yard touchdown pass to Marv Fleming. Every time Cleveland coach Blanton Collier looked up he saw another Packer crossing his goal line. At the end of the first *quarter* Green Bay led the Browns by the score of 35–0! The National Football League record for points in one quarter was 41, and that had been set by the 1945 Packers in a game against Detroit.

Cleveland finally found its way onto the scoreboard in the second quarter when Ernie Green ran 59 yards for a TD. Big mistake. On the next kickoff, Travis Williams took off again, this time for 85 yards. By halftime, Green Bay had piled up its lead to 45–7. The *Green Bay Press-Gazette* wondered what Blanton Collier might have said to his troops, or what remained of them, during the intermission. Collier shrugged. "I looked at the players and said, 'I can't explain it to you, men.' That was the pep talk."

Green Bay eventually wound up winning, 55–7. Such an explosion, just a week after the bitter ending at Baltimore, left fans wondering what Lombardi might have done to create such a rebirth. If Lombardi knew the answer, he was not about to supply it. But the coach wore his favorite "I told you so" expression when the topic of Travis Williams came up. "It's a question of speed. I warned the world about Travis Williams in training camp." Lombardi was beaming. Williams's brilliant explosive run on the opening kickoff energized and supercharged a team that had been waiting all season for such a spark. "Those kickoff returns were a thing of beauty," said Lombardi, hardly able to contain himself. "Two in a game. That is an accomplishment of a lifetime. This is a great club. I've never seen so many things go right."

This was not the Vince Lombardi that writers were used to confronting after big wins, the Lombardi who could be so terse and so insufferable. The coach appeared to permeate a feeling of complete relief now that the '67 Pack had at last demonstrated unmistakable thoroughbred form for the first time all season.

With the score out of hand, Lombardi let rookie quarterback Don Horn sample his first regular-season game experience in the second half. "You maybe saw the backfield of the future out there today," Lombardi told the writers. "Horn, Anderson, and Mercein."

* * *

Even though quarterback Zeke Bratkowski once noted that "the sixties *never* came to Green Bay," Vince Lombardi was hardly oblivious to the events that were more and more featured as lead items on the network newscasts. If the media were to be believed, an attitude of insurrection was becoming contagious.

"He was bothered by it and he talked about it," says Vince Lombardi, Jr. "In some areas, he was kind of liberal for a person who had been raised in that strict Jesuit background . . . politically liberal, at least. He campaigned rather actively for John Kennedy in 1960. So the idea of a protest demonstration, per se, did not bother him so much, but the concept of civil disobedience and breaking the law was something that bothered him a lot."

For professional reasons, Lombardi might not have been that enthusiastic about the black students who staged a forceful protest at Grambling University in Louisiana. Some students trashed the cafeteria and staged a "lie-in" at the football stadium, hoping to cause a postponement or even a cancellation of the homecoming. The topic of Vietnam or civil rights never came up during the outburst at Grambling. Students voiced indignation, in effect, because the college's football team was *too* good, and now they were disturbed over what the protesters described as a "second-rate atmosphere for learning."

The Grambling protesters noted that twenty alums of the college were employed on 1967 NFL rosters, more than any other school in the land except Notre Dame. Student body president Willie Zanders charged that the college "would rather turn out a pro football player than a Rhodes scholar," adding that there were no "academic pros on the Grambling faculty."

The protesters at Grambling would have the satisfaction of knowing that they had captured the attention of the college president, Ralph Waldo Emerson Jones, who in his spare time doubled as the school's head baseball coach. Jones summoned the National Guard, and twenty-nine students were expelled. This was a rebellion scene that Lombardi would have regarded as not only unlawful but mindless as well. Also, one of those Grambling alums in the NFL happened to be Green Bay defensive end Willie Davis. If Lombardi had been pressed to name a player on his roster that he regarded as indispensable, Willie Davis would have been the one.

WITH THE PACK now seeming to gel after their wholesale butchering of the Cleveland Browns, Lombardi was seeking defensive momentum to carry the team on to the championship. The San Francisco 49ers, with quarterback John Brodie, presented what Lombardi considered an ideal challenge for his team as it entered the stretch run of the regular season.

With Willie Davis supplying unrelenting constraint for Brodie, and Ray Nitschke obliterating the 49ers' running game, the result, for the second week in a row, was exactly what Lombardi had wanted—a defensive demolition demonstration. Green Bay's 13–0 shutout was the first posted by any team against San Francisco since 1961.

The coach expressed delight over another aspect of the show. Starting outside linebacker Lee Roy Caffey missed the 49ers game with a sore ankle, another result of increasingly rough play in the Sunday manslaughter that was becoming widespread in the league. "When you put all that payoff money on the line," rationalized Caffey, "it brings out the best in people. Also knees, elbows, and helmets."

With Caffey due to be missing only temporarily, Vince learned that he had more depth than he might have realized. Caffey's fill-in, Tommy Joe Crutcher (from where else but Texas with a name like that?) produced an all-pro effort when given a starting opportunity. Crutcher, who grew up not far from the farm where Audie Murphy spent his childhood, simply commented, "I don't know how well I played. I'd have been a lot more satisfied if I'd intercepted a pass or something."

After watching Lombardi's Green Bay team operate for an afternoon, San Francisco coach Jack Christiansen analyzed the two squads and determined what he felt might be the essential reason why the Packers seemed to win all the time and the 49ers of that era did not. "Our shortcoming," decided Christiansen, "is a lack of meanness."

IN THE FALL of '67, Southern Cal football coach John McKay watched a junior-college transfer playing halfback for the Trojans run 86 yards for a touchdown against Washington. "When I saw that run, I thought that whoever it was who recruited that kid is a genius." McKay was talking about himself, and the "kid" he was referring to was O. J. Simpson.

By early December, however, few Americans were tap-dancing at the cloudlike elevations occupied by Vince Lombardi. The preseason had been a difficult one for the Green Bay czar. Jim Taylor had become the first star Packers player to defect and seek asylum elsewhere, and for months Lombardi had been depicting Taylor to his team as a traitor for going to the New Orleans Saints. During some long portions of the regular season, just when it looked like things couldn't get any worse, all of a sudden, they did. Without Paul Hornung and Taylor, Bart Starr appeared out of sync with the newcomers, and that caused a torrent of turnovers. Then came a rash of injuries.

At the conclusion of the San Francisco win, the Packers could be assured that they had overcome this barrage of setbacks. With three games still to play, they had clinched their division championship and would coast into the playoffs, where Lombardi was now certain that his Pack would prevail. Lombardi kept a little plaque in his office that read: "I firmly believe that any man's finest hour is that moment when he has worked his heart out in a good cause and lies exhausted on the battlefield, victorious."

Lombardi, having felt that kind of rapture after beating the 49ers, turned his efforts to vengeance. Six weeks earlier he had been stung. Green Bay's 10–7 loss against Minnesota had left the coach seething. Not only had the Vikings limited the Pack to fewer than 50 yards rushing, Lombardi privately came away from the game with a rare sensation. He felt that he might have been outcoached. Afterward, the Vikes' new coach, Bud Grant, made those comments about how his team was not in awe of Green Bay, physically or otherwise, and about how determined he had been that his would not be the team to make the late mistake that lost the game.

Vince read something into those remarks, and in this case the print between the lines wasn't that hard to decipher. Lombardi's interpretation was that Grant, through the media, was telling football that if that old fart in Green Bay thinks he's the only person around here who can coach football, then he's in for a shock. So screw him. And that, essentially, was exactly what Grant had intended.

Appropriately, with the Packers once again functioning on most cylinders, the schedule called for Green Bay to travel to Metropolitan Stadium in Bloomington, the town between the Twin Cities. Since the

Vikings franchise entered NFL play in 1961, Green Bay had visited that stadium on six previous occasions, and Lombardi's team had never been beaten there. Green Bay *did* survive a close call in a game in Bloomington, and Lombardi had been so agitated at his team's play that he kicked a garbage can in the locker room with such force that he almost broke his foot. In the state of Minnesota, Vince Lombardi hadn't lost to Norm Van Brocklin, and he certainly did not want to establish any new and negative precedents against this impertinent Bud Grant. "All week Vince kept drumming away on the theme of how the Vikings hadn't seen the *real* Packers the first time around," recalled halfback Anderson, who had been enjoying his premier season as Hornung's full-time replacement. "Just because we had clinched the playoffs, he thought, was hardly a reason to lose intensity. Vince told us that the only thing more deadly to a football team than fatigue was complacency."

That Packers team that the Vikings had beaten earlier, the game that left Bud Grant feeling so cocky, had been quarterbacked by Zeke Bratkowski, and after three games as an emergency substitute Zeke had finally been overexposed and was showing his age. This time Bart Starr had returned, combat-honed and adequately healthy. Starr and the rest realized, though, that attitude alone might not be enough to beat Minnesota at home. After their 0–4 start, the Vikings had managed a 3–2–2 midseason run. If the Packers had improved since the first meeting in October, so, too, had the Vikings.

While the coach and his team had anticipated the same kind of playing conditions that Napoleon had faced on the Russian front, the sun was out in Bloomington, the weather unusually mild and almost balmy by Minnesota's December standards. A record crowd filled Metropolitan Stadium to witness the rematch. Minnesota fans were treated to a classic—not a classic by Lombardi's tastes—but a hilarious back-and-forth display of oscillating momentum, fluke plays, suspense, and a frenzied ending. On the whole, the spectators witnessed the sort of show that could only guarantee customer satisfaction.

Field goals by Don Chandler and Fred Cox left the contest tied after the first quarter. Minnesota running back Dave Osburn made the play that initiated the cannon fire. In the second quarter, Osburn, apparently trapped in his own backfield like a bug in a matchbox, somehow managed to elude the Packers' defense. Osburn, a freelance sub who worked behind Tommy Mason and Bill Brown in the Vikings running corps, slipped away and sprinted 43 yards for the game's first touchdown. The players' descriptions of that run reflected the degree of mutual dislike that had developed between the teams.

Said Osburn: "I had good blocking. We always have good blocking against Green Bay. They play it pretty straight and we like to play them."

Ray Nitschke remembered the play differently. "We were sloppy," he said. "I didn't tackle Osburn. If I had tackled Osburn, he wouldn't have done so well. We weren't as sharp as we should have been. Maybe that was good for us. We tackled better after that."

Lee Roy Caffey, back in the lineup after his ankle injury, backed up Nitschke's account of the play. "I should have had Osburn for a loss. I had him behind the line, but he got away. It was a poor job of tackling." Not, of course, a good job of blocking.

The Bart Starr factor surfaced quickly after Osburn's touchdown. He threw a 57-yard touchdown pass to Boyd Dowler, who scored only after he and Vikings' defensive back Ed Sharockman played ping-pong with a tipped ball. "Sharockman made a good play on the ball," said Dowler. "I tried to catch it, and his hand came between mine and deflected it. I kept running and the ball came back down to me. It was a good bounce."

Earlier in the season the direction of excruciating bounces had produced Packers turnovers in wholesale quantities. At the time, the coach had painstakingly pointed out that if those fortunes did not somehow reverse themselves, the Packers hadn't a prayer of winning that championship the coach so coveted.

Now the bounces, for sure, had taken a cheerful new direction for the Pack. After Dowler had gotten *his* on the 57-yard touchdown, the Packers got another on the next kickoff. Minnesota rookie Bob Grim, who would not commit such a botch for the next decade, bobbled the kickoff. Special teams whiz Steve Wright, who had already recovered three enemy kickoffs during the season, this time flopped down on top of Grim, pinning his face to the Minnesota turf, while the newest Packer, Chuck Mercein, recovered the ball. One month after his stint with the Westchester Bulls, Mercein, the former Yalie, had returned to prime time. That recovery led to another Chandler field goal, and the Pack led at the half, 13–10.

Joe Kapp, the quarterback who was built like a linebacker and often threw the football with about as much touch and finesse, completed just two passes in the Vikings' earlier 10–7 upset of the Packers. Kapp did not demonstrate noticeable improvement in the rematch, hitting six of seventeen. One of the completions, though, went to John Beasley for a six-yard touchdown that put the Vikings back on top in the third quarter, 17–13.

Again, Bart Starr fired a rapid counterpunch, finding Carroll Dale alone in the Vikings' secondary for a 34-yard TD. And shortly, a play that could have been re-created only on a pinball machine led to another quick score. Cornerback Bob Jeter tipped a Joe Kapp pass in the direction of linebacker Crutcher, who batted the ball in the direction of Nitschke, who grasped the interception. That play set up a Ben Wilson touchdown. The Packers now led 27–17.

Minnesota came grinding back. Ed Sharockman, wiped out earlier on the Boyd Dowler touchdown, neutralized the damage with a fourth-quarter interception of a Starr pass. The Vikings scored when another of Kapp's six completions went to Red Phillips for a touchdown.

A Green Bay fumble gave the Vikings additional opportunity, and Cox tied the game late with a 27-yard field goal. Green Bay's offense faltered, and the Pack was confronted with fourth and long, pinned down inside their own 20. Earlier, Donny Anderson had shanked a punt. Even with a more reasonable effort, Minnesota still figured to secure reasonable field position, and a couple of first downs would set Fred Cox up nicely for a game-winning kick. Anderson, however, hammered a career punt, a towering left-footed spiral, that sent Grim, the Viking safety, in rapid retreat.

Grim, perhaps uptight over his earlier fumble, mishandled this one, too, and the ball rolled another thirteen yards toward the Minnesota goal line. "I finally got some foot into that one," Anderson said. Grim recovered it this time but was nailed in his tracks by Mercein and Doug Hart. On that one Anderson kick, the Packers gained 72 yards' worth of field position. Bud Grant, finally, sampled the real taste of Green Bay fourth-quarter football.

After Bratkowski had been victimized on the late interception that had cost the Packers the game in the earlier meeting, Grant had been preaching the "let the Packers cut their own throat" gospel. The flaw in that approach was that, historically, the Packers seldom did that. Now came time for the payback.

From the Vikings' 15 they tried to run their version of the Packers' power sweep. But one of Minnesota's pulling guards collided with Joe Kapp and jarred the football out of the quarterback's grasp in what Lombardi might have described as "a lapse of execution." Now the ball was on the ground, but nobody was sure where. According to Kapp, "I never did get the snap under control and then someone hit me and I lost the ball. I was looking all over for it, but I couldn't find it. I don't know where it went."

Green Bay tackle Ron Kostelnik realized that the ball was loose, but he didn't see it either. "I kept watching Kapp," Kostelnik said, "because I figured he knew where it was."

What had happened was that fullback Bill Brown had inadvertently kicked the thing. Defensive back Tom Brown, the same player who had intercepted Don Meredith's pass on the fateful fourth down in the 1966 championship game, located the football rolling upfield, picked it up and, in his own words, "returned the ball about a quarter of a yard."

Now Bart Starr's job was to hand the ball off to Anderson and Wilson, run as much off the 1:47 left on the clock as he could, and position the ball for an easy Chandler field goal. Chandler's field goal traveled 19 yards, and the Packers had beaten the Vikings at last, 30–27.

Not only had both teams each registered fifteen first downs, they had gained an identical 274 yards in total offense. Vince Lombardi seemed more like the old Vince after the win, meaning that his post-game behavior with the media was terse and cold.

Lombardi's in-depth analysis of the really terrific game: "We scored more points than they did, so we won."

An hour and a half later, the Packers assembled at General Billy Mitchell Field in Milwaukee to catch a chartered flight. Their destination would be Santa Barbara and the same workout field where they had prepared for their championship game against Kansas City eleven months earlier.

This time, with the division title already locked up, the Pack would be practicing for a meaningless regular-season game against the Rams at the L. A. Coliseum. With Lombardi thirsty for an encore, he felt that now was a good time to expose his team to some Super Bowl atmosphere.

CHAPTER

11

Paul Cézanne wrote that every time he applied his brush to the canvas he could hear a chorus of angels rejoicing in heaven. He also said, "There are two thousand politicians in every legislature, but there is a Cézanne only every two centuries." Viewed from the context of artistic achievement, the game that the Dallas Cowboys played to clinch the championship of the Capitol Division in 1967 would gain no critical acclaim as something that resembled in its own fashion a masterpiece by Cézanne. Praying hands on velvet was more like it. After demolishing St. Louis in a game that Tom Landry hoped would establish a winning cadence that would sweep the team into the playoffs and beyond, the offense conked out almost totally in the second half at Memorial Stadium in Baltimore.

Dallas's defense played proficiently against the Colts. That, at least, qualified as a first. The Cowboys squeezed four turnovers out of Baltimore, rare largesse from a Don Shula team, but the Dallas offense hissed and gagged and squandered almost every opportunity. Stymied by a zone defense in the deep secondary, Don Meredith pitched up four interceptions. He managed to connect with Bob Hayes for a 35-yard touchdown in the second quarter, and Dallas actually led the Colts, 14–10, at the half. Then Dallas curled up into a self-destructive little knot and second-half pickoffs by Bobby Boyd and Rick Volk destroyed any hope of defeating the Colts. Baltimore wound up winning, 23–17, and Dallas's record fell to 8–4.

"Disgusting." That was the word Landry used to describe his team's offensive showing. He almost spat it out. Landry ripped his quarterback. "You can't throw the ball up in the air on their three deep," he fumed. "That's just what they're waiting for. Meredith should have taken his losses when he was under pressure."

True, Landry had not been the man standing midstream in a collapsing pocket and hearing the clippity-clop of the onrushing Bubba Smith and cohorts. Meredith, though, presented an account of the action that coincided with the coach's. "I didn't call a good game. I threw badly and I panicked," he said.

"After beating St. Louis the way we did, I really hoped that we could come here and finally establish some momentum," declared the frustrated Landry. "We haven't played good games back to back all season, and to think that you can pull it all together, just in time, when the playoffs start is not very realistic. Now look at Cleveland, the team that we're likely to play in the first round of the playoffs. They've won three straight now. That's the momentum that we're looking for and don't have.

"But while we didn't beat Baltimore, we beat the Baltimore image. This is the first time we've stayed on the field with them, and I think the team realizes now that we are certainly capable of beating them."

This would be a day when even Bubbles Cash would be upstaged. Down in Houston a woman ran onto the field at the Oilers game. At first, everyone thought she might be Bubbles. Instead, the woman identified herself as Terri Tail and outscored Bubbles in a key stat, 43 to 40. At least Bubbles and the Cowboys fared better than another Dallas team on that same day. The Dallas Tornado soccer team got stoned, literally, in Singapore. One Dallas player, Jan Book, was bonked on the head with a rock while the others scurried for cover. Vince Lombardi just *thought* those Baltimore fans, with their drunks leaving the stands and all, were nasty. Dallas also fared better than the man who founded the New York franchise in the AFL, Harry Wismer, who died that Sunday. While losing, though, Dallas became the beneficiary of events elsewhere. The Redskins and the Eagles, the teams that were attempting to catch Dallas in the four-team Capitol Division, played to a 35-all deadlock, thus mathematically eliminating each other.

The absence of blaring trumpets and drumrolls from the Cowboys' title-clinching weekend was altogether appropriate. At least owner Clint Murchison, Jr., probably felt that way. What the Cowboys had been accomplishing on the field in 1967 seemed quite subordinate to events happening far behind the scenes in Murchison's playground of big-time finance. It might not be inaccurate to state that Murchison was a man genetically inclined to get what he wanted out of life. Compare the recollection of William Randolph Hearst's father that his son, as a tot, "had insisted that we buy him the Louvre. Other than that, he always got everything he wanted."

At the beginning of the century, Clint Murchison's father made his living by trapping raccoons and selling them to Sears, Roebuck. Then Murchison Senior decided that oilfield speculation might offer faster and bigger profits than the raccoon-trapping business. Maestro of the handshake deal in those production reservoirs in East Texas that had so awed Admiral Yamamoto, the Murchison family proceeded to build one of the great American fortunes. Murchison Senior became impatient dealing with banks in the Yankee provinces. "Trouble with you guys up here, you're too slow," Murchison was once quoted as saying. "[In Texas] we make the deal and let the paperwork catch up later."

Clint Junior's approach to the world of commerce was similar. One Dallas business analyst noted that in the era that gave birth to the Cowboys franchise, "big oil ran Texas. They owned the banks. They owned everything, essentially. When it comes to clout, Jerry Jones could never even begin to compare with the power and influence of a man like Clint Murchison in those days."

In terms of flamboyance, with his horn-rim glasses and his hair chopped down in a flattop, Murchison made Ross Perot look like Mick Jagger. Modest and impeccably mannered, Clint certainly worked in defiance of the stereotypical bombastic Texan. But Murchison also brandished widespread influence. When Clint Junior decided that he wanted to marry Cowboys scouting director Gil Brandt's wife, that had been accomplished with little delay. And when Clint decided that he wanted a new ballpark for his football team, he got that, too, though that project took a bit longer.

By the mid-sixties the Cowboys had taken on a swashbuckling personality with their shiny silver uniforms and touchdown-on-demand attack. The Cotton Bowl had been an ideal showplace for Doak Walker and the SMU Mustangs back in the 1940s, and it was great for the manic crowd scene at the once-a-year Texas-Oklahoma game. But the neighborhood surrounding Fair Park had been getting South Chicago–tough. Skirmishes like the one that happened in the end zone at the Rams game, when the drunk fan snatched the policeman's pistol, would only be happening with more frequency. The North Dallas swells whom Murchison had been courting as the ticket base for his team had been growing reluctant to travel down around Fair Park, where "Brother, can you spare a dime?" was getting replaced by "Hand over your wallet, motherfucker."

Clint Murchison wanted something more polished for his Cowboys, something in the downtown area among the brilliantly illuminated, blandly designed Dallas skyscrapers that were all shaped like cereal boxes. His eventual nemesis in this plan became Dallas mayor Erik Jonsson, whose ambitions for the city did not include the Cowboys as a priority. The mayor told Murchison that inserting the proposed downtown stadium as part of a civic-bond package did not mesh with his own top priorities for the city. Jonsson, who ran a company called Texas Instruments that owned the patent to a device called the computer microchip, fit the image of a Scandinavian devoted to the scientific ideal. Erik Jonsson would not be found among the Dallas big shots with season tickets on the 45-yard line who whooped and drooled when Bubbles Cash came jiggling down the aisle. The mayor, in fact, didn't know a first down from a potato pancake.

"Clint scheduled a meeting with Erik Jonsson, who told him that the Cowboys 'are not in my plans right now' or words very close to that," revealed Tex Schramm, who was a keenly involved bystander to the stadium saga. "The new stadium had been Clint's big dream, his big push. So when the mayor told him that the best the city of Dallas was willing to do for the Cowboys was to put a couple of million dollars' worth of improvements into the Cotton Bowl, that was a blow.

"But Clint had also been anticipating that possibility and had been gathering land just west of the Dallas city limits in Irving—site of what is now Texas Stadium," Schramm said.

Clint wanted a new football tabernacle, and a renovated Cotton Bowl with bigger washrooms hardly fit his vision. Murchison's idea included an innovation that called for private boxes—football presidential suites, actually, something called sky boxes. He could lease or sell these, no matter how much the price tag. Murchison well understood the grazing habits of the rich. The amenities included in the sky box, with the comfortable seats and the open bar, remained secondary to the actual appeal of the privacy.

The big allure would lie with the subliminal concept, the illusion of separation. People entered those boxes via private elevator. No longer would they need to rub bellies with the tired and huddled masses *down there.* But the proletariat could look up and gaze upon the aristocracy, reclining behind the glass and swapping Dom Perignon–enhanced profundities. What a place to be seen. Box holders gazed at one another through binoculars. Such fun. Years after construction, Highland Park High School, also billed as America's Rich School after the America's Team concept finally popped, was involved in a playoff game at Texas Stadium. Some of the high school kids, lolling in their fathers' boxes, actually pitched cash out of the windows and down onto the riffraff assembled beneath them.

While *that* kind of activity might not have been what Clint had in mind, the sky box novelty became an overnight success. That strange Texas Stadium design, the semi-dome effect with the big hole in the roof, did present problems. Don Meredith, who retired before Texas Stadium had been completed, pointed out, "The place looks like it ain't finished yet." The hole in the roof created a bizarre sunlight-and-shadow effect on the field, making games difficult to televise.

"Well, the architect anticipated that problem and tried to prevent it," said Tex Schramm. "He built a little model of the stadium and put a wire arc over the top to simulate the path of the sun. And then he'd tilt the stadium in this direction and that, attempting to minimize the lighting problem down in the stadium. But somethin' got screwed up and I'm not sure why." What didn't get screwed up was the fortunes of the football team. After the Cowboys assumed occupancy of Texas Stadium at midseason in 1971, they would advance as far as the NFL championship game in fifteen of the next twenty-five seasons and win that game nine times.

With the division title wrapped up after the Baltimore game, with two games still left on the regular-season schedule, Schramm and Murchison pulled the trigger and announced that the Cowboys would be moving to Irving. Murchison, the futuristic owner, also made public the scheme by which season-ticket holders would be required to purchase a revenue bond. In order to sit between the 35-yard lines, fans were obliged to cough up a grand a seat, a considerable sum in the 1960s. A $500 bond would be required to purchase season tickets elsewhere in the stadium.

John Q. Public howled. The working stiff now faced exclusion from the Cowboys' home games. Jack Lowe, chairman of the Fair Park

Association, facing the painful fact that the NFL's matinee-idol franchise would be abandoning his Cotton Bowl, did raise some hell. "What that stadium in Irving will be," he said, "is a private club."

Time would demonstrate that Jack Lowe knew what he was talking about. Whether in the private suites or in the Texas Stadium stands, the fans displayed gentrified dress and behavior. Indeed, the audience appeared better suited for a ballet or at least a modern-dance recital. Cowboys touchdowns were received with polite applause.

THE FINAL TWO games of the team's 1967 season—with the playoffs locked up—took on the pace of exhibition games. The Cowboys did manage to avenge their earlier embarrassment against the Eagles; Philly got bounced, 38–17, and Craig Morton played most of the game at quarterback. If anything, the game became noteworthy for one play. Halfback Dan Reeves—the ex-college quarterback—took a pitchout, took off on what appeared to be a routine end run, then stopped, planted his foot, and heaved a deep pass to Lance Rentzel. The play worked for a 45-yard touchdown.

The same play had generated the same results two weeks earlier against the Cardinals, Reeves to Rentzel for a 70-yard TD. It would have worked against the Redskins, too, but Rentzel dropped the pass. "It's amazing how accurate Reeves is with that pass," Tom Landry marveled. "In practice he seldom misses."

If Green Bay Packers scouts were not taking copious notes about Cowboy Danny Reeves and his halfback pass, they should have been, because it was this play that was so significant in the Ice Bowl epic.

TEN DAYS INTO the month of December, the populace of eastern Wisconsin hadn't seen a cloudless day. Antifreeze and brandy sales approached *Guiness Book of World Records* numbers. On Sunday, in Madison, volunteer skin divers attempted to locate the remains of 26-year-old Otis Redding. His private plane had slammed into icy, fog-shrouded Lake Menona with "tremendous impact," and four other members of Redding's band, the Bar-Keys, died with him.

The Green Bay Packers had skipped town for the week, inhaling the hydrocarbons down in Southern California. Vince Lombardi's football team had been evacuated to Santa Barbara on a working vacation.

On Saturday the Pack would face the Los Angeles Rams. While Lombardi continued to prevail in the throne room of national football, another jealous prince, George Allen, had joined the gang of Tom Landry, Don Shula and Bud Grant—all intent upon seizing the crown.

Allen—nervous, manipulative, and too brilliant to work forever as George Halas's underpaid and overworked assistant—achieved instantaneous results in L.A. For the first time since the Bob Waterfield–Crazylegs Hirsch peak years during the Truman administration, the Rams were smoking. L.A.'s roster, top to bottom, was composed largely of less-than-ordinary talent. The Rams' best linebacker, Maxie Baughan, back in his prime, had starred for the Eagles in the only playoff game Lombardi ever lost. That had happened seven years earlier.

George Allen constructed a team around two assets—his Deacon Jones, Lamar Lundy, Roger Brown, Merlin Olsen Fearsome Foursome—and a hot quarterback, Roman Gabriel. The rest of the roster was an assembly of spare parts that worked in excellent harmony. The Rams, heading into game thirteen of a fourteen-game regular season, could win the Coastal Division championship in the finale at home against the Baltimore Colts. But first, they needed also to beat the Green Bay Packers. The Pack already had clinched its playoff slot, but Lombardi guaranteed the onlooking gallery that his Packers would enter the Coliseum in Code Red status. Women and children, clear the streets.

"Who the hell cares that you've won the division?" Donny Anderson remembers Lombardi telling his team during the practices in Santa Barbara. "This is a Saturday game, the only game on TV, and the whole country will be watching this. You're the Green Bay Packers, you're the world champions of football, and you're damn sure not going to play dead."

Fresh off the roster of the Westchester Bulls, Chuck Mercein now felt unable to conceal the elation that he felt when he saw his name printed in chalk on Lombardi's pregame blackboard as the starting fullback. Jim Grabowski's hurt knee would not respond to therapy, and Ben Wilson had joined the casualty list on a temporary basis. "What an experience," Mercein recalled. "I'd been leading rusher for the New York Giants. So what? Who wants to be remembered as a leading rusher on a team that didn't win a damn thing? Now, because Jim Grabowski had gotten hurt in Baltimore, I found myself in the starting lineup with this—this juggernaut." Educated in the Ivy League, Chuck Mercein decided that life was fair.

One week earlier, UCLA Heisman Trophy winner Gary Beban had played the game of his life, and that still wasn't enough to beat O. J. Simpson and USC. Sports-page critics largely agreed that the game might rank as the greatest ever played in the L.A. Coliseum. After the Packers-Rams showdown, they changed their minds. While a paid audience of almost 80,000 enthralled witnesses cheered the Rams' every move, the two teams traded touchdowns throughout the afternoon. Lee Roy Caffey, the erstwhile South Texas watermelon farmer, blocked a Bruce Gossett field-goal attempt in the first quarter. Future Hall of Fame cornerback Herb Adderley grabbed the blocked kick and returned the football to the L.A. 43. Then Bart Starr threw a 30-yard TD to Carroll Dale.

Green Bay's defensive secondary included two Hall of Famers, Adderley and Willie Wood. But the other defensive backs, Bob Jeter and Tom Brown, took the field with journeyman-type credentials. All season the Packers had forged a winning record against a procession of mediocre quarterbacks—Larry Rakestraw, Karl Sweetan, and so on.

Johnny Unitas, however, knew how to exploit the soft spots in the Packers' secondary, and he'd done that in the final quick drive when the Colts had beaten the Pack back in early November. Roman Gabriel, enjoying his premier season, came equipped with advanced stalking instincts similar to Unitas's. Here was a contest offering a full table of spicy ingredients. Some people intent on filming a documentary on the primeval aspects of pro sports had wired Lombardi for sound. Those experiments customarily bring embarrassing results. This one certainly worked out that way. One of the few snippets that could have been marginally acceptable for family viewing came early, when the Packers' line opened a huge hole, but fullback Mercein was tackled after gaining only nine yards.

"Holy Christ!" shouted Lombardi. "Who was that? Mercein? Jim Taylor would have run forty yards on that play! Oh, well. Mercein's a hell of a kid, and he's all we've got. You've gotta go with who you've got."

As the game progressed, Gabriel pitched two touchdown passes to Jack Snow, and the Rams claimed a lead in the third quarter. Travelin' Travis Williams supplied the boomerang effect on the very next play. After fielding a kickoff four yards deep in the Green Bay end zone, Williams ran up the middle of the field, spun away from one tackler, cut back, hesitated to pick up a block from Gale Gillingham, and then sprinted down the sideline to score. This was Williams's fourth kickoff return TD of the season, breaking an NFL record held by Verda T. "Vitamin" Smith of the 1950 L.A. Rams. Williams's fantastic voyage brought joy to the heart of Vince Lombardi. Paul Hornung, bless his proud heart, had been a brave soldier. But this Travis Williams looked more like Gale Sayers all the time.

Chuck Mercein then scored a Packers touchdown, running four yards in the fourth quarter. When Green Bay, leading 24–20, stopped the Rams on fourth down, it appeared that the game—and the Rams' season—was about over. Dave Robinson blocked a Gabriel pass on the fourth-down play. Had Robinson intercepted the ball, and he should have, the linebacker would have scored. "That ball had 'Dave Robinson' written all over it. I would have scored for sure," he said, "but maybe it was not meant to be that way. I don't know." At that moment, it seemed unimportant.

When the Packers couldn't move, Anderson dropped back to punt. Less than a minute remained to play. But a split second after Anderson's left foot hit the ball, he heard another thud. Tony Guillory, one of an even dozen NFL players (including Bubba Smith) from Beaumont, Texas, who had the same grandfather, had rushed through the middle of the Packers' line and blocked the punt. From the Packers' viewpoint, the football now was bouncing in the wrong direction. Claude Crabb, a Rams defensive back, picked up the ball and ran it all the way down to the five-yard line. With twenty-six seconds left, Bernie Casey caught a pass from Gabriel and the Packers were beaten, 27–24.

When Guillory blocked Anderson's punt, he delivered the play of the decade for the L.A. Rams. "It was about time we made a big play," Guillory commented. "I went right between the center and the guard. I thought an 'up' back would get me, but no one even touched me. I was there and I got the ball. That was all."

Packers receiver Boyd Dowler said, "As the offensive team was coming out, we were all hollering, 'They'll try to block it!' I was hollering from the sideline. So were the others. They had nine men on the line for the ball—I counted them—nine men and two safeties."

Both coaches blew some serious smoke at the assembled media after it was over. "What a credit to pro football the Packers are," proclaimed Allen, whose finest hour was still a week away, when the Rams destroyed the Colts to win the division championship. "It shows you, the way they played today, what a great coach Lombardi is." What else could George Allen say? If his master plan gelled, his Rams would meet Green Bay in the playoffs in two weeks, and his remarks had been aimed to leave the Pack tranquilized.

Lombardi, in defeat, delivered a courtly and polished critique of the event. "I am as proud of this football team as I can be. Their performance was a credit to the profession and to football, the way they went out and played as hard as they did with the division already clinched."

While Lombardi uttered those words, he must have been thinking, What in the hell is going on here? Against the two best teams, Baltimore and the Rams, the Green Bay God Almighty Packers gave away the lead in the final two minutes and were beaten because it appeared that Lombardi's kicking teams had fallen asleep. The Colts won by recovering an onside kick. Now this blocked punt nonsense.

When the team returned to the frigid streets of Green Bay, Lombardi lashed out at his Packers and pumped a season's worth of frustration into the invective. The unfortunate primary target of Lombardi's late-season diatribe became none other than the newcomer, Chuck Mercein. The Rams' Tony Guillory had been talking about Chuck after the game. Mercein had now been identified as the mysterious vanishing 'up' back who never touched Guillory while he breezed through and blocked Anderson's punt in the final minute.

Mercein had been relaxing in the whirlpool—a bad place to be—when Lombardi cut loose with his barrage. "Vince started in on me for letting the guy in there—tore into me good. 'You didn't do anything! You didn't block *anybody*!' The whole team overheard it, of course. I wanted to sink down in the water and drown.

"But later on, in a meeting, we were watching the film of the play, and Lombardi conceded that the Rams were pouring in there from every direction and that I didn't have much of a chance. Nobody out there knew what in the hell his assignment was supposed to be. He didn't apologize necessarily, but he did tell the team that I hadn't been the only one to mess up. For a newcomer, that meant a lot to me because if he'd left things the way they were after that whirlpool encounter, it would have been devastating. From the edge of despair, I felt almost elated."

THE FINAL GAME of the regular season was against Pittsburgh. The fourteen-game grind had been the most grueling ever during the Lombardi tenure. The players had been battered. Jim Grabowski, the coach had learned, was through for the year because of his bad knee. This team that relied so heavily on its ground game now found itself seriously low on stallions. Anderson, Mercein, and Travis Williams remained as the only healthy running backs. One more injury and Lombardi himself might have to suit up.

Many of the regulars, including Bart Starr, had been granted a furlough for the final game against the Steelers. Don Horn, the man that the coach envisioned as the quarterback of the future, played most of the game. Even using the fill-in players, the Packers still figured to beat the dead-end Steelers. But Pittsburgh won, 24–17, behind Kent Nix, the man who almost beat the Cowboys at a point in the season when the game meant something. "We did everything we planned to do today, except that we didn't plan to lose," Lombardi said. Meanwhile, out on the West Coast, Dallas duplicated the Packers' feat, enjoying the scenery at Kezar Stadium and going through what seemed like the motions in a 24–16 loss to the 49ers.

The real news took place down in the L.A. Coliseum. Baltimore traveled there with plans to finish as the NFL's first unbeaten team since 1942. Instead, the Colts were handed their heads when the Rams routed them, 34–10. Both teams finished the season at 11–1–2, but because the Rams prevailed in the head-to-head series, 1–0–1, they advanced to the playoffs while Baltimore, with arguably the best team in pro football in 1967, was eliminated.

"Our offense put some points on the board early," said Deacon Jones, "and so we were able to dictate to Mr. Unitas what we wanted him to do, and that was to pass." Or attempt to pass. Unitas, who had thrown for career yardage that surpassed eighteen miles, was harassed and beaten up by the Fearsome Foursome. They sacked Johnny U. seven times, and in desperation he threw two fatal interceptions.

Now the children of Lotus Land would travel to Wisconsin looking for more scalps.

CHAPTER

12

Nobody who had occasion to cross paths with Vince Lombardi would describe the coach as boringly predictable. In so many ways, Lombardi stood out as a composite of contradictions. Some might partially explain it by Lombardi's birthday—June 11—which students of the zodiac recognize as a Gemini. Characteristics of persons born under that sign primarily involve a duality of personality. Inconsistencies that arise from what often progresses into a Jekyll and Hyde syndrome serve as the root cause as to why most Gemini people carry such labels as "ne'er-do-well" and "no account." Also "card-carrying nut case." But Lombardi defiantly violated the Gemini archetype with his almost Teutonic obsession with structure, preparation, punctuality. If you worked for Lombardi, you set your watch to "Lombardi Standard Time." Football players soon learned that when they arrived five minutes early for a team meeting, in Lombardi's book that was five minutes late and it cost them $50.

To Lombardi, the best part of the day happened at five o'clock in the afternoon. That was when the Gemini facet seemed to kick in. At five o'clock a transformation took place. Lombardi, the supreme commander of allied forces, became Vince the happy-hour raconteur. A major element of Lombardi's life centered around what he called the "five o'clock club," when he would collect friends, associates, and various hangers-on, throw down a few pops, and unwind. Lombardi could and would pontificate on myriad topics. That was how Lombardi and all of those around him helped maintain their sanity.

"Every year, when Vinnie and I were on the NFL competition committee, we would meet for a week in Hawaii," recollected Tex Schramm. "Lombardi always insisted on having a hotel room with a balcony that faced west. And he insisted that we all gather there in that five o'clock social hour and he'd watch the sun go down and talk about some of the goddamnedest topics you could imagine. Philosophy. Religion. Quite the contrast from the popular image of the hard-hearted, tyrannical Green Bay football coach."

The gathering of Lombardi's five o'clock club on the Friday evening before the Saturday rematch against the Los Angeles Rams in the division playoff game occurred in his suite at the Pfister Hotel in Milwaukee. The Pfister offered the kind of ornate amenities that Lombardi was inclined to appreciate. When Vince took over at Green Bay, his first edict called for the Packers to go first class in every way possible. Which meant the team would be billeted in the kinds of hotels that chased all the hookers out of the lobby. The Pfister qualified in that regard, and the people who stayed there and patronized the lounge seemed more inclined to sip good cognac than Pabst Blue Ribbon and Everclear.

So the Pfister met Lombardi's test as his kind of place, and the gathering in his suite for that Rams game included some of his kind of people. Lombardi enjoyed the company of the big-time syndicated columnists from both coasts—Jim Murray from L.A., Red Smith from New York. He always felt that the reporters from Milwaukee and Green Bay were too local, maybe parochial.

Writers with a national following had assembled in Milwaukee two days before Christmas to witness what the smart money insisted would be Lombardi's downfall. While completely dismantling those tough Baltimore Colts to win the Coastal Division, George Allen's Rams had looked like, well, the old Green Bay Packers. Now Green Bay entered this contest with zero momentum, having suffered back-to-back losses to Los Angeles and Pittsburgh. Because of the multitude of injuries, Lombardi would be starting what the media were describing as "third stringers" at running back against the red-hot Rams.

But none of that seemed to matter at the five o'clock club on that Friday, where Lombardi was telling Red Smith and some others that he'd never actually said, "Winning isn't everything; it's the only thing."

What he had actually said, the coach was insisting, was that winning isn't everything—and that the maximum 200 percent all-out, do-or-die effort was all that mattered. Somehow, some sportswriters had bastardized the quote during the translation, Lombardi was saying now. Then Lombardi gazed at the ceiling and intoned, "As Saint Paul wrote in the Epistles, 'Know ye not that those who run in a race run all, but one receiveth the prize? So run, that ye may obtain.' "

Nothing can break up a gathering of sportswriters more quickly and more effectively than a hard dose of Scripture. The writers stumbled out of the hotel suite, one of them muttering, "How about that? The gospel according to Saint Vincent de Paul." Red Smith, an inquisitive type, decided to further investigate Lombardi's quotes. "I went back to my hotel room, looked it up in a Gideon Bible and sure enough, Vince had it right," Smith wrote. "The coach who worshiped a God of peace taught a game of cruel violence, with total devotion to both."

That's a Gemini for you. When Red Smith, much later, retold the incident to Jerry Kramer, the guard noted, "Vince has a way of making saints sound like they would have made great football coaches."

If Lombardi seemed unperturbed on the eve of the Rams game, the coach had undergone another complete personality transplant by the time the Packers arrived at County Stadium on game day. "I wasn't there in those early years, of course, but I had never seen Lombardi so absolutely intense before a game," said halfback Donny Anderson. "And that included the championship game against Kansas City the year before."

Lombardi told his Packers, in effect, that he was sick of reading all the crap about the invincibility of the Fearsome Foursome. After a decade of achievement, Lombardi was furious that his Packers were appearing in the newspaper obituaries. George Allen's Rams were not the team attempting to win a third straight championship. The Packers were. The Rams hadn't been winning long enough, and they hadn't paid their dues yet. The Rams seemed a little too damn cocky for Lombardi's taste, and he wanted them destroyed. Annihilated. That was Lombardi's pregame message to his football team.

"He called it a crisis game," said Bart Starr. After the warm-ups on a fast field at County Stadium—temperature at game time a jolly plus-20 degrees—Starr thought back to a spring day in 1959. "It was the first time I had ever met Vince Lombardi, and he had brought in about eight or nine of us for what they now call a minicamp," Starr said. "He talked to us for about an hour and a half, but after only twenty minutes I could tell what was going to be happening.

"After that first meeting, I ran down the hallway to a pay

phone and called my wife—we were still living in Alabama in the off-season—and I said, 'Honey, we are going to begin to win.' He made everything seem so clear. He was a teacher and a brilliant communicator."

Since getting hurt in the third regular-season game against Atlanta, Starr had attempted to conceal the extent of the damage to his right shoulder—even from the coach. "Well," says Starr retrospectively, "he told us from the outset, in that first season back in 1959, that once you establish the goal and the price you're willing to pay to attain it, you must ignore the minor hurts, the opponent's pressure, the temporary setbacks. So if ever there was an occasion to adhere to all of that, here was the time."

All-pro offensive tackle Forrest Gregg recalls being emotionally ready to take on the challenge of his career. "The Rams were a hot team—*the* hot team going to the playoffs. That Fearsome Foursome was all that it was billed to be, too. Those were great players. But it was cold in Milwaukee. Not by our standards but by theirs, and during the pregame warm-ups, George Allen was on the field in a white shirt and necktie, presumably to show his team that the cold wasn't all that bad. But when they came back out, George was so bundled up that you couldn't recognize him."

The Rams scored first on a Roman Gabriel to Bernie Casey pass for 29 yards. This happened after Merlin Olsen recovered a fumble. The Fearsome Foursome appeared back on the job. Gabriel, at six four and 235, looked like Goliath standing back in the pocket behind enormous Rams linemen like Charlie Cowan, Tom Mack, and Joe Scibelli. If Los Angeles had come into the game cocky, it seemed early on that they had a right to be.

Then a Tom Brown punt return put the Packers in good shape, and Travis Williams, now heralded as "the Roadrunner" in the revamped Green Bay offense, sprinted 44 yards through the Rams' defense, Fearsome Foursome and all, to tie the game. Williams's run seemed to stimulate a mean streak in the Green Bay defense that had lain dormant in the game against L.A. two weeks earlier. When the official called for the chains to measure what looked like a Rams first down, Ray Nitschke snarled at the official: "Just give 'em the damn first down. Let 'em have it. We aren't finished with them yet, and we don't want to get out of here until we are."

Late in the first half, Willie Wood made the play that snuffed the

Rams for good. Bruce Gossett attempted a field goal that would have put L.A. back on top, but his kick misfired. Wood picked up the football at the Green Bay one-yard line and ran it back 44 yards before L.A. halfback Les Josephson could catch him. Starr, despite the bad shoulder, pitched a 17-yard TD to Carroll Dale with only thirty-three seconds left in the half. Lombardi's spirits must have zoomed. The Rams were on the slab.

In the third quarter the Rams made one more run at the Packers and the game was over. George Allen acknowledged: "The cold weather had nothing to do with it. We just got outplayed, that's all.

"We got down to their 21, had a chance to tie the game and if we did it's a brand-new game. Instead we got nothing, and then here they came back again and scored again." For their efforts, the Rams would play the loser of the next day's Cowboys-Browns playoff in an NFL fiasco event that was known as the Playoff Bowl. Allen called it "warmed-over stew. Boy, will that ever be an anticlimax. Funny thing, we played twenty-one games, counting the preseason, and lost only two. But it wasn't enough."

He also said that his team offered no excuses for the pounding that they had taken from the Packers—and then proceeded to offer one anyway. "We reached an emotional peak against the Colts last week, and it was not humanly possible to get that high again," Allen said. "When we led 7–0 and moved within five yards of another touchdown, if we scored at all down there, we'd have won. We had the momentum and Starr has got to come to us. But Dave Robinson blocked a field goal, and that picked them up; you could see it. It's like when you have the bases loaded and nobody out, you need a run and you can't get one."

A Rams assistant, Ray Prochaska, said, "We just didn't play well and that's the whole damn thing. We scored one touchdown, and there was no more enthusiasm for the rest of the game." According to Roman Gabriel, the Packers "were better prepared than we were and more inspired."

Deacon Jones bitched that "Forrest Gregg did some things that I didn't go for. He held me on seven or eight occasions, and they only called it once. Oh, well. What the hell. The Fearsome Foursome chose today to play its worst game of the season." By missing out on a shot at the Super Bowl, one compassionate writer pointed out to Olsen that each of the Rams had "blown $20,000." Olsen bristled a little. "Money is never a part of my objective for wanting to win," said the future spokesperson for a floral delivery service. "Some guys said the money gave us tremendous incentive, but I say baloney. I think we have too much class and pride to sell ourselves for dollars."

Chuck Mercein, one of the media-maligned "third stringers," battled his way into the L.A. end zone from six yards out in the third quarter, and Williams completed the rout with another touchdown, a short one, in the closing minutes. Meanwhile the Packers' defense was playing stomp-butt throughout the entire second half, soiling Roman Gabriel's uniform. A newsman suggested that special stunts might have created express lanes into the Rams backfield. "Nuts," countered Henry Jordan. "Consistent winners don't use trickery. In order to win, you just have to play more football than the other guy."

After a newsman suggested to Bart Starr that the turning point came in the second quarter, when Gossett missed the field goal and Willie Wood ran it back, the quarterback quoted from Lombardi's pamphlet of football disciplines: "There's no turning point. You play sixty minutes and every one of them counts. We didn't particularly pick their defense to pieces. We just had a lot of blocking."

When the game was over, Vince Lombardi was in a mood to talk. People involved in professional motivation like to say that the ultimate benefits that come from the accomplishment of a long-term goal are derived from whatever has been gained during the journey to get there. What the Green Bay Packers had accumulated in this forced march to the NFL championship round largely consisted of cracked ribs, wrecked knees, busted heads, and bad press.

In the process of trying to defend their championship, the Packers, like the hunting jacket that they'd given the coach, had a target painted across their backs. Every team in the league wanted a piece of the Pack. Not since 1963, when Paul Hornung had been kicked out of football for a season for gambling, had Lombardi experienced a more trying, demanding campaign than this one. The nadir, for Lombardi, concerned something that happened off the field. A feature about the coach that appeared in *Esquire* depicted Vince Lombardi as a raging tyrant and a terminal bully and compared his politics to those of a "South American general." The worst part, for Vince, happened when his mother called him, upset to the point of tears. The article quoted the coach using coarse language, and Mama Lombardi was embarrassed.

"There is a special satisfaction in winning this one," the coach said. "Everybody had been saying that we were dead, that we were in a patsy division with the Bears, Vikings, and Lions, that we weren't the Packers that we once were. They were saying that we were too old. We had something to prove, and we proved it.

"We've handled the Rams' front four before and we handled them today. Yes, we had some special pass patterns today, and that might have been why Bart Starr completed seventeen out of twenty-three passes. Our defense was superb. Defense is mostly a matter of reaction, and we were quick off the ball all day. When the highest-scoring team in football needs two fumbles to score seven points, you must be doing quite a job. We're still the champions, and maybe we're still improving with age. If some of our veterans have a little less hair and a lot more experience—well, we've got some youngsters who are getting more experience, too."

Lombardi came forward with praise for everyone and everything, even the condition of the playing field at County Stadium. That might have been due to a run-in earlier that had involved Lombardi and the groundskeeper in Green Bay. Vince had chewed the guy out in front of the team. Later he attempted to apologize. It didn't work. "You eat me out in public and apologize in private, so I refuse to accept your goddamn apology," the groundskeeper told the coach.

The coach rattled off the names of his offensive linemen: Gregg, Kramer, Bob Skronski, Gale Gillingham, Ken Bowman, who had first neutralized, then dominated the game so that by the end the Fearsome Foursome had been reduced to the Quarrelsome Quartet. "I think it's imperative that I give the offense the credit they deserve. The newspapers and broadcasters never will. I know. I played in the offensive line myself once upon a time."

Then, almost instantly, Lombardi dismissed the "crisis" win over the Rams as yesterday's news. He shouted over the heads of the assembled reporters, over to the locker area where his assistant coaches were changing clothes. "Meeting tomorrow at nine-thirty! Meeting tomorrow at nine-thirty!" Tomorrow was Christmas Eve, but the Packers had an Ice Bowl coming up and needed to prepare.

Peace and joy prevailed throughout the whole fooball-besotted state of Wisconsin, where they rescheduled Halloween if it conflicted with a Packers game. Almost the whole state, that is. A resident of Mercer, Wisconsin, experienced a bad day when, one day before

Christmas Eve, the IRS filed a lien against him, seeking more than $920,000 in taxes and interest on the profits from the sale of distilled spirits from 1921 through 1932. ABC had been running a sensationally popular television series called *The Untouchables,* based on the activities of the man's late brother, and he had never seen a nickel from that. "Where's the justice?" wondered the man in Mercer, Ralph Capone.

EXACTLY A WEEK to the day before the Packers-Rams playoff game in Milwaukee, one team from a high school in Abilene, in West Texas, played another team from Austin for the upper-classification state championship football title. The contest attracted considerable media attention throughout Texas, primarily because the team from Abilene featured a quarterback named Jack Mildren. In 1967, Mildren rated as the most highly coveted high school football player in the United States. *Sports Illustrated* published a long feature story about the coast-to-coast recruiting frenzy over Mildren.

That championship game was played at TCU Stadium in Fort Worth during a sleet storm. Mildren's team trailed by a point, 20–19, in the fourth quarter, but the quarterback sensation drove the ball the length of the field into the teeth of the strong north wind. With seconds remaining and the Abilene team facing third down on the Austin school's one-yard line, Mildren called his last time-out. With a slick ball on a slick field, facing that stiff wind, Mildren and his coach, Merrill Green, decided not to risk a kick. Instead, Mildren attempted a quarterback sneak between his center and right guard.

But Mildren's feet seemed to skid when he took the snap and he was stopped short of the goal, and before the offense could line up again, the game was over. The unbeatable high school team had been beaten after all. Fortunately for the Green Bay Packers, Bart Starr hadn't seen that play. Otherwise, he might have made a different choice with the game at stake in the Ice Bowl.

PROSPERITY, AS USUAL, was the password in Dallas as 1967 came to a close. With LBJ continuing to ink the presses to finance his war in Vietnam, inflation prevailed throughout the worldwide economy. The price of oil seemed certain to zoom straight up. For the petro barons of Texas, the outlook could not have been rosier.

On Christmas Eve Sunday, the mood in the Cowboy Club's tent saloon near the front steps of the Cotton Bowl was especially festive. The Dallas fans felt confident that the Cowboys could move past the Cleveland Browns for that long-awaited and much discussed championship rematch against the Packers. Dallas had beaten the Browns on the road in the first game of the year, and they should handle them again in the raucous Cotton Bowl.

Despite a season riddled by inconsistent performance on both sides of the football, Tom Landry felt confident as well. The week of practice had left the coach with the impression that the team was solidifying at exactly the right time. In the locker room at midweek a player in the bathroom noticed Landry standing at an adjoining urinal. "Tom, how long have you been bald?" the player asked the coach. Landry, his outlook brightened by the productive week of practice, simply cackled and said, "I like a guy who lives dangerously." The coach was similarly unperturbed when he found another player's yellow Volkswagen parked in his own private slot at the practice facility, though he was less than thrilled by the bumper sticker on the car: "America: Fix It or Fuck It." But the preparations for the important Cleveland game left no room for distractions from lesser concerns.

Dandy Don Meredith's household had acquired a new occupant—a pet ocelot. Meredith, after his miserable showing against the Colts, had played rather sparingly in the final two regular-season games. Now, in the pre-playoff workouts, Landry conceded that his quarterback had never appeared sharper. Bob Hayes looked quick too. The bullet man had pulled up lame on the last play against Baltimore, sprinting deep on a Meredith version of a Hail Mary play. His leg felt good now. "I love this game," Hayes said shortly before the kickoff against the Browns. "I love money, too. And this game today, this is a money game."

In the press box before the kickoff against Cleveland, Tex Schramm had been grousing to reporters that television executives in New York—Schramm still dealt with those characters on a daily basis for the same reason that Willie Sutton dealt with banks—were warming to the idea of calling the NFL-AFL championship the "Super Bowl." Schramm shook his head. "I don't like it. It sounds hokey."

Tex's chagrin did not last long. The Cleveland game was over a little after it started, and Bob Hayes was at his gold-medal best, clearly intent on operating at a performance level that surpassed any other effort of the season. Early in the contest Dallas pulled away to a 21–0 lead, and one of the touchdowns came on an 86-yard Meredith-to-Hayes completion that left the Browns' secondary appearing as if they were running in wet concrete.

Later, Bob Hayes set up another touchdown with a 68-yard punt return. For the game, he gained 144 yards in pass receptions and 141 more on kick returns. Ernie Stautner and Ermal Allen, two of Landry's assistants working upstairs in the press box and relaying information back to the field via the phone, wound up working a short day. With the Cowboys in front 38–7 in the third quarter, Landry told them, "If we score again, just come on back downstairs."

"What do you mean 'if'? I'm calling it quits," laughed Allen. The part of the contest that Landry found most pleasing had been the work of his offensive line, particularly Ralph Neely, who was developing some all-pro skills at tackle. During the AFL-NFL bidding wars, the Cowboys had gone to court to secure Neely's services after they disputed a contract he'd signed with the Oilers. Tony Liscio, an ex-Packer who couldn't beat out either Bob Skronski or Forrest Gregg, had come to Dallas and was developing some all-pro skills of his own. Dave Manders was solid at center and John Niland, the player whom the Cowboys had selected when they realized that they could not afford Jim Grabowski, now played at a level that made that choice seem prudent, too.

After the championship game of 1966, Landry had felt the offensive line had been the one element of the game where Dallas was clearly inferior to the Packers. Dallas still was not as good up front as the Pack. But the line was closing the gap. It ripped some big holes in the Cleveland defense all afternoon, and Dallas finally wound up winning, 52–14. Green Bay just *thought* it had played impressively against the Rams.

Even Tom Landry seemed a little awed by the Cowboys' onslaught. "You'd have to say it was our greatest game ever, considering the quality of the competition," the coach said. His players realized that those words represented strong commentary because Tom Landry had never been one for overstatement. Landry liked his game plan for the Browns, too, and said as much. "We had a sound game plan and the players believed in it. You have to establish a running game against Cleveland."

One thing dampened Landry's afternoon. Pete Gent, healthy again after his bad back injury against the Giants, had entered the game while Bob Hayes caught his breath after another huge gain. While throwing a block on a Cleveland linebacker, Gent hit the ground and heard a crunching sound when backup fullback Walt Garrison was knocked on top of him. Gent's right ankle had been dislocated and his right leg broken. "En route to the hospital, I made a mental note to save up my pain pills for next week," Gent recalled. "I knew I'd be watching the Packers game on TV, and if we lost, I'd need the pills."

"Ohh," Landry said when told of the X-ray results on Gent. "I hate to hear that. With the Packers coming up, you need all your players. That's a bad break for our team." Not to mention the rotten break it was for Gent.

Across the tunnel, in the Browns' dressing room, the players stuffed equipment into canvas bags as quickly as they could. After a day like this one everybody wanted to make a hasty exit. Owner Art Modell, clad in a fur coat, seemed especially shell-shocked. "I've never, *never* seen a Browns team thrown around like that in an important game," Modell said, wearing an expression that seemed to say, "One of these days I'm going to move this team to Baltimore."

Cornerback Ben Davis quietly explained that covering Bob Hayes had not been the happiest experience of his life. Angela Davis, the antiwar activist accused and later acquitted of terrorist activities, was the Cleveland cornerback's sister. Another Browns defensive back, Mike Howell, said, "I got burned all day, but I don't feel too badly. It's to be expected with that guy [Hayes]. You can't compare him with anybody."

Frank Ryan, the Browns' cornerback with his doctorate in physics, offered this analysis: "Obviously we had a game plan. It just didn't work too well." Blanton Collier, the Browns' coach, echoed Ryan and then spoke the obvious: "We didn't contain Hayes at all. He had a fantastic day and he really hurt us."

Dallas also scored on a long interception return by Cornell Green, which the Dallas cornerback felt had been particularly gratifying. Published reports earlier in the week included quotes from

Browns receiver Gary Collins, who said, in effect, that he planned to eat Green's lunch, just like he always had.

"I don't think I said that," Collins said. "You don't say that about an all-NFL man. Not if you're a sane man, and I think I'm sane. I've had my good days, and Cornell has had his. He had the better one today."

OVER ON THE Cowboys' side, the players began to drift out into the chilly Texas December air. Tom Landry stopped Don Meredith at the dressing room doorway.

"Merry Christmas, Don," the coach said.

"Yeah. I think it's gonna be all right," the quarterback answered.

CHAPTER 13

Long-range meteorological forecasters gazed at their upper-atmosphere-pressure charts and determined that the temperature in Green Bay for the one o'clock kickoff against Dallas should hover around seventeen degrees. That estimate hardly conformed to the fabled coach's ideal for Packer Weather. On New Year's Eve, in that region where the Fox River connects into the bay off Lake Michigan, those seventeen degrees amounted to bikini weather. Season-ticket holders at Lambeau Field could not be sure what to bring to the game—brandy or coconut oil.

Another forecast, the one from Las Vegas, pegged the Green Bay Packers as a six-and-a-half-point favorite to beat Dallas and move from there to the Super Bowl to play the Oakland Raiders. Oakland was playing Houston for the AFL title, but that contest would be a formality. Al Davis clearly had the superior team. With the Cowboys and Packers, however, pregame suspense was expanding quickly.

Packers scout Wally Cruice had sat in the Cotton Bowl press box and watched as Dallas demolished the Cleveland Browns. Cruice did not feel he was disclosing any military secrets when he said, "If the Cowboys play like that against us, it will be too bad for the Packers." Vince Lombardi had watched the rout on television and agreed that against the Browns, Dallas "was unstoppable. It looks like they're going to be rough to handle."

L.A. coach George Allen said that his Rams had left all their emotion on the field after their big win over Baltimore, that his team was psychologically drained and flat against Green Bay. After displaying such a passion for the kill in beating L.A. 28–7, would the Packers show up a little less hungry against Dallas? Lombardi doubted that would be a problem.

The teams uttered all of the proper platitudes as the week progressed. Bob Lilly was looking for a "dogfight" on Sunday. Said he: "The Packers are clutch players, and they play like champions are supposed to play." Lee Roy Jordan worried about the Cowboys' mental aspect, now that the team was again being called onto the center stage of the football universe. "The tension is really building," Jordan said. "Here it is, only midweek, and we're sky-high already." Linebacker Chuck Howley was somewhat more specific as he outlined his concerns about the title game: "The Packers always have the best game plan that we face. They attack our defense better than any other team in the league."

Twenty-nine years after the fact, Bart Starr would agree. "Coach Lombardi always enjoyed preparing for the Cowboys—more than any team. That's because he felt that Tom Landry, and that containment defense that the Cowboys used, were a special challenge. He had all the respect in the world for Landry," Starr said.

When Lombardi and Landry had coached together with the New York Giants, the two assistants literally ran the team for head coach Jim Lee Howell. "The Giants didn't have a head coach. They had a head smile," said sportswriter Jerry Izenberg. "Jim Lee Howell had a great personality and took care of the media. Lombardi and Landry were clearly the people in charge of football operations. Lombardi with the offense, Landry with the defense. The Giants in those days were like two separate teams."

Lombardi, understanding Landry's theory of defense because of the men's association in New York, tried to read the other coach's mind whenever he prepared to play the Cowboys. But he knew, too, that their previous working relationship could very well act as a double-edged sword. What worried him most about Landry and the Cowboys entailed some events in the championship game of the season before. In Lombardi's nine seasons as head coach, the Packers would participate in ten postseason games. Of those ten games, Green Bay's splendid and ever reliable defense yielded three rushing touchdowns. One had come in the only postseason game Lombardi ever lost, when Philadelphia beat the Pack in 1959. Ted Dean scored from five yards on the play that won the game for the Eagles.

The other two running touchdowns had been scored by Landry's

Cowboys in the game at the Cotton Bowl when Don Perkins and Dan Reeves raced in with first-half long gainers. Lombardi never said so until after he had retired, but those two runs—with Dallas attacking Green Bay's strength—had troubled the hell out of him. So Landry, Vince feared, might have located other soft spots in the Packers' defense for this rematch.

THE DALLAS ENTOURAGE arrived on Friday afternoon via a chartered 727 that landed in Green Bay. The Cowboys players appeared relaxed and ready. "I thought that this time Dallas would probably beat Green Bay," said Frank Luksa, who had been covering the team for the *Fort Worth Star-Telegram* since its early years. "This Dallas team had tremendous speed and Green Bay—well, they were playing at home but had been getting old. For Dallas, a lot of us just sort of felt a suspicion that its time had finally arrived."

"Even back then, never had there been a professional franchise of such excesses," Luksa continued. "They won big and lost even bigger. They had a quarterback in Don Meredith who liked to sing in the huddle. And they had the basketball player, Cornell Green, starring at cornerback. He's the one who put his tight pad into his pants backwards and almost became a soprano after his first practice.

"Then you look at the guys running the thing—they could not have been more opposite. Tex Schramm—gregarious. He liked to socialize with sportswriters, for God's sake. And then Landry—aloof, private. No time for small talk or idle chatter. He was always lost in thought, like he was concentrating on something that might be happening next week, or next year. What a cast of characters. This was a different kind of football team. You know, nobody ever wrote any books called *North Cincinnati Forty* or *North Atlanta Forty.*

"But before the Packers' game, up there the day before the game, I thought they were ready to beat Green Bay."

The team boarded two buses at the airport for the drive over to Lambeau for a loosening-up session. The Packers had just finished. The Dallas media corps got into rented cars to ride to the stadium. Lombardi would be holding a press conference. Since the NFL championship was at stake, a national assembly of media had flocked into Green Bay. Many had arrived in Wisconsin for the Rams game of a week earlier and had stayed on. Lombardi, like most successful coaches, tended to regard his dealings with the media as a necessary nuisance, but through the years, he'd learned to become more tolerant of the needs of reporters. In one-on-one sessions with certain journalists Lombardi was sometimes more open and cooperative than many other coaches. Those mass-interview situations—like the prechampionship-game press conferences or any postgame scene in the dressing room, when he faced a firing squad of twenty or more quill pushers throwing out questions—had been the ones that made Lombardi often behave like a saber-toothed tiger with a case of hemorrhoids. He also felt that some reporters, in a group setting, tossed out questions just for the sake of asking questions. Dumb questions, often, although Lombardi deemed himself sole arbiter of what did or did not qualify as a dumb question.

Just off the Cowboys' charter, the Texas-based reporters had trouble with the icy streets in Green Bay en route to Lombardi's big press conference. "The roads were slippery as can be and—horror of horrors—we arrived five minutes late for this scheduled press conference," said Luksa. "I tried to slink into the back of the room, hoping that Lombardi hadn't seen me or that nobody had even noticed our arrival. Everybody knew his attitude about being on time. Five minutes late—might as well have been five hours as far as Vince was concerned.

"Toward the end of the press conference I finally asked a question, and that's when Lombardi nailed me for being late. 'I've already answered that,' he snapped. But when the thing was over, his mood lightened considerably. He escorted some of us—Tex Schramm was along—down into the basement of the stadium. He wanted to show off his technological marvel."

Before the season, Lombardi had invested in an underground heating system designed to prevent the turf at Lambeau Field from freezing in the late-season games—like this one. Electric coils, about a foot apart, ran the length of the field, six and a half inches beneath the surface. Lombardi had bought the apparatus from a sales rep named George Halas, nephew of Green Bay's longtime rival from the Chicago Bears. Not only had Lombardi agreed to buy the underground heating rig, the world's largest electric blanket, from a man named Halas, he'd appropriated $80,000 of Packers funds for its purchase and installation. In those days, for that eighty grand, Lombardi could have bought a new front four, plus maybe a reserve tight end and a placekicker.

"The reason that he bought the thing," theorized Tex Schramm, "was that he always wanted optimum playing conditions for his team and the other team as well. Frankly, an ice-hardened field would probably work to the Packers' advantage in a game like this against a team like ours. But Vince, as everybody knows, was a person of genuine character, and he had real strong feelings about taking unfair advantage of a situation. He didn't think that should be a part of normal competition." What Schramm was saying here served as a denial of Cowboys' visions of Vince Lombardi tiptoeing through some lower cavern at Lambeau with a flashlight at 3 a.m. and unplugging his field-warming device. Lee Roy Jordan and George Andrie, in fact, both claimed that they could see Lombardi ordering the plug pulled on the underground gismo.

Through the years, Tex Schramm said that he felt he knew Lombardi better than he knew Tom Landry. "I never really *knew* Tom Landry. I don't know that anybody did," Schramm said.

"Anyway, Lombardi was sure proud of that heating system and he was clearly having fun down in that control room, showing off the gauges and dials and all that goddamn stuff," Schramm said.

"When Dallas took the field to practice at Lambeau Field, the underground system was turned on and the smoke or steam was pouring up from the field like the mist coming off moors," remembered Frank Luksa. "It looked like a scene from the *Hound of the Baskervilles.* It looked sort of eerie. But the field conditions were fine and the weather was all right. About twelve degrees and not much wind. With those circumstances, I liked Dallas's chances even better."

Another member of the Dallas press troop, Steve Perkins, picked the Cowboys to win by fourteen points in the Saturday *Times Herald.* (Steve Perkins, during World War II, had worked as a reporter for *Stars and Stripes,* the U.S. military daily newspaper. At a cocktail party in Honolulu a woman introduced Perkins to Edgar Rice Burroughs. "*The* Edgar Rice Burroughs?" Perkins is said to have blurted out. "Well . . . I'm the writer," Burroughs confirmed. Perkins said he was a writer, too.)

The traveling Dallas press corps had acquired a certain reputation around the league. One of them, Gary Cartwright (working in New York by the time of the Ice Bowl) at a press reception before a Dallas-Minnesota preseason game in Birmingham, asked Vikings coach Norm Van Brocklin about rumors that the "Dutchman" might be gay. *No* such rumors ever existed, of course, but Cartwright was just interested to see what might happen if he asked the question. Eyewitnesses recalled that several peace-makers were required to remove Van Brocklin's fingers from Cartwright's throat.

THE NIGHT BEFORE the championship game against the Packers, the Texas reporters had gathered at a big table at Fuzzy Thurston's restaurant. "We involved ourselves in many hours of deep research, and, as I recall, spirits were served," said Frank Luksa. When he returned from Thurston's to his hotel late in the evening, the sportswriter vaguely recalls detecting a chill in the air. . . .

While the press corps remained in Green Bay, the Cowboys players and coaches took buses over to Appleton, about 25 miles outside Green Bay on Highway 41, where they spent the night. Landry predesigned the arrangements, thinking that Appleton might offer a quieter surrounding than Green Bay, where loud and excited Packers fans would be pouring into town like lemmings from other locations around the state. Party time had commenced full steam, and Landry didn't want his players disturbed.

While some pro coaches like to sequester their teams in out-of-the-way hotel settings even before home games, Vince Lombardi liked to leave his players to their own devices. He felt that they'd be better rested spending the night in their own beds at home with their families.

Donny Anderson had flown his parents and his brother and sister-in-law in from Texas to see the game. "It was a spur-of-the-moment thing. I thought that maybe this might be the last time ever that a championship game would be played in Green Bay. You never really know, and I wanted them to be here to see it," Anderson said.

"We'd had a good workout at the field that afternoon. A light workout but a good one. The weather seemed fine. I ran some wind sprints and worked up a good sweat. My jersey was wet. I knew that we were ready to play Dallas," said Anderson, by then turning out nicely as the million-dollar bonus boy. "That night I went to dinner with my folks, I don't remember where, and then I sent them back to their hotel and I went home to the town house that I was renting with Jim Weatherwax and went to bed early."

During the workout, Bart Starr's shoulder felt as pain-free as it had at any time since he'd been belted by Tommy Nobis back in the third game of the season against Atlanta. "It wasn't too cold but, more important, there was no wind to speak of," Starr said. "I thought the team was relaxed and ready."

Starr's parents had traveled from Montgomery, Alabama, to watch the rematch with Dallas. "I stayed home and had a quiet dinner. We could have gone to a restaurant, even on a big night like this one, in Green Bay. The fans were great and enthusiastic, but really unobtrusive when it came to respecting the privacy of the players. But I wanted to stay home and review the game plan one last time. That was my routine. I slept very well that night. But then, I always did, for some reason, before a big game."

Tackle Forrest Gregg remembers leaving the Saturday practice at Lambeau Field just as the Cowboys were arriving for their warm-up session. "I remember going over to Don Meredith—we'd both grown up in towns in East Texas not far from each other. I was older but we were sort of kindred spirits. Frankly, I was very worried about the Cowboys. They had really matured as a team and I was grateful that we were playing them in Green Bay. I commented to Meredith about the weather and how the playing field looked all right. There wasn't much grass left, but it seemed passable. Meredith looked around and said, 'Yeah, man. This ain't half bad.' A lot of our players went out and had a few the night before the game, but I stayed home. They had apartments in Green Bay by then. I figured that I would be able to stand up and play football, that the conditions would allow the best team to win, and I went to bed with visions of sugar plums."

Chuck Mercein spent the night by himself. His wife, expecting a second child soon, was visiting her parents down in the Chicago area.

Vince Lombardi, Jr., with his wife and two children, had traveled from Minnesota to watch the game. The coach's son, then twenty-five, was attending night law school. "The setting at my parents' house was the same as it was before any home game. My father was relaxed by now and upbeat. If you were going to be around him, the day before the game was the time to do that," Lombardi says. "Early in the week he'd be tense, preoccupied. But after Thursday the game plan would be installed, there wasn't much else he could do about the preparations, and [he] was inclined to unwind some. That was the mood before this game against Dallas. He had some people over, I don't recall exactly who they were. He had a couple of scotches with the guests, and then they all went to dinner someplace. I didn't accompany them. One of our kids was sick, and we were up all night with him."

After midnight, things began to change in the world outside the Lombardi house. Like Sam Houston's Texas army sneaking through the woods to prepare its sneak attack on General Santa Anna's Mexican army at San Jacinto, a powerful, unexpected and silent force was cascading down from the Arctic and across the skies above upper Wisconsin. With the temperature at plus eight degrees around midnight, the winds picked up, and then the mercury began a harsh descent.

CHUCK MERCEIN, ALONE in his apartment, had set the alarm on his clock radio for 7:00 A.M. "I was still in a not-quite-awake state after the radio came on, and I thought I heard the announcer say something about thirteen degrees below zero," said Mercein. "I knew, actually, that I had heard that, but I wasn't sure exactly *where* it was thirteen below. But I knew that *if* he was talking about Green Bay, then it was important as far as the football game was concerned.

"I called the weather bureau at the airport, and the man there confirmed it. Yep. Minus-thirteen and due to get *colder.* I got up, went to church, and got to the field as quick as I could because I knew this was going to be a different kind of football game."

In the motel in Appleton, where the Cowboys were headquartered, George Andrie heard a chirpy voice at the other end of the line when he picked up his wake-up call. "The lady said, 'Good morning, it's seven o'clock and the temperature is fourteen degrees.' Then she paused for effect and said, 'below zero.' Well, I thought it was funny," the Cowboys' defensive end recalled.

"So I hollered over to Bob Lilly. He was my roommate for eleven years on the road with the Cowboys. I said, 'Hey, Bob. Watch this.' Then I took a glass of water and tossed it against the inside of the window. The water turned to ice, froze solid, before it could drip down to the windowsill.

"See, I was from that part of the world, remember, and had played in stuff like this, or at least similar to this before, and Lilly, he was a Texas guy. All this time, I'd been playing down there in all that damn heat—*his* kind of weather—and now I felt sort of glad that we were turning the tables.

"But . . ." said Andrie, "when Lilly saw that water freeze there on the window, I thought that I'd just pulled a *dumb* stunt. All of the color just drained right out of his face. I got dressed quickly and went off to church. I was a Catholic and they held a special mass for us. I don't know what Lilly did the rest of the morning—maybe they had church for guys like him, too, although he sure as hell wasn't Catholic—but when I left the room, I knew that he was going to be plenty worried about what it was like outside."

In another part of the motel, linebacker Lee Roy Jordan received the same wake-up call. "I didn't know if I heard her right, then the phone rang again and it was one of our players, and I don't remember who, and he said, 'Did you hear what the damn temperature is?' All I could do was go to the window and look outside. I just stared. I wanted to see what thirteen below actually *looked* like.

"The motel where we stayed there in Appleton was sort of horseshoe-shaped. From my angle I could see most of the other rooms in the place," says Jordan, now reciting what might be his most vivid Ice Bowl recollection after twenty-nine years. "In almost every window I could see somebody just like me—a Dallas football player staring outside, wondering what it would feel like when we finally went out there."

When the news reached Tex Schramm, he said that the crackerjack minds of the Dallas Cowboys' executive force, smartest young franchise in the history of pro sport, lapsed into a panic mode. At least, that happened to Tex Schramm. "I knew two things—first that I was worried about how or if the team might make it to the stadium back over in Green Bay in time to make the kickoff. I didn't know what the highway conditions might be. So I had somebody get on the phone and try to get us a police escort. And with the traffic and all, I was thinking our buses might need an alternate route."

That priority handled, Schramm then found himself digging through the Yellow Pages, searching under "Sporting Goods Stores." Surely, he figured, there would be plenty of retail outlets in Appleton open on a New Year's Eve Sunday and selling wholesale supplies of golf gloves. So what if the temperature was approaching what might be a record low for the planet Neptune? Back in Texas, everybody played golf on Sunday.

"We knew that we might not be equipped to play a game in weather like that," Schramm concedes now. "The Cowboys had never played in anything like that, and we didn't have any idea what to expect. We were completely unprepared. We found a hardware store that would open up and sell us some gloves, but they sure as hell weren't golf gloves. But what the hell, I remember thinking then. At least Vince had installed the underground heating system, so I knew that the field, at least, would be all right."

Back down the road toward the east, in Green Bay, lifelong locals awoke surprised, concerned, and even alarmed at what had happened so unexpectedly during the night. This was the coldest December day in Wisconsin since 1924. *Press-Gazette* sportswriter Lee Remmel received a phone call before 7:00 a.m. "We were a good paper but had a small staff and so practically everyone who worked at the paper, even on the Metro side, would be at Lambeau Field with some kind of assignment. I was going to hitch a ride with a city-side reporter, and he called and said, 'Guess what the temperature is outside? Just guess.' I looked at the thermometer outside my kitchen window. Well, that was a shock. Temperatures like that were not unprecedented in Green Bay. But I knew that there had never been a football game played in it here. That thirteen below had been the official temperature at the airport. Other thermometers around town were registering a minus-twenty."

Bart Starr woke up early. He was going to attend services at the Green Bay First United Methodist Church downtown. "I always went to the early service, but in Green Bay, churches even scheduled the second service to let out in time for the game." Starr's father, visiting from Alabama, planned to accompany him. His father had been a career military man who had fought in General Douglas MacArthur's troops in the Pacific. The Green Bay quarterback had been taught hard-line lessons by his father about the importance of confronting adversity. The father had served as an excellent warm-up act for the son's eventual exposure to life under Vince Lombardi. "I hadn't heard what the temperature was, but when my father and I went outside for the drive to the early church services, it was apparent to both of us that conditions for the game were going to be absolutely brutal. But neither of us even mentioned the weather on the drive to and from church," Starr remembered. "It was a non-topic." . . .

Forrest Gregg received an early-morning call from Jim Grabowski. "Jim lived in the same apartment unit as I did, with my wife, Barbara, and our little kids. Grabowski said his car wouldn't start, and then asked me how cold I thought it was. I looked out the window and the sun was out. I told Jim that I figured it was around zero and would probably get up to twenty by the afternoon. Then he told me the news, that it was minus-fourteen and wasn't going to get any better. I went outside to see if *my* car would start. It did, but I knew then that it was going to be a *bad* day."

Donny Anderson, now in his second season, had established a pregame morning ritual before home games in Green Bay. "I'd get up and drive over to the Downtowner Hotel and eat a light breakfast in the coffee shop. I was kind of a regular there. This place where I lived had a heated garage. I hadn't listened to or watched any newscasts during the morning, and as I drove through town to get my breakfast I still didn't know that anything out of the ordinary might be happening," said the Texan. "But then I noticed quite a few people in the driveways, starting their cars with jumper cables. That was unusual, because those folks knew how to keep their cars running in cold weather.

"When I got to the hotel, I saw a couple of guys I knew in the parking lot and they yelled at me: 'Good luck, Donny. It's gonna be cold today.' And I said, 'Yeah. It'll be about like last week down in Milwaukee.' And one of them said, 'Uh-uh. It's going to be *real* cold. It's already about fifteen below.' I went into the coffee shop and asked a waitress who I knew if that was really true. She told me that not only was it true but that the chill factor was going to be about minus seventy.

"I wasn't due at the stadium until eleven a.m. to get taped, but I figured that today it might be a good time to show up a half hour early."

If Vince Lombardi had been calm and convivial the night before the game, his mood altered when he learned about the unheard-of temperatures that strangled the town on the day of the championship game. His son, Vince Junior, drove the coach to Lambeau Field on the morning of the Ice Bowl. "He was agitated. Really concerned. I'd never seen him quite that way on game day," the son said. "The reason? He was worried about the heating-coil apparatus at the stadium. He was afraid that the thing might not work in temperatures like this. And he worried that if the thing didn't work, he'd be accused of tampering with it to make the field worse for Dallas."

Sportswriter Frank Luksa woke up at a reasonable hour to make the one o'clock kickoff. He left the hotel and rode to the stadium on one of several press buses provided by the NFL. "I had plenty of time that morning and didn't need a wake-up call," he said. "Or, if I did get one, they didn't mention the temperature. So I didn't realize that anything was particularly out of the ordinary when I climbed on the bus carrying a portable typewriter, a briefcase, and a hanging bag with all my stuff inside.

"But I was on one of the last press buses to leave the hotel. Heavy traffic was clogging the entry to the stadium, and the bus was going to have to go down to the end of a street, and make a U-turn to reach the press gate. I had some work to do early and decided to get off the bus and walk the rest of the way, thinking that would be quicker.

"So I jumped from the bus, carrying my typewriter and the rest of my stuff, walked about fifteen feet and slipped and fell on my ass—and then landed on my back in a ditch. *That's* when I found out how cold it was. I thought I was going to freeze in place and that they wouldn't find me until the next spring thaw. I'd never—ever—experienced anything like that in my life."

Somehow, the displaced Texan climbed from his predicament and advanced, stunned and sputtering, toward the press gate at Lambeau Field. "That was the first and only time, in about thirty-five years' worth of covering NFL football games, that I walked through the gate and nobody asked to see my press pass. Nobody stopped me. Nobody asked me for a ticket. I had ice and crap all over me, and I guess they thought I was the Abominable Snowman."

Luksa, like the CBS-TV technicians and other working news people, remembers hoping that the Lambeau Field press box "might offer *some* warmth. What I found instead was coffee that froze in paper cups in a matter of seconds.

"They were busy with some kind of squeegee device, scraping the frost off the press-box windows from the inside. I had some things to write to transmit back to the paper, and I remember the ice crystals falling off the windows and into my typewriter. And I remember that I kept thinking, I'm inside, thank God. And I wondered how those poor devils out in the stadium seats and down on the field were ever going to survive."

CHAPTER 14

On New Year's Eve in Wisconsin, 1967, the iceman cometh. Then the iceman looked around, inhaled deeply, and promptly booked himself onto the next available flight to the Fiji Islands. Late in the autumn of 1967 Charles de Gaulle presented his worldview to an inquiring essayist. Among other offerings, de Gaulle opined, "You may be sure that the Americans will commit all the stupidities they can think of—plus some that are beyond the imagination."

So de Gaulle would have felt justified, perhaps even pleased, by the spectacle unfolding on an early Sunday afternoon amid the deepest interior province of the Great American Heartland. Normally stable adults accompanied by good numbers of children filled a vast arena in defiance of climatic conditions unfit and dangerous to any living organism. They had come, and actually paid to come, to witness an exhibition in which men wearing odd padded regalia knocked one another down and on this day also earned style points for falling down on their own.

Down in Milwaukee, the sunrise temperature reached the lowest December reading since 1924. In the Green Bay Packers' locker room Donny Anderson had been thinking the same thing. "I arrived there early, after I heard about the chill factor. Most of the other players had already arrived and were having their ankles taped and were sipping from cups of hot beef bouillon. Vince—you could always recognize his handwriting—had made the usual notation on the blackboard. It read, '12:10 kickers; 12:20 team.' Which meant that the people doing the kicking—Don Chandler with Bart Starr, the holder, and Willie Wood, the return guy—went out a little early to warm up, and then the rest of us would follow. Although I was the punter, of course I played offense, too, and usually went out with the second group.

"Well, on this day," Anderson remembered, "those three went out and then came trotting back inside. They had ice in their eyebrows. You know, there were about ten Texans on that Packers team, and three of us had lockers together, me and Lee Roy Caffey and Tommy Joe Crutcher. And when the kick guys came back we just sort of stared at each other, and I said, 'They're crazy if they play this game. It's just too cold. People are going to get frostbit and we're going to break our legs.' I was concerned about the people who were sitting down in the stands, too. Of course, those fans in Green Bay, they'd all come out if it was a hundred below."

Come out, of course, they did, although the customary pregame bar-hopping activity was toned down. Most of the spectators took extra precautions against the fierce elements and came bundled in gear suitable for a prolonged ice-fishing expedition. Of course, it might have felt like springtime for some pilgrims from areas like Eau Claire and Park Falls, where the cold reached minus 24 degrees. But when the wind blew hard through Lambeau Field, the crowd realized that they were seated in the great and fierce outdoors. If these fans wanted to see the game, the inhumane natural setting inside the stadium provided the only recourse. Also in 1967, Green Bay and the surrounding territory remained subjected to the TV-blackout regulations.

"Most of the fans, or a lot of us at least, brought sleeping bags and tucked ourselves into those to watch the game," said one Packers fan. "One person I'll never forget, a young woman, came to the game wearing high heels, a short cocktail dress and a lightweight jacket. Even before the game this woman had turned purple. I'm sure that she was from Dallas."

TEX SCHRAMM'S WIFE, Marty, customarily joined Alicia Landry in the stands at Dallas Cowboys road games. "Alicia and I tried to buy a hot dog at a concession stand beneath the stadium before the game started," said Marty Schramm, "but the catsup and mustard were frozen solid in their little packets. Inside the stadium, when we got to our seats, some of the Green Bay fans recognized who we were—or at least they recognized Alicia. We were wearing topcoats, appropriate for a cold day in Texas, and the Green Bay fans realized that we were underdressed for a day like this. We weren't prepared. Conditions like that were foreign to us.

"So they gave us plastic bags to literally wrap around our bodies, and if it had not been for that I think we might have frozen to death. When the game started it was so cold that when I got any moisture in my eyes, my eyelids actually froze tightly shut."

In the press box, Tex was busily scraping the ice off the window in front of him with the wooden stirrer from his coffee cup so that he could see the game. Earlier, he had prowled the field while the team warmed up—relieved that the Cowboys' buses had arrived safely from Appleton in time to make the kickoff. The game would proceed on schedule, all right. They could hardly call the thing off, else the beer, cigarette, and automotive sponsors of the national telecast would loudly protest. Schramm made a note to meet with Pete Rozelle still to discuss a contingency plan for future occasions like this, when some unforeseen calamity created a circumstance that was potentially hazardous to players, officials and spectators. That meeting would be at a later time. On this day Pete Rozelle, the NFL commissioner and an intelligent man, had chosen to bypass the contest in Green Bay and devoted his day to the AFL championship match in Oakland.

In the television booth, not far from Schramm, Ray Scott was preparing to describe this Cowboys-Packers collision to the American viewers. Scott's assignment from CBS required him to call the first half. Jack Buck, who then was assigned to all Cowboys telecasts (after three seasons, Buck had still not mastered the reality that the Dallas tight end was named Pettis Norman, not Norman Pettis), would take over for the second half and Scott would retreat downstairs to conduct postgame interviews. A third person working in the CBS booth, Frank Gifford, would act as the color man for both halves. The window of the television booth had been pulled open because Scott insisted on working in an open booth, no matter the weather, to get a better feel for the stadium atmosphere outside.

"Jack Buck brought a bottle of whiskey to the game and poured us all a big shot into our coffee cups just before the kickoff," remembered Ray Scott. "Even strongly laced with the booze, the coffee still froze. Just after we went on the air Gifford said, 'I just took a bite of coffee.' I wasn't sure that the viewers knew what Frank was talking about. God almighty, it was cold and I was simply grateful that we were at least not perched up on a rooftop, like I'd been for that Packers-Giants game in 1962."

Green Bay sportswriter Lee Remmel recalled: "Usually the Packers would bring in a college band or a good high school band for the halftime show, and the Packers had their own band that played 'The Star-Spangled Banner' before the games as well as the Packers' song. But best I can remember, the bands were silent for this game. They were afraid the instruments might stick to the musicians' lips and they'd rip the skin off after they played."

During pregame preparations, while Tom Landry retained his normal pose as the human computer, the rest of the team, if not in turmoil, had been completely distracted by the unexpected severe winter conditions. "There was no talk of strategy. All that we concentrated on was how to dress for weather like this," said George Andrie. "And in the pregame warm-up I knew that heated-field machine wasn't going to work. Being from that part of the country, I'd seen it before. The ground was getting hard, and it was obvious that it would freeze and the footing would be a nightmare.

"We had some gloves, but then Ernie Stautner, the defensive line coach, came to me before the game and said he didn't want me wearing the gloves. He thought there might be fumbles and stuff and that the gloves would keep me from maybe recovering one."

In the pregame workout Starr recalled, he tried to ignore the wind and the weather. "But it was . . . oh, boy . . . it was *cold* out there. Still, the job was to ignore that. I could grip the ball just fine. This had been a tough year for me earlier in the season and for a lot of the other players, too. No season, ever, had we gone through a tougher year with injuries, but we were now exactly where we had worked to be. That was all that would matter."

One Packer, Jim Grabowski, put on a uniform and, despite his bad knee injury, was hoping to make a heroic effort to get into the game. But he slipped on the risky turf and reinjured the knee.

Chuck Mercein, clopping around the field in the pregame drills, recalls being almost more curious than cold. "The condition of the field was strange—getting hard but not smooth like an ice surface," the fullback said. "Here's the best way to describe it—imagine a stucco wall laid horizontal. The actual surface of the ground was rough and pointy, with thousands of little clods of dirt and clumps of mud already freezing solid to the turf. And the field was already getting hard. It was *dreadful.*

"I hadn't dressed any differently than I would for any other game. I mean, I didn't put on any rubber suit underneath my uniform or anything like that. What stood out to me in the pregame warm-up was Bob Hayes, over on the Cowboys' side of the field. He had his hands jammed down the front of his pants and that's how he played practically the entire game. That's how the defense knew for sure before a play that Hayes wouldn't be involved in a pass play. He'd come up to the line of scrimmage with his hands tucked into his pants.

"Well, I hadn't been with the team that long, but I knew all about the Packer Weather attitude and that had a lot to do with how I dressed. This was the Packers' home field and I was like the rest of the players, all prepared to go do this macho thing out in that meat freezer. My contacts had frozen solid to my eyeballs, but I was ready and willing to show as much or more mettle than any of the old veterans.

"And I realized one thing: We were cold, but it was colder for the Cowboys, and you could see it. They were over there cutting holes into stockings to make face masks, or ski masks. Before it started, they weren't focused on the football aspect of the game at all."

Donny Anderson, who would start at running back alongside Mercein, had decided to remember that while he was a Texan, he had been brought up on what amounts to the Texas polar ice cap, in the northernmost reaches of the Panhandle, where the cold wind loves to howl and torture all of humanity. "Back in Texas as a kid, working outdoors on the farm, or the ranch or whatever it was, I learned that as long as your feet are warm, then you can stay warm. I wore some kangaroo-skin football shoes laced up tight as a glove. Underneath my uniform I wore long handles, but they were cut off above the knees and above the elbows. That probably wasn't enough, but we had heaters—those blower-type things—behind our bench. I stayed away from those, and out on the field, when the game started, I kept my hands from freezing by sticking them in the front of my football pants or, in the huddle sometimes, I'd also stick them under the armpit of Gale

Gillingham, one of our guards. After a while, I quit noticing the weather."

After all, according to the Lombardi ideal, if pain is simply a state of mind, who can be bothered by a little bite of the real thing?

THE OFFICIALS ASSEMBLED the captains at midfield. The National Football League had selected veteran Norm Schachter as the referee for the championship game. Schacter had been involved in two rather controversial games for both teams during the season. He had worked as the head official in the Packers' opener against Detroit, when Lombardi had raised a ruckus at the end, claiming the game ended two seconds too early and therefore cheated the Packers out of a field-goal attempt that might have won it. And Schachter had been the referee at the Cowboys' fracas at New Orleans, when Dallas couldn't run a play for nearly fifteen minutes, unable to hear signals over the boos and shouts of 83,000 enraged fans.

Dallas won the coin toss and Don Chandler prepared to kick off. The Packers would own a marginal wind advantage for the first quarter—although that wind, blowing steadily at nearly twenty miles an hour from the northwest, felt unbearable, like onrushing death. On the Green Bay sideline, Lombardi wore a long overcoat and one of those fur hats favored by Soviet premiers en route to make a speech at the Kremlin. As Tom Landry stood facing Lombardi across the field, he was clad in something that looked like a mink coat.

When Chandler's toes met the football, he felt as if he had just kicked a shotput, but the ball connected with a wind current and Sim Stokes fielded it at the Dallas five-yard line and returned it to the Dallas 33. On the first scrimmage play, with the Packers' defense poised to stop fullback Don Perkins, Don Meredith faked in that direction and flipped a sideline pass to Hayes. The play gained exactly 10 yards and a first down. That was clearly a hopeful beginning for the Dallas offense, but it also proved to be the last meaningful contribution of Bob Hayes, the famed game-breaker, for the day. If the Dallas Cowboys came into the contest with a distinct advantage in any particular area, it was the constant threat of an insta-touchdown from Hayes. The week before, in the playoff game against the Browns, Hayes rampaged for 281 yards on receptions and returns. Hayes, however, was not enthusiastic about Packer Weather. Hated it. Already defeated by the minus-70 wind chill, Hayes, after that first 10-yarder along the sideline, would contribute only six additional yards total offensive for the remainder of the Ice Bowl.

After the initial first down, Dallas rapidly swallowed a large gulp of what reality would be offering to the streamlined Cowboys offense for most of the remainder of the game. After Dan Reeves ran for four yards on Dallas's initial try from the ground, Meredith looked for Lance Rentzel on a slant pattern downfield and missed his receiver badly. On third down, Reeves tried another run, but Herb Adderley, coming up quick from his cornerback post, nailed the runner for no gain. From the Dallas 47, punter Danny Villanueva kicked the ball to Wood, who returned it two yards to the Packer 18.

"When I went into the huddle for our first offensive possession, I no longer felt the cold. I couldn't hear the crowd. We had prepared all season for this and I was eager to get started," recalled Bart Starr. On the Packers' first offensive play, Starr handed the ball to Donny Anderson, who gained five yards but lost the football when hit by Chuck Howley. The first real break of the game went in Green Bay's direction, though, when the fumble bounced at the feet of Chuck Mercein, recently of the Westchester Bulls and now recovering a Packers fumble in the NFL championship game. Starr, needing a confident Donny Anderson running the ball, ran the halfback again, this time for four yards, and then called the same play. Anderson gained four more yards, and the Packers, seemingly ready now to roll, had a first down.

Starr began to mix his offensive calls, but his first effort to throw the ball downfield to Boyd Dowler never left the ground. Both Bob Lilly and Andrie, finding some good traction on the rapidly hardening field, penetrated hard through the Packers line, decking Starr for a nine-yard loss. On second down, Starr finally got the football airborne. Tight end Marv Fleming, running a medium-length pattern across the middle, couldn't catch the pass, but Dallas was flagged for interference. Green Bay owned a fresh set of downs at its 31.

Green Bay knew that Dallas owned data on a printout sheet that showed the Pack tended to run the power sweep in a situation like this. Starr further realized that Tom Landry, knowing of Lombardi's long devotion to the running game, would gear his defense to stop that because the Cowboys had no chance of winning here if they couldn't.

So on first down, Starr pumped a pass to Donny Anderson, who outran a linebacker and gained 17 yards. Starr wanted to establish an early offensive rhythm and figured he could best accomplish that by forcing the Cowboys' defense to start guessing before every play. Now Green Bay pounded the Dallas midsection, first with Anderson and then with Mercein, but those two visits into the meat grinder gained only five yards. On third down, though, Dallas picked up its second defensive penalty of this early drive, a holding call that gave Green Bay yet another first down, now in Cowboys territory at the 42.

Starr stuck with the running attack now, but Bob Lilly, the all-pro and on fire early in the Ice Bowl, was totally dominating Packers guard Gale Gillingham, and he buried Anderson for a two-yard loss. Linebacker Dave Edwards tackled Mercein after a short gain. Starr, looking at third down and nine, searched the field for another key component in the Packers' offensive repertoire, Carroll Dale, and for the first time in the game the Packers connected with a wide receiver on a slant-in pattern.

The play gained 17 yards. Now Starr looked for his other wideout, the six-foot-five Dowler, and when that failed to connect, the quarterback went back to Carroll Dale—not over the middle this time but on a sideline route. Dale caught the pass and by the time Cowboys safety Mike Gaechter pushed him out of bounds, the Packers had control inside the ten. After Anderson picked up another yard, Starr, noticing man-for-man coverage on his split end, changed his play at the line of scrimmage and fired a quick shot to Dowler, slanting inside, and the veteran star, a half-foot taller than three members of the Dallas secondary, pulled down an eight-yard touchdown pass.

That opening drive contained all of the enviable characteristics of Green Bay's artistic offensive pedigree. The march contained sixteen plays—eight running and eight passing. Better yet, it covered 82 yards and chewed almost seven minutes off the clock. Bart Starr's Act I drew a standing ovation. After the Cowboys' defense returned to the sideline, Lee Roy Jordan went for the box that contained the gloves that Schramm had ordered that morning. "The coaches didn't want the defensive players wearing the gloves, in case we might miss out on a turnover. They were these cumbersome canvas work gloves, the kind that I used back on the farm when I was carrying a hoe in the cotton field. I didn't care what the damn things looked like. I put 'em on and wore them the rest of the game."

Even more disturbing to Jordan than the ease with which Green Bay had scored on its first drive was something he saw on the Dallas sidelines. "Tom had icicles an inch and a half long sticking down from either nostril," Jordan said. "He looked a little . . . weird."

With that opening-drive touchdown, it looked as though Green Bay had delivered a staggering psychological blow to the freezing Cowboys. One touchdown, in the minds of some of the thundering Lambeau Field fans, probably seemed enough. The Packers received another nice break on the next kickoff. Chandler appeared to mis-hit the football. It rolled downfield, bounced off Cowboys' special-team player Larry Stephens, then went out of bounds before anybody else touched the ball, and now Dallas was stuck back at its own fourteen. Don Meredith handed off to Don Perkins for five yards and then threw the little sideline pass to Hayes for five more.

Perkins, who had scored one of those so-rare playoff rushing touchdowns against the Green Bay defense the year before, got the call on the next three plays. Those three carries gained an even 10 yards and another first down. But Meredith clearly looked like he was groping. Between two incomplete passes, Ray Nitschke blasted Perkins down for no gain. Two Dallas possessions, two Dallas punts. Green Bay got the ball back at its own 34.

Now the Cowboys' defense became surly. Lee Roy Jordan, feeling more comfortable in his Farmer Brown work gloves, leveled Mercein for no gain on first down. Starr looked for Dale again, but burned twice on the last drive, the Dallas secondary double-covered the Packers flanker. Starr overthrew him intentionally, and when Jethro Pugh smothered Mercein after a three-yard gain it was the Packers' turn to punt. Anderson launched a high kick and the odd spin that the left-footed punter put on the ball seemed to confuse Rentzel, who was set back to field the punt opposite Bob Hayes. Rentzel appeared momentarily hypnotized by the falling football, staggering beneath it like a member of the 1962 Mets infield who'd lost a pop-up in the sun. Finally Rentzel fielded the ball after signaling a fair catch. Ron Kostelnik and Lionel Aldridge, alerted to Don Meredith's growing tendency to hand the ball to his fullback, smacked Perkins down for no gain, and the first quarter ended with that play, Dallas on its own 33 and down 7–0.

* * *

After two Meredith passes fell incomplete, Bart Starr took the field in the second quarter with two new backs, Travis Williams and Ben Wilson. Right away, Wilson banged into the Dallas secondary and ran 13 yards before Mel Renfro could pull him down. Next Williams ran seven yards and into Cowboys territory. If the rocketlike Williams, hottest of the Green Bay backs over the second half of the season, could somehow maintain his footing on the treacherous turf, Dallas figured as precertified DOA. Williams now pounded ahead for two more and, facing third down and one, Starr decided again to try to outguess the Dallas defense. He faked the ball to fullback Wilson, whose simulated plunge into the middle caused safety man Renfro to hesitate for the nanosecond required for Dowler to slip away downfield. Starr's perfectly timed 43-yard throw resulted in Dowler's second touchdown of the afternoon. Green Bay now led, 14–0, and with 12:10 still to play in the first half, the main challenge the Packers faced appeared to be merely avoiding pneumonia.

An eternity remained on the game clock, but Meredith seemed frustrated already and pressed the issue. A first-down pass to Hayes, whistling down the field on a deep route, was nowhere near complete. Hayes had been so tightly covered that Meredith then gave up any hope that a one-punch TD to the Bullet would be a possibility. Perkins again gained nothing on second down, thanks to Nitschke, and Adderley intercepted Meredith's pass on the next play and counterpunched 15 yards to the Dallas 32. Not only was Dallas freezing on the outside, it appeared that internal hemorrhaging had set in as well.

Wilson gained nothing on the first down, though. Linebacker Dave Edwards knocked down Starr's next pass and then Andrie knocked Starr himself down for a 10-yard loss. Instead of transforming the game into a 21–0 laugher, Green Bay found itself punting. "Even after we jumped out 14–0, I was concerned about Dallas," Starr said. "Their front four was playing hard. I had a sort of feeling that Dallas was going to come back somehow." Frankly, after a 1967 season full of bad hops and wall-to-wall contusions, in weather like this a cakewalk seemed too much to ask, Starr was thinking. Still, after Anderson's punt died at the Dallas nine, the Cowboys' offense was looking more and more feeble. Aldridge, Kostelnik, Nitschke, and Robinson brutalized three Dallas running plays. Punt time, Cowboys.

From exactly midfield, the Pack's replacement backs, Williams and Wilson, went nowhere on three plays. That sadistic arctic wind now had shifted slightly from northwest to north and had intensified. On a normal day, Donny Anderson could have kicked a pumpkin farther than he did his next punt, which traveled, counting the roll, 16 yards. Two Dallas running plays gained a net three yards. Meredith looked for Hayes in the flat and completed the third-down pass. Caffey and Bob Jeter knocked Hayes down after an advance of only one yard—and *that* was the final occasion that the most potent missile in the Dallas attack arsenal would advance the football as much as one inch for the remainder of the afternoon. Now, six Dallas offensive possessions had resulted in five Danny Villanueva punts and one Meredith interception.

Starr's premonition that Dallas could and might shortly create some unpleasant sensations in Packerville became real. After Willie Wood ran Villanueva's punt back to the Green Bay 31, the Packers received their first penalty of the game, a five-yarder for illegal motion. A small but unwelcome omen. On the next play Starr attempted to drop back deep on a pass play and turned to discover that Willie Townes, Dallas's left defensive end, had slipped a block. Starr retreated further, and as his footing faltered, Townes advanced like a leopard stalking a baby antelope. When the defensive end finally grabbed his prey, the football bounced loose.

George Andrie, firing into the Packers' backfield from the other side of the line, picked up the football at the seven-yard line and carried it across the Green Bay goal line. "Cold weather did not affect that play," said Starr. "I should have tucked the ball away when I saw Townes coming, but he simply batted the thing loose."

Andrie clearly recalled the reception he received on the Dallas sideline. "Old Ernie Stautner, the line coach, came running over and yelled, 'See! See! If you'd been wearing gloves, you wouldn't have made that play!' I just said to hell with that. With or without the gloves, I was going to score that touchdown."

Now the Cowboys looked pumped up. The next Packers offensive series quickly stalled. Travis Williams gained a yard; then Ben Wilson couldn't hold Starr's pass. Even after Dallas jumped offside on third down, Jethro Pugh rumbled over the Packers center and threw Starr down onto the cold hard ground for a five-yard loss.

Dallas had the ball now in Packers territory for the first time in the game, but again, the Cowboys' offense looked even more futile than Green Bay's. After Reeves gained two yards on first down, Dallas—obviously willing to attempt anything, no matter how foolish—tried a flanker reverse on the ever hardening Lambeau Field surface. Henry Jordan threw Frank Clarke down for an eight-yard loss. Meredith, who'd thrown for 16 yards against the Packers' defense, took a third-down stab at Rentzel, but that only brought Villaneuva back onto the field.

His high kick seemed to paralyze the reliable Packers safety, Willie Wood, who flubbed the catch, and Phil Clark recovered for the revitalized Cowboys at the 17-yard line. "I misjudged the ball for a moment, then tried to catch it anyway, because if I didn't I could see the thing rolling dead at our one- or two-yard line. Obviously, when I blew the fair catch, the outcome was much worse than that."

Dallas's offense advanced three yards in three plays. Villanueva, though, kicked a 21-yard field goal. Now the score stood at 14–10 as the first-half clock ran out. Dallas hadn't made a first down in the entire second quarter—didn't come close—and still somehow had scored those ten points.

As Chuck Mercein watched from the sidelines he was thinking, "Boy, that's not like us. The Cowboys hadn't done a damn thing all day, and then they pick up that fumble and they're only a touchdown behind. And then Willie Wood, always sure-handed and who never fumbles, he fumbles one, too."

As halftime neared, Forrest Gregg, anchor of the Packers' offensive line, worried that the Pack attack might have landed its only blow and now wondered if Green Bay's 14 points might have to suffice. "The wind . . . the cold . . . the conditions of the field. Everything was deteriorating fast," he said.

"The effort to block anybody became very difficult. The sweep, which was the play that set up our entire offense, wasn't working anymore. The guards couldn't get the footing that they needed to get in front of the ball carrier. The field was hard as a rock, and it was treacherous. I worried about falling down on every play. Not from fear of being hurt when I hit the icy surface. But you don't play football flat on the ground.

"When the game started, the Cowboys looked colder than we did, and they were. You could tell. But they really fooled us all. They had made a great effort to stay that close, and by the half we had all gained great new respect for the Cowboys."

Vince Lombardi trotted behind his Packers into the halftime dressing room and muttered to his defensive coach, Phil Bengtsen, "The pendulum just swung Dallas's way."

CHAPTER 15

Before this Cowboys-Packers football epic that contained so many elements of triumph and despair, of suffering and salvation, the term "frozen tundra" maintained a standard definition in the geological texts. It meant "a level or undulating treeless plain characteristic of arctic or subarctic regions—consists of black mucky soil with a permanently frozen subsoil—supports a dense growth of often conspicuously flowering dwarf herbs."

In the post-1967 era, after NFL Films got hold of the term, "frozen tundra" came to mean "once-in-a-century football game played on a surface like greased asphalt with a substructure of electric heating coils that conked out in the clutch."

After both teams sat through almost identical halftime seminars that were somber and etched with anxiety, they returned to the field. "We thought we were still in charge," said Green Bay's Chuck Mercein, "but we knew we still had football to play and that it was time to hunker down."

The players were not certain whether the winners would be claiming the National Football League championship or the Stanley Cup. Between periods, they should have brought out the Zamboni machine. While some traction remained available in the center of the field, between the hash marks, the real estate along the sidelines had become frozen and forbidding. Instead of blowing that $80,000 on his underground dirt-warmer, Vince Lombardi probably should have installed guardrails. Any activity beyond the middle of the gridiron resembled the practice runs by the Jamaican bobsled team at the Calgary Olympics.

Players from both teams realized that a huge crowd must be

watching all of this because they could hear deafening cheers, punctuated by groans and growls. From where the teams were situated on the field, though, they couldn't actually see the fans, who were hidden in a dense veil of frosted breath.

Barbara Gregg, whose husband Forrest's playing career encompassed eleven seasons in Green Bay, was one fan who decided that she had endured enough. At the start of the third period she and another Packer's wife abandoned the stands. They would take in the second half in the Lambeau Field parking lot inside the Gregg family automobile and absorb the action on the car radio. "But we ran the battery down, and so we kept track of the game watching the stadium scoreboard, screaming and cussing," Ms. Gregg said.

Green Bay had the option to receive the second half kickoff, but Lombardi could not be sure if that was any advantage. The Packers' offense had generated two picture-perfect scoring incursions on their first three possessions of the game. After that, the offense looked like something choreographed by Sir Charles Chaplin. But the Pack got a break on the kickoff. Dallas was intent on kicking the ball away from Travis Williams, with his handsome TD résumé. But Danny Villanueva, perhaps too cautious, fired off a kick that Lee Roy Caffey, playing on the front perimeter, fielded at his 37-yard line. Linebacker by trade, Caffey trudged ahead to the 44 before he was tackled, and the Packers opened the second half advantageously positioned.

Right away, however, the Cowboys' defense displayed its second-half intentions. If tackle Bob Lilly had been psyched out earlier that morning when roommate George Andrie had thrown the glass of water against the windowpane to illustrate the cold, he'd gotten past that. On first down, Lilly stuffed Donny Anderson after a three-yard run. On second down, Jethro Pugh leveled Bart Starr for a four-yard sack, and on third down Dallas cornerback Mike Johnson, burned on the Packers' first touchdown, retaliated when he knocked a pass away from the much taller Boyd Dowler. Anderson then hit a mediocre punt, and for the second time in the game receiver Lance Rentzel, standing at his 23-yard line, "let the ball play him" instead of vice versa. Rentzel missed the catch, and Phil Clark, who recovered Willie Wood's fumbled punt near the end of the first half, landed on top of this one, too, but not until the football had rolled down to the Dallas eleven.

Don Meredith launched Dallas's second-half offensive with a seven-yard completion to halfback Dan Reeves, and when fullback

Don Perkins followed that with an eight-yard gain the Cowboys made a first down for the first time in twenty-three consecutive plays going back to the first quarter. After enduring an afternoon's worth of frustration and battering from the Packers' defense, Dallas had found a little spark. On the next play, Meredith passed to Frank Clarke, now substituting at split end for the ineffective Bob Hayes, for fourteen yards. For the first time in the football game the Cowboys had made consecutive first downs.

The assault continued. Reeves ran for 8, then 20 yards before Caffey pulled him down at the Green Bay 32. Reeves lunged to the 29, then Meredith probed the middle of the Packers' defense and connected with Rentzel for 11 more. But it was the Pack's Caffey, one of those frozen Texans who had been so apprehensive about playing in this ridiculous cold before the show began, who now took command of the football game. Seeing that Meredith was becoming ever more reliant on Reeves, perhaps the one player who could instinctively maintain his balance on this ice floe, Caffey anticipated a running play and tackled the halfback for a four-yard loss. Meredith missed Rentzel on second down, looked for his flanker again on third down but took a fierce rush. For the first time that afternoon, Meredith left the pocket and took off. It appeared that he had successfully scrambled for a vital first down, but Caffey again rescued Green Bay. The linebacker tackled Meredith *and* the football, which rolled loose. Herb Adderley recovered the fumble at the 13-yard line.

Anderson tried to bang ahead to place the Packers in safer range from their own end zone, but two plays gained one yard each. First Lee Roy Jordan, then Pugh, tackled Anderson violently. Now Green Bay appeared stuck in a prolonged offensive drought. The Packers had not made a first down of their own for seventeen straight plays. Since Starr had thrown his second TD pass to Dowler early in the second quarter, the Packers had not run a play that had gained more than four yards. In fact, after Dowler's TD, Green Bay's run-pass production chart indicated no profits but an appalling minus-34-yard deficit. Starr, though, now corrected the downward spiral and hit Carroll Dale for a 12-yard first down. But that prosperity proved only temporary. On the next play, with Lilly occupying both guard Gale Gillingham and center Ken Bowman, Andrie, from his end position, rumbled past tackle Bob Skronski and pinned Starr to the Lambeau concrete for a massive 16-yard loss.

"If it was cold, I didn't know it," said Andrie. "With the adrenaline pumping like mine was, you didn't feel any cold." With the Cowboys' defense back to avoid long throws to either Dowler or Dale, Starr handed the ball instead to Anderson, who gained 16 yards on two carries, but Green Bay was still nine yards short of a first down.

Anderson, who might have been feeling some foot fatigue, punted the ball once again, and Rentzel eyed Anderson's punt as if it were Cleopatra's asp. He dropped the thing. This time, at least, he fumbled forward three yards and Rentzel himself fell on the ball at the Green Bay 46.

On first down Reeves, handling himself on the ice like Wayne Gretsky, ran through the Packers' defense for another 11 yards. Caffey, again, had to haul Reeves down. This Reeves act was turning into a one-man show. Meredith threw to Reeves and then handed off to him, but Ray Nitschke and Caffey had forecast what was coming. With Dallas facing third-and-five at the Packers' 30-yard line, Meredith got sacked by the blitzing Caffey, who by now was earning MVP stripes.

Landry decided now that Dallas should attempt a long, 47-yard Villanueva field goal. What a strange call. Villanueva couldn't have made that kick under optimum circumstances, and even if through some divine intervention he did it now, Dallas would still trail. Willie Wood caught Villanueva's dead quail at the four-yard line and returned it to the Green Bay 27. Two runs by Anderson presented a third-and-four situation. By now, however, Dallas's defense was decisively whipping the Packers' line on virtually every play. According to Landry's computerized actuarial tables, it was time for Starr to throw. Dave Edwards blitzed and dumped the quarterback for a four-yard loss. Anderson punted and Hayes made a fair catch at the Dallas 45. With a shadow moving across the football field, the ice on the "tundra" began to sparkle as the afternoon wore on. As the chill factor grew more cruel by the moment, both teams appeared to adopt a tactically conservative approach. On first down, Perkins jabbed the football five yards, and the third quarter ended with the football resting squarely on the 50-yard line.

From the first day that undrafted free agent Dan Reeves reported to Cowboys training camp in 1965, Landry had been impressed. The coach overlooked the fact that during the annual rookies skit Reeves had mooned an audience that included Landry's wife, Alicia. Landry detected that the former South Carolina quarterback offered all kinds of nice intangibles. Reeves was versatile, resourceful, owned an uncanny knack for the end zone, and was endowed with football smarts that rivaled those of the coach.

Between quarters, with the teams switching ends, Reeves offered a tip to Meredith, who was open to any suggestion by now. Since nothing else seemed to work, Reeves told the quarterback, why not try the halfback-option pass that had clicked to Rentzel for long touchdowns against St. Louis and Philadelphia? Yeah, thought Meredith. Why not?

On the opening play of the fourth quarter, Reeves took the pitch from Meredith. The Packers' defense bit nicely. Here he comes again—the ice-skating whiz. Willie Wood came up quick from his safety position to provide run support. Flanker Rentzel had played the entire Ice Bowl in a sleeveless jersey. Out there in agonizing thermal cold that could permanently damage human flesh, this Rentzel presentation truly qualified as indecent exposure.

For an instant, Packers defensive backs Tom Brown and Bob Jeter noticed Reeves with the ball but did not anticipate what was coming. Willie Wood did. As Rentzel broke on his deep-pass pattern, he heard Wood yell, "Oh, shit!"

Reeves, who had so often awed Tom Landry with his accuracy on the option pass in practice, heaved another bull's-eye. Rentzel was alone, behind the secondary. He might have dropped two straight punts, but this time he caught the ball cleanly at full stride, just as he entered the Green Bay end zone. With eight seconds elapsed in the fourth quarter, Dallas had taken the lead, 17–14. "When that happened, it seemed to get colder over on our sideline. Damn right it did," said Chuck Mercein.

Again Villanueva kicked the ball away from Travis Williams. Tommy Joe Crutcher fielded the punt and Green Bay owned the ball on its 34. Dallas was immediately flagged for pass interference, and the Pack moved ahead to the 48, only to watch the savagely efficient Dallas defense assert itself once more. Mercein got tackled for no gain. Pugh sacked Starr. Lee Roy Jordan batted down a pass. Anderson punted again. Green Bay was running its Rockettes offense. One, two, three—kick.

Dallas returned the favor. Two short runs and a long pass, no good, to Hayes. Reeves probably should have tried the option pass again. This time, though, Dallas got stuck with a 15-yard face-mask penalty on Wood's punt return—the only flagrant-foul call of the entire game. In a contest where brutal intensity ruled the day, with combat ferocious along the front lines, no player was flagged for holding, clipping, or unnecessarily rough play.

Starr completed a pass to Dowler for 13 yards, and the Packers now were at the Dallas 34. Lambeau Stadium started to erupt. Green Bay was behind, and while the team was not about to panic, some fans were starting to clutch their chests. Three plays generated nothing, though, and Don Chandler missed a 40-yard field goal. "By now, the field was causing us problems to the extent that some players were getting better footing, or better traction, than others," said Starr. "And it was difficult for me to determine who was and who wasn't, so we might have been out of sync a little."

Now starting from its own twenty, Dallas put together two first downs. Green Bay's defense jumped offsides to give the Cowboys the first one. Meredith connected with Clarke again for ten more yards. If Dallas were to mount a scoring drive here, it would be curtains for Green Bay. The defense could not allow that to happen. But Dallas stalled once more, and for a final time Villanueva put his proud old foot into the ball. Wood caught the punt and returned it nine yards.

Bart Starr took his offense onto the field. The goal line beckoned in the distance, now 68 ice-choked yards away. The Lambeau Field clock read 4:45, all the time that remained for Vince Lombardi's proud ambition to claim a third straight championship. On the sideline Vince Lombardi, Jr., began edging toward the Packers' dressing room. "I figured that it was over . . . that they'd lost the damn thing, that there was no way," Lombardi Junior said. He wanted out of the cold.

Bart Starr thought about making a quick speech in the huddle but couldn't think of anything meaningful to say. Damn the torpedoes, full speed ahead? Give me liberty or give me death? Remember the Alamo? Get serious.

"I just looked into the eyes of some of those guys—Boyd Dowler, Jerry Kramer, Bob Skronski, Forrest Gregg—we'd been working together for ten years, and it all came down to this drive. We all realized what had to be done," said Starr, "and there was no point in putting it in words."

"Yeah, yeah. There was definitely a feel of urgency now in that huddle," said Mercein. "But there was calm, no panic, no desperation. I looked at some guys and nobody was looking downward, nobody's eyes were frantic. We were single-purposed, focused and determined. There was no feeling that we would not succeed."

Jerry Kramer, who had been playing guard for the Packers while Mercein was still in junior high school, wasn't so sure. When the Pack offense took the field for the final drive, Kramer recalls thinking to himself, Maybe this is the year that we *don't* get it done—that it all ends. . . .

Halfback Anderson put his faith in Starr for this drive. "I had confidence that Bart would do something, find something, that would get us down there," he said.

So the drive began. Starr threw the ball to Anderson in the right flat for a six-yard gain. "The condition of the field by now was really poor," Anderson said. "I don't think any of us had ever had any practice playing on something like *this.* Now the players with better athletic instincts, the lighter guys, started taking over. The bigger guys were having trouble just standing up. And because the field was *so* hard and *so* slick, as an offensive player I felt I had an advantage now because I could anticipate what I was going to do." The players with better athletic instincts that Anderson described also realized that lateral movement would be impossible.

After the swing pass to Anderson, Mercein bolted forward for seven more yards and a Packer first down at the 38. "That was a big play for me, personally," said Mercein. "I got tackled near our bench. That first down was a confidence-builder, and the guys were shaking their fists and yelling encouragement."

In fact, that first down seemed to energize the whole offense. Starr said he felt like he might be at the control of what physics calls "the irresistible force." Quickly, he rifled a 13-yarder to Dowler; Green Bay had crossed the continental divide of Lambeau Field and moved to the Dallas 42. Vince Lombardi, Jr., stopped his slow retreat to the Packers' dressing room and headed back toward the bench.

Disaster came. Starr called the famous Lombardi sweep, and Dallas end Willie Townes broke through the stampede of Packer blockers and tackled Anderson for a nine-yard loss. "Let's just say it like it is—or was," commented Mercein. "That was my fault. On the sweep, the tight end and the tackle block down, the guards pull, and the fullback's job is to block the end. On this particular play I went straight at him, but Townes made a sudden inside move. He got by my left shoulder and I didn't get my helmet on him. Townes read the play and he made a helluva play, and believe me, I felt absolutely *terrible.* That's a key block. That's what made Jim Taylor great. Any fullback who plays up here *has* to make that block. And most of the time I did. But every play isn't perfect. I went back to the huddle knowing that Chuck Mercein didn't do a good job on that block."

Second and 19. The drive appeared to be in serious jeopardy, and with it the outcome of the Ice Bowl game *and* the reputation of the entire Vince Lombardi dynasty.

As the players returned to the huddle, Anderson approached Bart Starr. "I'm open over here if you need me." Anderson had been watching the positioning of linebacker Chuck Howley. "On pass plays my job is to block Howley if he blitzes," Anderson said. "But now, after we hit Dowler downfield on that pass, Howley was dropping back and giving support to the weak-side safety. Dowler was a big target, and with Howley moving downfield I had about five or six yards of open space."

Consecutive passes to Anderson, who maintained his balance and ran upfield for 12 and 9 yards, enabled the Packers to overcome the second-and-19 problem. "On both plays, Anderson was a secondary receiver, and on one of those plays he had to turn and make a good play just to get the ball—and then take off down the field. Those plays to him weren't called in the huddle," said Starr. "But Anderson and Mercein are both smart players who can think out there on the field, and Mercein came to me with the same suggestion that Donny had given me." With less than two minutes now remaining, Green Bay had moved 38 of the 68 yards to the Dallas goal line.

Starr then threw another first-down pass, his third straight, to a player coming out of the backfield. This time it was Mercein. "I had a situation on my side of the field that was the same as it was on Anderson's side," Mercein said. "The linebacker, Edwards, was dropping straight back. Bart was aware that he could get away with those swing passes. They were safe plays and they were good plays. I saw the pass coming to me, to my inside shoulder. I was wide open, and when that happens the quarterback often lays it in there differently. Maybe that happened, maybe the wind blew the ball off-course a little—anyway, I always had good hands, and I had to make kind of a heck of a nice catch."

Mercein ran past two defenders who couldn't maintain enough leverage to make the tackle. "I was running at about eighty percent speed. If I ran at a hundred percent I just wouldn't be able to keep my feet underneath me," said Mercein. Certain Dallas defenders, notably Howley and Cornell Green, would not discover that until it was too late. Mercein "ran out of field" but not until he had gained 19 enormous yards. "And I made it out of bounds and stopped the clock, and that didn't hurt us any, either," he said.

Eleven yards now separated the Packers from the end zone, a mystic little chunk of land that for the eleven men on the field, along with twenty-nine others on the bench and one well-known coach, now came to symbolize a divine place in the eternal hereafter.

The remaining passage to the end zone would not be a simple task, though. Green Bay had run out of room. Those swing passes to Anderson and Mercein would not work anymore. Starr had one play up his sleeve that might take the place of the passes to the backs. "George Andrie, the defensive end, lined up a little off the scrimmage line, and I asked Bob Skronski, our tackle over there, if he thought he could get to Andrie and maybe seal him off," said Starr. "Bob said he thought he could."

So Starr made the call: "Fifty-four give." Later, Lombardi referred to Starr's decision as "one of the most inspired calls in championship history . . . it was superb." In the nomenclature of most coaches, the play that Starr called on first down from the eleven is known as the Old Sucker Play. "Coach Lombardi would never demean an opposing player as a sucker, so he just called it the give play," said Starr. Fifty-four give is designed to first appear to be a sweep in progress. The guard, in this case Gillingham, pulls to his right and the tackle, Lilly, moves with the guard in pursuit of what he thinks will be the sweep. Instead, Starr then hands the ball to the fullback, Mercein, who runs into the area that Lilly would have vacated. "It's a play we run a lot but hadn't in the Ice Bowl until that point," said Starr.

"The play was set up to take advantage of the exceptional talent of Lilly," Lombardi would say later. "Lilly had been tearing us up all day. He was the heart of the Dallas defense. That just shows you what a team can do when it takes advantage of the opponent's strength."

Mercein located the defensive void created when the unblocked Lilly chased Gillingham down the line. "Also, Skronski got the necessary shield against Andrie, who then slipped down," said Mercein.

Fifty-four give gained eight yards. Now the Packers were at the gateway to the championship. Anderson took a straight handoff from Starr and reached the one, where the Packers had a first down. The clock showed less than a minute to play and was running, while Lambeau Field seemed to rock and sway underneath the screaming frenzy in the stands. Bart Starr said, "I knew we had reached a point where we could not afford any setbacks."

Starr gave the ball to Anderson on first down. "Well, I think I scored," Anderson says now. "I was under a stack of players, and I was on top of the football and the football was on the goal line. Lee Roy Jordan was yelling, 'Fumble! fumble!' I think hoping to distract the officials from seeing where the ball was. Anyway, they didn't give me the touchdown and placed the ball right there at the goal line," said Anderson.

Starr called the same play, and this time Anderson slipped on the ice as he came out of the starting blocks and barely managed to clutch the handoff. "At first Donny seemed like a guy running and tripping over some marbles," said Mercein, who had an excellent view of the whole play. "That could easily have resulted in a fumble. My heart almost stopped." Green Bay still needed that final foot—the world's longest foot—and the clock now showed less than twenty seconds. Nineteen. Eighteen. With thirteen seconds left, Bart Starr signaled for Green Bay's last time-out. "In situations like this before, I knew what Lombardi liked to do," said Forrest Gregg. "So before Bart went over to the bench, I told him to tell Lombardi not to try that sweep. We'd get tackled in the backfield for sure if we did."

Starr trotted to the sidelines to visit his coach. Green Bay faced three alternatives. Kick a field goal to tie the game and force an overtime. Throw a pass. If that didn't work, the clock would stop and the Packers could run, pass, or kick again on fourth down. Or the Packers could roll the dice and attempt a running play, knowing that if they did not penetrate the goal stripe against the compressed Dallas defense, no time would be left available to reassemble and run another play.

Starr knew what he wanted to do. "I told the coach, 'I can make it in on a sneak. Kramer and Bowman can get underneath Pugh on a wedge block, and I've got good footing.' We had to go to that side. Jethro Pugh had a tendency to stand up at the snap. On the other side, Lilly stayed low and he would have buried me alive. There have been many different reports about what was said during that time-out and who actually called the play," said Starr. "But I presented the case for the sneak, and the coach said, 'Do it and let's get the hell out of here.' And that was all that he said."

Back in the huddle, Starr called, "Brown right, thirty-one wedge, on one." Brown right, thirty-one wedge is *not* a quarterback sneak. That's a dive play to the fullback. But the blocking assignments remained the same.

Anderson said, "The sneak call made complete sense. I'd nearly fallen down on the play before, and now we had a situation where the backs were four yards from the goal line and the defensive linemen were one *foot* from the goal line. I was supposed to block down on the end, and when I heard the cheer, I figured it was Chuck who had scored. I didn't find out it was Bart until I got back to the bench."

"Well, I was very excited when Bart called thirty-one wedge. That was *my* play," said Mercein. "So I was rather astonished when I plunged ahead to take the handoff and saw Bart carrying the ball in instead. I had to put the brakes on quick because if I'd run into him from behind, the official could have penalized me for trying to help advance the runner."

Starr not only scored, but scored with ease. The double-team block by Kramer and Bowman was executed with perfection. They pushed Pugh back from the goal line like he was a big sled.

"I hadn't thought about the weather all day," said George Andrie, who had played the game of his life. "But when I looked over there and saw the official with his hands raised, signaling touchdown, I remember thinking, God*damn,* it's cold out here. That was the first time I noticed it."

Bart Starr now says that people constantly question the wisdom of attempting that sneak with no more time to play. If the effort had failed . . . "We could have run that play ten times, and it would have worked all ten times," he believes.

Announcer Ray Scott remembers the moment. "After the first half, Jack Buck was to call the second half, and my job was to go to the sideline and interview the winning team. There was no press-box elevator at Lambeau Field at the time, so I walked through stands and stood next to the Packers bench.

"I still say that final Packers drive," Scott declares, "was the greatest triumph of will over adversity that I have ever seen in *any* football game. No pass was dropped, nobody fumbled, and you cannot *imagine* the condition of their hands. They were like bricks. After the game somebody told Lombardi that some of the Cowboys might have suffered frostbite, and he said, 'Losers get frostbite.' But lemme tell you something. In the Packers' dressing room I saw players shaking their fingers and shaking their hands. The Packers were frostbitten, too. They were *cold.* It's hard to imagine a game filled with so many ifs and so many ironies being played in those conditions. It was terrible."

Dallas sports columnist Blackie Sherrod, leaving the press box well after the game was over, noticed that crews had already been at work sweeping out Lambeau Field. "What I remember most vividly about that game was that the cleanup crew had stacked up the damnedest collection of pint bottles you ever saw in your life."

Unfortunately for the Dallas team, they'd had no access to any elixirs that might have better enabled them to brave the chill. Even Tom Landry admitted that he and his players "suffered all day" in the dreadful Wisconsin cold. Don Meredith was furious. "That wasn't a fair test of football," he said. After the game George Andrie said, "I cried. I swear. Actually shed tears. That's the only time I ever did that after a football game. I was that devastated. I truly was. But it was like when somebody close to you dies, you just go on. I mean, it wasn't like the end of everybody's careers. We were all going to come back next year and do it again. So we all went and climbed back on the plane. And then we all got loaded."

Tex Schramm walked over to the Packers' side to congratulate Lombardi. "Vinnie was joyous, and I think surprised that we had come as close as we did," Tex said.

"We felt elation but more than that, we felt relief," said Forrest Gregg. "We knew that the next game we played was the Super Bowl in Miami, and we knew that we would be in the *sunshine.*"

Donny Anderson recalls Lombardi's "coming up, putting his arm around me, hugging me, and saying, 'Today, you became a man.' But that game, in that last drive, was the best I ever played for the Green Bay Packers. All the hard work. All the discipline. All the good and all the bad were right there in my lap. You know, the guy [Lombardi] just pushed you past every limit that you thought you had. That's what it's all about and that's what every Packer went through.

"Bart. Hornung. Taylor. McGee. Just name 'em. Vince brought you to another level. After the game I remember sitting in front of our lockers and talking. We thought right then that we might have just played in the greatest football game of all time."

When Lombardi Junior drove the coach back to the house, father told son, "We've got the Super Bowl coming up, and you just watched me coach my next-to-last football game." What a time to schedule an exit. But no man ever recognized and appreciated the value of timing in the sport of football more than Vince Lombardi did.

EPILOGUE

AFTER THE THAW

The eleven little men who ran out on the field at the last were like bewitched figures in another world, strange and infinitely romantic, blurred by a throbbing mist of people and sound. One aches with them intolerably, trembles with their excitement, but they have no traffic with us now. They are beyond help, consecrated and unreachable—vaguely holy.

—F. Scott Fitzgerald in his short story THE BOWL, published in the *Saturday Evening Post* in 1928.

IF BART STARR'S NINE-AND-A-HALF-INCH TOUCHDOWN—"one small step for man, one giant leap for the Green Bay Packers"—gave birth to an everlasting football legend, survivors of the Ice Bowl fell into a postpartum malaise moments after the ordeal had come to an end. Players felt as if they had just been aroused from a cryogenically induced coma. The sensation that their joints were lined with ground glass told them that all of this had not been a strange dream.

In the sanctity of their dressing room, the Green Bay Packers felt cranked up on the dark adrenaline that flows after one has experienced the fright of having narrowly dodged a bad traffic accident. This had been too close a call, and only after the game did the Packers begin to realize how very close they had come to losing. That final scoring drive had put the team on a precarious tightrope. One bobble, one blown assignment, one flop on the ice—and the championship was lost.

Halfback emeritus Paul Hornung watched the Ice Bowl from the Packers' sideline. "I'm just glad Bart scored," he said. "Otherwise, there would have been hell to pay."

Vince Lombardi talked about Bart Starr's touchdown: "We gambled. We won. It was as simple as that. Everybody loves a gambler, but not when he loses. Want to know the real reason why we went for the touchdown instead of the field goal? Because I didn't want all those freezing people up in the stands to sit through a sudden-death overtime. I've been accused of lacking compassion. But that just shows I'm not without compassion."

Broadcaster Ray Scott, Lombardi's old friend, stood nearby holding a microphone when the coach made the comment about the fans in the stands. "I just laughed. The reason that Vince didn't want the overtime was because he was freezing too and he just wanted to get his fanny out of there!" Scott said.

If the Packers were marginally shaken by their narrow escape from the infamy of defeat, the Cowboys' frustration in losing was amplified by the gnawing awareness of how tantalizingly *close* they had been to winning the Ice Bowl. "We could have won. We *should* have won," said Lee Roy Jordan. What made it worse was that the Cowboys did not know until the game was over and they had boarded their chartered jet back to Dallas that Green Bay had been out of time-outs when Starr scored the touchdown.

Sports columnist Blackie Sherrod remembers the amazement on the face of linebackers coach Jerry Tubbs when he heard that. "Tubbs said, 'What? They were out of time-outs? God. What a ridiculous call.' Clint Murchison was sitting in the front of the plane. He didn't usually offer much critical commentary about the football games, but Clint acted flabbergasted that Green Bay would gamble on that sneak. He just shook his head and called it dumb luck."

Professional football players—unlike their major league baseball counterparts—are rarely known to offer excuses after big losses. Most of the Cowboys, however, had been vocal in expressing their opinions that the weather conditions at the Ice Bowl prevented them from winning the game. Wrote Jim Murray of the *Los Angeles Times:* "The theory could be advanced that neither team had the advantage because it was cold for the Packers, too. That's like saying that the shark had no advantage over the swimmer because both were in the water."

IF THE PACKERS answered the ultimate challenge in the fourth quarter of the Ice Bowl, so too did many of their fans. Impaired by antifreeze of the soul that had been ingested during the game, many brave spectators encountered difficulty finding their cars in the Lambeau Field parking lot. And when they did, the cars often refused to start because of the cold. Auto repair shop owner Paul Massulini, in his service truck, stayed busy outside Lambeau Field past nine that night, reviving dead engines. He cleared $425 for his efforts—a handsome day's payoff by 1967 standards for a man and his jumper cables.

Green Bay bar owner Ray Bilotti said his customary postgame profits did not reach expectations after the Ice Bowl game due to the condition of the fans. "There had to be an unbelievable number of drunks sitting out in that cold drinking brandy," said Bilotti. "They were on the floor by the time they entered here. They would be stone sober because of the cold, and the minute they hit the heat inside our place—wow! They just started to pass out all over the place."

IN LOMBARDI'S LAST game on the Packers' sideline, Green Bay flattened the Oakland Raiders, 33–14 in Super Bowl II. His intentions to retire as the coach had been made public by Ray Scott's brother, Hal, on a television newcast in Minneapolis. In an odd twist, Hal Scott said that Lombardi's decision to quit had coincided with the appearance of the hatchet-job feature article that appeared earlier in the fall in *Esquire*. Vince Lombardi, Jr., closer to the source than Hal Scott, offered another suggestion: "I think he just felt his veteran players had heard all the same speeches so many times through the years that maybe they wouldn't work anymore and it was time to let somebody else give it a try. There's no doubt that he was awfully fatigued."

With Vince Lombardi serving as head coach from 1959 through 1967, the Green Bay Packers posted ninety-eight wins, thirty losses, and four ties. Somebody would write: "Vince Lombardi retires as the greatest coach of all time—one foot better than Tom Landry."

After the Ice Bowl season, the Packers and Cowboys franchises ventured off in opposite directions. It required a quarter-century for the Packers to resurrect the greatness. But in Dallas—"The outcome of that Ice Bowl game had been a tremendous disappointment, but I know that the game provided a big turning point for the Cowboys," says Tex Schramm now. "If the America's Team concept for Dallas ever had any validity, that all started with the Ice Bowl. The way Dallas played Green Bay that day, even in losing at the last, won the admiration of the whole country."

Sportswriter Frank Luksa said, "Dallas got its britches shot off by Cleveland in the playoffs in the two years following the Ice Bowl, and then the Cowboys took off. What a cast of characters. They bring in a Bible-totin' halfback from Yale—Calvin Hill—and after that Duane Thomas, one of the all-time characters. They lost to the 49ers on the famous catch by Dwight Clark, but they beat the Vikings on the amazing Hail Mary pass, Roger Staubach to Drew Pearson. What a ride."

Jerry Jones pulled the plug on the Landry-Schramm merry-go-round in February 1989, proving that, eventually, nobody lives happily ever after. Jones fired Landry and made it evident that he was taking over Tex's job . . . so Schramm soon quit. At the press conference that left Cowboys fans gasping, Jones said that he was in charge of the whole operation, "from jocks to socks." One visiting sportswriter from Philadelphia wrote that Jerry Jones reminded him "of the banjo player in *Deliverance*."

Landry now makes a happy mint on the value of his face and name, endorsing health-care-insurance plans and other ventures that are largely associated with the senior population. Tex Schramm owns two houses, one in Dallas and one in Key West, Florida, and he spends the majority of his time at the latter.

LOMBARDI LEFT GREEN Bay to coach the Washington Redskins in 1969. Washington finished 7–5–2, the 'Skins' first winning record in fourteen years. It looked as if Lombardi might establish a new football dynasty on the Potomac. But the coach was diagnosed with colon cancer in June of 1970. The cancer spread elsewhere unchecked, and Vince Lombardi died shortly after seven o'clock in the morning on September 3, 1970.

Ice Bowl participants from both teams are now flung throughout the United States. Don Meredith felt deflated emotionally after the Ice Bowl, but he did realize at the time that God was soon going to give him Howard Cosell. With ABC's *Monday Night Football* serving as the platform, the comedy duo of Meredith and Cosell became even hotter than Dean Martin and Jerry Lewis. Meredith now lives in Santa Fe, New Mexico, a mountain art colony occupied mostly by Texans and Californians. He tells most inquiring journalists where to stick it and plays golf almost every day.

Lee Roy Jordan got rich in the lumber business and lives in Dallas. Bob Hayes served a little time in the Texas state pen on drug-related charges, but he overcame that and, as of spring 1997, was living in Jacksonville, Florida. Lance Rentzel was arrested for "flashing" a Dallas girl late in the 1970 season, when the Cowboys were en route to their first Super Bowl. Rentzel never played another game for the Cowboys, but he wrote a book about his experience. Rentzel lives in the Washington, D.C., area and is involved in a computer business.

Dan Reeves coached successfully in the NFL, particularly at Denver, where he took the Broncos to a couple of Super Bowls. After writing *North Dallas 40,* Pete Gent moved to what is known as the Texas Hill Country to continue his literary career. He now resides in western Michigan and is involved in turning out scripts for a television sitcom about a sports agent and writing novels. Gent recalls bumping into Tom Landry a couple of years ago at an NBA basketball game in Dallas: "I said, 'Well, Tom, how's life outside football?' and he said, 'Ah, it's not so bad, Pete.' Then he laughed and said, 'I think you've been trying to tell me that for years.' He was very cordial and while a lot of guys thought Tom was difficult to play for, he *was* a father figure, and he made you think twice about the things you were doing off the field."

Four players on the Packers' Ice Bowl team are deceased. Henry Jordan died of a heart attack at age forty-two. The man who played next to Jordan in the Packers' front four, Ron Kostelnik, was killed in an auto accident, but it was determined that he, too, had suffered a heart attack before the wreck occurred. Lee Roy Caffey, possibly the best player on the field on that particular Ice Bowl Sunday, died in 1994 of a cancer very similar to Lombardi's. Travis Williams, the rookie Roadrunner who displayed such immense promise in 1967, never seemed to develop his talents as a halfback. According to a teammate, Williams became a "street person" and later died.

Fuzzy Thurston still resides in Green Bay, and his Fuzzy's Shenanigans sports bar thrives there. Don Anderson runs a cellular communications company in Dallas. Those students who engineered the demonstration at Grambling in 1967, complaining about the college's image as a football factory, might have been surprised to learn that even products of the professional gridiron assembly line can make good outside the jock realm. Willie Davis earned his M.B.A. at the

University of Chicago while still playing at Green Bay. He then moved to California, bought some radio stations, got rich, and has sat on the boards of Sara Lee and MGM.

Forrest Gregg was inducted into the National Football League Hall of Fame on the same day as Bart Starr, Frank Gifford, and Gale Sayers. He then coached the Cincinnati Bengals to a Super Bowl. Gregg has the distinction of having participated in the three coldest pro championships played in the modern era, if not ever—the 1962 Giants-Packers game, the Ice Bowl, and the 1981 Cincinnati–San Diego championship game that he coached for the winning side. "Actually, the wind chill at that game in Cincinnati was colder than the Ice Bowl," he said. "But the players had better cold-weather equipment, like electric hand warmers inside their jerseys, that was not available when I played. Also, the game was played on artificial turf and the footing was all right.

"That 1962 game was bad, too," Gregg said. "The wind was blustery and there was no grass at all on the field at Yankee Stadium. But for overall miserable conditions—the cold and the slick, ice-solid field—that Ice Bowl game was the absolute worst. Nothing will ever top that, I don't think."

After Phil Bengtsen and Dan Devine failed in their efforts to restore the Packers to glory, banners appeared at Lambeau Field: A NEW START WITH BART! But Starr's head-coaching experience in Green Bay ended badly, too. Starr found prosperity back in his home state of Alabama, and he now owns a Birmingham-based company that specializes in health-care-oriented office real estate nationwide.

In the winter of 1997, Starr declared that scarcely a day goes by that he *does* think about the Ice Bowl game. "No. I have put that in the back of my mind," he said. "I'm proud that I played in that game and proud of my Packers career. But once that is over . . . it's in the past, and that's where it should remain. What matters in life is what is taking place *now* and not then."

If the players from the Ice Bowl share one common postcareer characteristic, it is this: Professional football leaves a lasting impression on the skeletal frame. The shoulders. The knees. The back. All these guys might as well have gone over Niagara Falls in a washtub. George Andrie aches in about four key locations whenever he brushes his teeth. "Pro football is not like golf. I used to like to hit guys on every play and try to make them suffer," says Andrie. "And look how it affects me now!"

Vince Lombardi, Jr., has four children of his own. The youngest of those, in early 1997 a first lieutenant in the U.S. Air Force at Wright-Patterson in Dayton, Ohio, has had some experience coaching football at the prep school level and thinks he might want to coach somewhere full-time after leaving the military. Imagine the grandson of the everlastingly celebrated Lombardi someday prowling the sideline of Lambeau Field. Lombardi Junior cautioned his son about the realities of coaching football, stressing that this is a tough, overly competitive, and often cruel profession.

"I wouldn't know about that," the kid responded. "I've never lost a game."

SCORING • LINEUPS • MISC.

DATE December 31, 1967 DAY OF WEEK Sunday STARTING TIME 1:11 P.M.
HOME TEAM Green Bay Packers VS. VISITOR Dallas Cowboys AT Green Bay
WEATHER Clear, Cold TEMPERATURE –13 WIND AND DIRECTION Northwest at 15
OFFICIALS REFEREE Norm Schachter UMPIRE Joe Connell LINE JUDGE Bill Schleitaum
LINESMAN George Murphy BACK JUDGE Tom Kelleher FIELD JUDGE Fritz Graf

LINEUPS

DALLAS

Offense		Defense	
LE	Hayes	LE	Townes
LT	Liscio	LT	Pugh
LG	Niland	RT	Lilly
C	Connelly	RE	Andrie
RG	Donohue	LLB	Howley
RT	Neely	MLB	Jordan
TE	Norman	RLB	Edwards
QB	Meredith	LH	Green
HB	Reeves	RH	Johnson
FB	Perkins	LS	Gaechter
FL	Rentzel	RS	Renfro

Walker, Hays, East, Boeke, Wilbur, Stephens, Stokes, Banham, Garrison, Villanueva, Clark, Shy, Daniels, Rhome, Clarke

GREEN BAY

Offense		Defense	
LE	Dowler	LE	Davis
LT	Skoronski	LT	Kostelnik
LG	Gillingham	RT	Jordan
C	Bowman	RE	Aldridge
RG	Kramer	LLB	Robinson
RT	Gregg	MLB	Nitschke
TE	Fleming	RLB	Caffey
QB	Starr	LH	Adderley
HB	Anderson	RH	Jeter
FB	Mercein	LS	Brown (Tom)
FL	Dale	RS	Wood

Crutcher, Williams, Flanigan, Long, Chandler, Hart, Weatherwax, Hyland, Rowser, Brown (Bob), Wilson, Wright, Thurston, McGee

DID NOT PLAY

Dallas: Morton, Tubbs, Gent

Green Bay: Bratkowski, Horn, Grabowski, Brown (Allen)

INDIVIDUAL SCORING

DALLAS		GREEN BAY
Andrie (1), Rentzel (1)	TOUCHDOWNS	Dowler (2), Starr (1)
Villanueva (2)	P.A.T.'S	Chandler (3)
Villanueva (1)	FIELD GOALS	
Villanueva (1)	FIELD GOALS MISSED	Chandler (1)

	1	2	3	4	Total
Cowboys	0	10	0	7	17
Packers	7	7	0	7	21

SCORING PLAYS

TEAM	PERIOD	ELAPSED TIME	DETAIL ON SCORING PLAYS	SCORE Visit	SCORE Home
Packers	1	8:50	Dowler, on eight-yard Starr pass	0	6
Packers	1	8:50	Chandler, PAT	0	7
Packers	2	2:41	Dowler, on 46-yard Starr pass	0	13
Packers	2	2:41	Chandler, PAT	0	14
Cowboys	2	10:56	Andrie recovered Starr fumble and ran 7 yards	6	14
Cowboys	2	10:56	Villanueva, PAT	7	14
Cowboys	2	14:28	Villanueva, on 21-yard field goal	10	14
Cowboys	4	:08	Rentzel, on 50-yard pass from Reeves	16	14
Cowboys	4	:08	Villanueva, PAT	17	14
Packers	4	14:47	Starr on one-yard quarterback sneak	17	20
Packers	4	14:47	Chandler, PAT	17	21

ATTENDANCE 50,861 TIME OF GAME 2:30

CITY Green Bay, Wisconsin

FINAL TEAM STATISTICS

DATE Dec. 31, 1967

Green Bay Packers Vs. Dallas Cowboys	DALLAS	GREEN BAY
TOTAL FIRST DOWNS	11	18
First Downs Rushing	4	5
First Downs Passing	6	10
First Downs by Penalty	1	3
TOTAL YARDS GAINED (NET)	192	195
Yards Gained Rushing (Net)	92	80
Yards Gained Passing (Net)	100	115
Gross Yards Gained Passing	109	191
Times Thrown & Yards Lost Attempting to Pass	1—9	8—76
Passes Attempted	26	24
Passes Completed	11	14
Average Gain per Pass Attempt	3.8	4.8
Passes Intercepted by & Yards Returned	0–0	1—15
Number and Total Yardage of Punts	8—313	8—230
Average Distance of Punts	39.1	29
Number and Total Yards Punts Returned	0—0	5—19
Number and Total Yards Kickoffs Returned	3—43	3—10
Number of Penalties and Total Yards Penalized	7—58	2—10
Number of Fumbles and Fumbles Lost	3—1	3—2
Number of Rushing Plays	33	32
Average Gain Per Rushing Play	2.8	2.5
Total Offensive Plays (Inc. times thrown passing)	60	64
Average Gain Per Offensive Play	3.2	3.1

INDIVIDUAL RUSHING

DALLAS							GREEN BAY						
Player	Att.	Net Yards	Avg.	Long Gain	Yds Lost	TD	Player	Att.	Net Yards	Avg.	Long Gain	Yds Lost	TD
Baynham	1	–2	–2	–2	2	0	Anderson	18	35	1.9	9	11	0
Clarke	1	–8	–8	–8	8	0							
Meredith	1	9	9	9	0	0	Mercein	6	20	3.3	8	0	0
Perkins	17	51	3	8	0	0	Starr	1	1	1	1	0	1
Reeves	13	42	3.2	11	13	0							
							Williams	4	13	3.2	7	0	0
							Wilson	3	11	3.7	13	2	0
Totals	33	92	2.8	11	23	0	**Totals**	32	80	2.5	13	13	1

INDIVIDUAL PASSING

DALLAS							GREEN BAY						
Player	Att.	Comp.	Yds. Gain	Long	TD	Int.	Player	Att.	Comp.	Yds. Gain	Long	TD	Int.
Meredith	25	10	59	14	0	1	Starr	24	14	191	43	2	0
Reeves	1	1	50	50	1	0							
Totals	26	11	109	50	1	1	**Totals**	24	14	191	43	2	0

PASS RECEIVING

DALLAS					GREEN BAY				
Player	No.	Yards	Long	TD's	Player	No.	Yards	Long	TD
Baynham	1	3	3	0	Dowler	4	77	43	2
Clarke	2	24	14	0	Anderson	4	44	17	0
Hayes	3	16	10	0	Dale	3	44	17	0
Reeves	3	11	7	0	Mercein	2	22	19	0
Rentzel	2	61	50	1	Williams	1	4	4	0

PUNTING

VISITORS						HOME					
Player	No.	Yards	Average	Blkd	Long	Player	No.	Yards	Average	Blkd	Long
Villanueva	8	313	39.1	0	44	Anderson	8	230	29	0	38

PUNT RETURNS

Player	No.	Yards	Long	Fair Catch	TD's	Player	No.	Yards	Long	Fair Catch	TD's
Hayes	0	0	0	2	0	Brown	1	–2	–2	0	0
Rentzel	0	0	0	3	0	Wood	4	21	10	2	0

KICKOFF RETURNS

Player	No.	Yards	Long	TD's	Player	No.	Yards	Long	TD's
Stokes	1	28	28	0	Crutcher	1	3	3	0
Stevens	2	15	15	0	Caffey	1	7	7	0
					Weatherwax	1	0	0	0

INTERCEPTIONS

Player	No.	Yards	Long	TD's	Player	No.	Yards	Long	TD's
					Adderley	1	15	15	0

INDEX